Why the JFK Assassination Still Matters

"As a man of science, Dr. Buyer is in an excellent position to be a dispassionate evaluator of medical evidence and related information.

"As a loving father, Dr. Buyer isn't willing to 'look the other way' when teaching his daughter the history of our great nation. As a proud citizen, Richard Buyer feels duty-bound to set the record straight.

"This book is well researched, well written, and will help to enlighten all those who have a deep and abiding regard for the truth.

"It's my pleasure to commend it to you."

—Marilyn Pincus, president of Marilyn Pincus, Inc.
Author and ghostwriter, Tucson, Arizona

"*Why the JFK Assassination Still Matters* sets forth the arguments against the Warren Commission Report in a cogent and well-organized fashion. A dynamic review and analysis of the true facts and conspiratorial fictions involved in the murder of JFK."

—Cyril Wecht, MD, JD

"Dr. Buyer's solid research and analysis clearly supports for all time the truth. JFK's assassination was a conspiracy!"

—Andrew Thomas Greeley, MA
Managing member Literary Partners Group LLC
Tucson, Arizona

Why the JFK Assassination Still Matters

The Truth for My Daughter Kennedy
and for Generations to Come

RICHARD BUYER MD

Why the JFK Assassination Still Matters
The Truth for My Daughter Kennedy and for Generations to Come

Published by Wheatmark®
610 East Delano Street, Suite 104, Tucson, Arizona 85705 U.S.A.
www.wheatmark.com

Publisher's Cataloging-In-Publication Data
(Prepared by The Donohue Group, Inc.)

Buyer, Richard.

Why the JFK assassination still matters : the truth for my daughter Kennedy and for generations to come /¬ Richard Buyer.

p. : ill. ; cm.

Includes bibliographical references and index.
ISBN: 978-1-60494-193-7

1. Kennedy, John F. (John Fitzgerald), 1917-1963--Assassination. 2. United States. Warren Commission. 3. Conspiracies--United States--History--20th century. 4. Oswald, Lee Harvey. I. Title.

E842.9 .B89 2009
364.1/524/0973   2008942427

I dedicate this book to my wife, Kris, the bravest and most courageous person I have ever known. Throughout my writing, she has always been a constant inspiration. She continues to inspire all who know her.

Contents

The primary reason this case has never been solved (despite the government contention that it was) is the fact that there is an enormous amount of disagreement and discrepancy regarding the medical evidence. The direct observations made at Parkland Memorial Hospital where the President was first taken following the shooting are at complete odds with the autopsy results and subsequent Warren Report. The autopsy photographs and X-ray findings tend to disagree with both of these. Eyewitness reports are disregarded and ignored unless they tend to agree with what the government wants us to believe. It is not surprising that the American public has been confused.

Who was JFK? How did he get interested in running for the presidency? What role did his father play in his decision and how was he influenced by the death of his older brother? JFK had many obstacles in his way. He was Catholic and he was young.

This was considered Kennedy's biggest failure as president. The CIA during the presidency of Dwight Eisenhower had planned a potential takeover of Cuba and ouster of its communist dictator, Fidel Castro. Kennedy eventually backed out of this plot and refused to give much needed air support. The plan failed and Castro was victorious. This angered many factions especially the CIA, the anti-Castro Cubans, and organized crime. Their anger was directed toward the president.

This was considered Kennedy's biggest triumph as president. The Russians were supplying missiles to Cuba which were aimed toward the coast of Florida. The threat of nuclear war was imminent. Kennedy decided on a naval blockade of ships heading toward Cuba although many of his advisors wanted us to attack Cuba and remove the missiles. After much discussion between the two parties, Krushchev backed down and agreed to move the missiles out of Cuba. One of the concessions Kennedy had to make was that the United States would never invade Cuba. This again angered the Cuban exiles, CIA, and organized crime. It appeared that our prior interests in Cuba would never again be realized.

This was the only war that the United States truly lost. Kennedy saw the futility of the war as well as the corruption of the South Vietnamese government. The anti-war sentiment in the U.S. was reaching a high and Kennedy wanted to be reelected in 1964. As a result, he began advocating for the gradual withdrawal of our troops from this small country in Southeast Asia. It is a known fact that many people become extremely wealthy during wartime and our withdrawal from Vietnam would adversely affect this group. Among those would be members of the military-industrial complex.

Organized crime had a large financial interest in Cuba and wanted to reestablish their foothold by getting rid of Castro. In addition, the Mafia was being persecuted by the Senate Racketeering Committee led by Robert Kennedy and to a lesser extent by the president himself. The Mafia had also felt betrayed by the Kennedy brothers because of an earlier agreement reached with Joseph Kennedy Sr. that there would not be undue pressure exerted on organized crime if JFK was elected president.

Neither Robert nor Jack knew of this arrangement which their father had made with the Mafia. In any event, this all created much hostility and resentment toward both the president and the attorney general.

This was the last day of President John F. Kennedy's life. This date will remain infamous in our history as will December 7, 1941 and September 11, 2001. What were the circumstances surrounding the Kennedy assassination, both before and after that fateful day?

This was the alleged assassin of the president of the United States. Was he capable of orchestrating and carrying out the assassination of the president all by himself or was he part of a conspiracy plot and being framed as a patsy as he so desperately claimed? Who was using him as the fall-guy and why was the government so anxious to conclude he was the lone gunman?

Jack Ruby murdered Lee Harvey Oswald in front of millions on national television. Most people were never convinced of his story that he did it for patriotic reasons. Jack Ruby had a connection to organized crime and this raised the possibility (or probability) of his being a part of a conspiracy.

These were the two prime agencies which were supposed to protect the president during his trip to Texas. Obviously, they failed. There has been much speculation that police were told not to give close protection and that the shooters actually had Secret Service badges so as to avoid detection during all the chaos directly following the shooting.

No one gained more from the assassination of President John F. Kennedy than did his successor, Lyndon Baines Johnson. Following the assassination, Johnson appointed a commission (known as the Warren Commission) to allegedly investigate the assassination, but more importantly to prove that Oswald was the lone killer and there was no conspiracy. This appeared to be the preconceived conclusion. The Warren Commission did just that, despite the fact that it did not conduct its own investigation. It said what the true conspirators wanted it to say.

Hoover feared he would be forced into mandatory retirement by President Kennedy. The FBI had learned of death threats against the president but chose to ignore them. The FBI was the main investigating body for the Warren Commission. Only two days after the assassination, Hoover declared Oswald was the shooter and that he was a crazed lone gunman. The cover-up was obviously in progress.

Why has the media always professed to the lone gunman theory and refused to believe in the possibility of a conspiracy? Even today the media does not waver from its original premise. It must be remembered that the media is owned by big business conglomerates, certainly a vital part of the military-industrial complex. There was no love lost between the president and big business. Oliver Stone's movie "JFK" revitalized the interest of this country in the assassination. It re-informed the generation of the 1960s, but more importantly, it presented to the current generation of Americans (those people not here in 1963) the vital details of the assassination. Many were hearing this for the first time. Though it was mainly a movie (though part documentary), Oliver Stone was able to bring together many of those ideas which the authors on the assassination had been saying for years. It was more realistic than its critics would allow the audience to believe.

If it weren't for this book — the students of today who look up information on the assassination from sources such as textbooks, history books, encyclopedias, and the internet *would* come away with the conclusion that Lee Harvey Oswald acted alone in the assassination of the president. There is absolutely no proof that this is true. In fact, the evidence points to the contrary. There was a conspiracy to assassinate President John F. Kennedy and there was also a conspiracy to cover up the details behind the assassination. Unfortunately, both of these conspiracies have been successful in keeping the truth from the American public since 1963.

The actual killers of John F. Kennedy are probably no longer living themselves at this time. However, those people who planned the assassination may indeed be alive. It is this second group which holds the key to the assassination and a true historical account of what actually occurred on that tragic day of November 1963. History must be rewritten to reflect the truth. The gullibility of the American public must no longer be infringed upon. The government version of the assassination can no longer be believed, let alone accepted. If we can change history by saying John F. Kennedy was killed as a result of a conspiracy, then this would be a major step toward finding the truth.

Acknowledgements

November 22, 1963 is a day which I will always remember, not only because of its historic significance to our country, but also because of the personal impact which it made on my life. At that time, I accepted the report of the Warren Commission and subsequent conclusions of the government. It wasn't until several years later that I began doing my own extensive reading, listening, and research. I was shocked at what I discovered; throughout all these years I had been lied to and deceived into believing that Lee Harvey Oswald had assassinated President Kennedy and that he had accomplished this all by himself. I then realized that this deception was still prevalent and my children were also being taught false information. For four decades I was educated into believing that there was no conspiracy in the assassination and I fell for it, as did so many others. Thus, this book is written.

Although many people are responsible for the writing of a book, there are always some individuals who truly stand out. Foremost on my list is my wife, Kristin, who always was at my side and gave me the encouragement and positive reinforcement needed for a book of this significance. She agreed when appropriate and disagreed when she thought necessary. Without her support this book would not have been possible. Secondly, is Kennedy, my precious twelve-year-old daughter who happened to be born three weeks prematurely on the anniversary date of the assassination. She was my inspiration in writing this book and looking for the truth. Kennedy is proud of her namesake and certainly likes seeing her name in print. In 1993 following the release of Oliver Stone's monumental movie *JFK* I vividly recall having discussions with my two sons, Paul and Jason, both born after 1963. They were very interested and passionate about the subject and in later years strongly encouraged me to pursue my quest for the truth. Without the constant support of my family, you would not be reading this book.

There are certainly other people who warrant a large amount of personal gratitude and appreciation for the help they gave me. Marilyn Pincus, herself an established author, was always a cheerleader for this project. She helped to assure that this book was reader friendly. Andrew Greeley, a great lunch companion and managing member of Literary Partners Group, was instrumental in helping with public awareness. Finally, Wheatmark Publishing, specifically Grael Norton and Lori Sellstrom, were responsible for arranging the final presentation which you are now reading. My sincere thanks to all.

We live in a great country. Yet we must have faith and trust in our government or we cannot succeed. On the other hand, the government must also believe in its own people. Both factions must tell the truth. For this reason, the JFK assassination still does matter. History cannot be replayed but it can be rewritten.

Introduction

> We owe respect to the living;
> to the dead we owe only the truth.
> —*Voltaire*

Why **read another book** about the assassination of President John Fitzgerald Kennedy?

The answer is simple. The major crime of the twentieth century remains (essentially) unsolved.

In 1964 the Warren Commission, a commission appointed by the succeeding president, Lyndon Baines Johnson, to investigate the assassination, concluded that President Kennedy was assassinated by a single individual named Lee Harvey Oswald and there was no evidence of a conspiracy.

This conclusion remains the dogma of the government today, more than forty years later, despite a vast amount of information that points to the contrary. The majority of books written since that fateful day of November 22, 1963 deal with the probability of a conspiracy. The authors cite convincing evidence to support their conclusions.

The Warren Report is the official government version of the assassination in advocating the lone gunman theory. The members of the Warren Commission relied on the Federal Bureau of Investigation (FBI) for information without conducting their own inquiry. The head of the FBI, J. Edgar Hoover, decided within twenty-four hours of the assassination that Lee Harvey Oswald had committed this horrific crime by himself.

Two days after the assassination, Hoover sent a secret internal memo to his organization stating the following: "We will use the prestige of the FBI to convince the American public that Oswald is the real assassin." *Why?*

About two weeks later (December 9, 1963) Hoover reported to President Johnson that Lee Harvey Oswald was the lone assassin; there were three shots, three hits, no conspiracy, and the case was closed.

As a medical doctor, I find this especially difficult to accept. Furthermore, it's amazing how anyone, even the director of the FBI, could have formulated these conclusions so rapidly.

Layers Build over Time

In 1960 while attending the University of Illinois, I was fortunate to be in the audience to hear a speech by John F. Kennedy. At the time, he was campaigning for the office of the presidency of the United States. As he spoke I was completely mesmerized. To use an old cliché, the crowd was so quiet you could hear a pin drop. He captivated the entire audience with his charisma, youth, vigor, and eloquent way of speaking.

Do you remember where you were at the time of his assassination? Most Americans who were adults at the time remember. The nation couldn't believe what had happened.

For the second time, I was mesmerized; only this time, it was while watching a funeral procession. The man I respected and idolized was being put to rest—our youngest president was dead. John F. Kennedy was the very first president for whom I was eligible to vote, and I had voted for him. President Kennedy gave my generation the hope and courage that buoyed us to face the future unafraid. We were stunned when he was assassinated in broad daylight, right in front of our eyes. Our new spirit of optimism, hope, and confidence was fractured by the shot of a gun.

Time Moved On

For the next twenty years I didn't think much about the events leading to the assassination. But, several authors and researchers questioned the findings and conclusions of the Warren Commission. Among them were Josiah Thompson, David Lifton, Harrison Livingstone, Robert Groden, John Newman, Jim Maars, and Mark Lane. I read their work, which convincingly placed doubt on the findings and validity of the Warren Commission.

An Itch that Needed Scratching

I acquired a renewed interest in JFK, both in regard to his life as well as his tragic death. I deliberately obtained and read all related books and newspaper and magazine articles, and purchased all types of JFK memorabilia. I attended seminars in Chicago and Dallas that focused on the assassination.

At these seminars, I had the opportunity to meet and listen to Marina Oswald (the purported sole assassin's widow) as well as Oliver Stone, whose monumental movie *JFK* single-handedly pushed the Kennedy assassination forward into the public consciousness.

The movie, released in 1993, sparked an interest in that segment of our population that wasn't even born at the time of the tragedy. The more I read, the more I questioned the findings of the Warren Commission. I began to feel that my countrymen and women and all people had been outrageously deceived about what really happened on that fateful day.

Kennedy Buyer Is Born!

On November 22, 1996, my daughter, Kennedy Buyer, was born. It's not a coincidence that her first name is Kennedy; she was born on the anniversary date of JFK's demise. And, I adore her too much and have too much respect for her to permit her to be hoodwinked, misled, tricked, bamboozled, led astray, or taken for a ride by unscrupulous people when there's something I can do about it!

Much as a parent desires to ease the way for beloved offspring, it's often a one-step-forward, two-steps-backward type of challenge. But, here, I feel strongly that I can make a difference, and so I wrote this book.

Kennedy's edification is not the only reason I decided to write this book.

The population today is primarily made up of people born after 1963. As a result, the majority of Americans have no memory of 1963 at all. Great numbers of young people are in the same position as my daughter. When they ask *who* really murdered President JFK, the preponderance of answers they receive via the Internet and from other readily available sources is poised to hoodwink, mislead, trick, bamboozle—to lead them astray.

I'm not forgetting my contemporaries, either. I respect their right to know.

Here and Now

I feel obligated to do my part to reestablish history as the recording of truths. We live in the greatest country on Earth, and I want America to remain the greatest country on Earth!

We recently lived through the horrific events of September 11, 2001. A commission was set up to investigate the attack and to see if government officials were negligent in any way. Some blame was placed on our intelligence agencies and lack of communication. One hand did not know what the other hand was doing! Straight talk did not factor into the equation.

In 1963 the Federal Bureau of Investigation did not transmit vital information to the Central Intelligence Agency and vice versa. If this had not been the case, could the assassination have been prevented? If we had remedied the practice then, might the tragedy of September 11 been avoided? How else might the course of history have been changed if the sharing of information—full disclosure—had been standard operating procedure all this time?

Straight Talk

In 1963 few citizens thought to question government officials' modus operandi. In recent times, the public doesn't hesitate to question and second guess what they're told by officials and candidates for office. No doubt the flip-flop label that attached to presidential candidate Senator John Kerry was partly responsible for his November 2004 defeat at the polls.

We have a great regard for straight talk and for the truth, and we're in good company. William Shakespeare wrote, "No legacy is so rich as honesty." Thomas Jefferson wrote, "If a nation expects to be ignorant and free, it expects what never was and never will be." If you believe the truth helps to keep us free, then you further appreciate why I wrote this book for my daughter—for all daughters and sons.

* * * * * *

After much intensive reading and research, I concluded that a single assassin did not kill JFK.

There is too much evidence that points to the fact that he was killed by more than one individual, each shooting from a different angle. By definition, this would mean there was a conspiracy responsible for the death of President Kennedy. I believe there were two conspiracies:

- The assassination

- The post-assassination cover-up

During the past ten years, several books have been written about the assassination. Many of these have discussed the possibility of a conspiracy. In addition, newer books focus on different aspects of Kennedy's time in office (e.g., handling of the Cuban missile crisis), his wife, Jacqueline, and their children. These books are important when it comes to learning about the president's life and times. We especially need this information to help us find and make sense of motives.

But ... *who really murdered JFK?* The question begs to be answered.

I'll share with you what I've discovered during the past thirty years of interested-citizen research. I'm not a historian or scholar, though I'm a physician, and all physicians are trained to be researchers. You already know I accumulated a large amount of knowledge of these events through reading, viewing, and listening. I have documented and referenced my sources as best as I could. My earliest investigation was initiated because of personal interest. At the time, I didn't give a thought to writing a book, and although I accumulated materials, I didn't always record sources. You have only to turn to the back of this book, however, to see that reference citations and attributions fill more than a dozen pages. *Why the JFK Assassination Still Matters* is laden with verifiable straight talk!

Known and Undisputed

- JFK was assassinated on November 22, 1963, in Dallas, Texas.

- The governor of Texas, John Connelly, was wounded in the same attack.

- Lee Harvey Oswald, the alleged assassin of the president, was murdered by a man named Jack Ruby just two days later, on November 24, 1963.

Ignored, Altered, and Suppressed

We're told that documents regarding the assassination have been stored and locked away, only to be made available to the public many years from now. *Why?*

We're told if pertinent documents relative to the assassination got into the hands of certain foreign or domestic parties, this could compromise our national security. I believe this is a legitimate reason for restricting information, although I'm not sure how any such document could now affect our national security, because the assassination did occur over forty years ago.

Is there another reason for restricting information? I doubt if any document still contained in the archives will reveal all the details of what actually happened on November 22, 1963. Most of the pertinent information has already been released. I submit to you that this and other pertinent information has been misused and misinterpreted to fit the government theory of a lone gunman.

Allow me to prove it. To put it bluntly—It's time for me to put up or shut up!

Section One

THE CRIME AND THE VICTIM

Medical Evidence: Parkland vs. Bethesda

The primary reason this case has never been solved (despite the government contention that it was solved) is the fact that there is an enormous amount of disagreement and discrepancy regarding the medical evidence. The direct observations made at Parkland Memorial Hospital, where the president was first taken following the shooting, are at complete odds with the autopsy results and subsequent Warren Commission Report. The autopsy photographs and X-ray findings tend to disagree with both of these. Eyewitness reports are ignored unless they agree with what government officials want us to believe. It's not surprising that the American public has been confused. The greatest source of controversy in the John F. Kennedy assassination stems from the medical evidence and what was observed by two separate groups of physicians and other ancillary personnel at two different locations: Dallas, Texas, where the assassination actually took place, and Bethesda, Maryland, where the official autopsy took place a few hours after Kennedy died.

In 1963 the assassination of the president was not considered a federal crime in Texas. As a result, the jurisdiction for the investigation was within the state of Texas. By law, the federal government should not have been involved. In case of a violent death, Texas law prohibited moving the body from the state without a coroner's inquest or autopsy. This mandate could be overridden by the governor but in this case, Governor Connelly was unavailable because he had also been shot. As a result, the Dallas County medical examiner, Dr. Earl Rose, a highly qualified forensic pathologist, began to make preparations to conduct the autopsy. He met with a great deal of hostility, primarily from the United States Secret Service.

At the same time, Lyndon Johnson decided he should be sworn in as the new president on Air Force One in Dallas. He believed the people needed to know the transition of power could be carried out in an orderly fashion even in times of unimaginable shock and sorrow. In reality, taking the oath of office was not necessary since he automatically became president when John Kennedy died. Still, he wanted the formal induction ceremony and insisted that Jackie Kennedy be there at his side. He felt she lent dignity to the proceedings, and he believed her presence made the transition of power indisputably final.

He would not fly back to Washington D.C. unless President Kennedy's casket was aboard the plane. Jackie Kennedy, who was still in shock from the horrific events, wanted the body of her husband flown to Washington without delay. She did not want to wait in Dallas for an autopsy. Although it was clearly against Texas state law, the Secret Service insisted the body of the deceased President be removed from Dallas. After a rather rigorous and combative argument with the medical examiner, arrangements were made to fly President Kennedy's body back to Washington D.C. and have the autopsy performed there.

Bethesda Naval Hospital was chosen by the first lady because her late husband had been a distinguished member of the navy during World War II. In fact, he was considered a hero with the PT 109 episode. Mrs. Kennedy did not realize (and probably was never told) there weren't any trained forensic pathologists at Bethesda to conduct the autopsy.

Lyndon Baines Johnson took the oath of office aboard Air Force One at approximately 2:38 PM and was sworn in as the thirty-sixth president of the United States of America. Jacqueline Kennedy refused to change her clothes and was in attendance still dressed in her blood splattered pink suit.

"I want them to see what they have done to Jack," she lamented.

Could this simply be a statement from a shocked widow, or did she really believe there was more than one assassin?

The investigation into the assassination of JFK produced more questions than answers. The president of the United States had been assassinated in broad daylight in front of thousands of people. Yet the culprits and the motive for his killing have never been satisfactorily explained to this author, let alone the rest of the population. Government officials relied upon the "impossible" conclusions of the Warren Commission to convince the public this case had been solved. Though most people were initially very accepting of the government's lone gunman version, some immediately questioned the findings and were vocal about the likelihood of a conspiracy.

An Overview of Events

As this chapter unfolds, some information is repeated more than once. This has been done in an effort to untangle a profusion of material and make it easier for the reader to follow along especially when new information is added. Readers should expect some graphic descriptions to be upsetting.

- Immediately after the shooting, Kennedy was rushed to Parkland Memorial Hospital, at that time considered one of the leading trauma centers in the state of Texas.

- Once the limousine reached the hospital, Kennedy was seen by one of the hospital attendants who stated, "I knew the back of his head was blown out. I felt that Jackie shouldn't be getting her hands under there because there would be nothing but blood."

- Agent Clint Hill was the Secret Service agent responsible for the welfare of Jackie Kennedy, and he climbed onto the back of the presidential limousine right after the shooting. Jackie had climbed onto the trunk of the limousine in what appeared to be an effort to retrieve part of her husband's skull and scalp after it was blown out. Agent Hill attempted to stop her. He described the president's head wound as follows: "The right rear portion of his head was missing. It was lying on the right seat of the car. His brain was exposed."

Therefore, we have two eyewitnesses who by their direct observations indicated that the fatal shot to the president's head came from a location that was in front of the president. A large exit wound in the back of the head as described by both of these witnesses could only have been caused by a shot fired from the front. This would occur as the president was approaching the grassy knoll. A shot fired from behind or the side would have caused the exit wound to be in a different location.

- When he was first seen and examined in Trauma Room One at Parkland, the president was described as ashen, having agonal respirations (ineffective nonspontaneous breathing), having no voluntary movements, and having dilated pupils and no palpable pulse. This is virtually the description given to someone who is declared dead on arrival. Resuscitative measures were carried out probably because he was the president of the United States. President Kennedy was pronounced dead about thirty minutes after the actual shooting.

- It was while the physicians and nurses at Parkland were attempting to save the president's life that further observations were made of the president's nonfatal and fatal wounds. The Parkland Hospital physicians were the best eyewitnesses to the president's wounds. They were the only trained individuals to examine the president immediately following the shooting. Their observations should have provided the most reliable clues as to the shooters' locations and the bullets' trajectories. The primary point they all made was that there was a large gaping hole in the back of the skull on the right side. The size was estimated at 5 x 7 centimeters. Medically speaking, this would be in the location of the occipital-parietal area of the brain. In addition, several observers said that part of the cerebellum had fallen out. Everyone who observed the president when he was brought to the emergency room (probably at least twenty to thirty people) said the same thing—a massive wound at the back of the head.

You do not have to be a gun expert to know that the entrance wound of a bullet is very small and that as it traverses its course, the bullet explodes and leaves a very large exit wound. This fact would indicate that the president had to be shot from front in order to sustain such a large and fatal wound to the back of his head. This knocks out the lone gunman theory and supports the conspiracy theory, because all agree that Oswald was always located behind the presidential limousine and therefore could not have fired from the front.

- The Parkland physicians' responsibility was to report what they observed. In addition to describing the "exit" wound in the back of his head, the Parkland physicians and nurses described a small oval wound at the front of the throat, near the area of the Adam's apple. They determined this was an entry wound. Remember, they were experts and took care of thousands of cases involving wounds from gunshots. It was described as a small 3 to 5 millimeter wound of entry. Because of its location over the anterior neck, it became the site for a tracheotomy performed by the physicians at Parkland as they valiantly tried to save JFK's life. The opening was widened for the tracheotomy.

- The Parkland personnel were all sworn to secrecy and told never to reveal their findings. This was at the threat of losing their jobs and possibly even their lives. This secrecy lasted until 1992 when Charles Crenshaw, a surgical resident at Parkland in 1963, came out and said emphatically that the bullets struck the president from the front. Dr. Crenshaw's book, similar to the movie *JFK,* seemed to again ignite the controversy about a conspiracy in the assassination.

On to Bethesda

JFK had been assassinated. Questions needed to be answered. Who would believe that the autopsy would create more questions than answers?

- The federal government chose three military physicians who never did a forensic autopsy before to perform the postmortem examination on the man who had been president of the United States. *This decision defies all logic, common sense, and rationality.*

- The three military physicians chosen were James J. Humes, Director of the Naval School Laboratories in Bethesda and Commander of the Medical Corp of the United States Navy; Thornton Boswell, Chief of Pathology at the Naval Hospital; and Pierre Fink, of the United States Army. Fink did have some experience in forensic pathology and wound ballistics, although he acted primarily as a consultant in this case. Humes and Boswell were the pathologists in charge of the autopsy, although they were probably taking orders from some of their military superiors. Not one of them was a full-time forensic pathologist, which by definition is an expert to determine the cause of death in criminal cases. In fact, when Dr. Humes testified before the Warren Commission a few months after the assassination, he said that his training was primarily in natural disease and death rather than in violence. He admitted to some dealings with cases of violent death and then added that he had taken a course in forensic pathology as part of his overall training in pathology.

- Surely there had to be other physicians available who were more qualified and experienced. Several renowned individuals have voiced their opposition to the selection of these pathologists, though unfortunately they did so several years after the autopsy was performed. Dr. Cyril Wecht, one of the nation's top forensic pathologists said, "Humes and Boswell had never done medical-legal autopsies in their careers. It was really inept." Michael Baden, chief medical examiner for the City of New York and the chair of the House Select Committee on Assassinations Medical Panel stated, "Humes had never autopsied anyone with a gunshot wound. The three doctors didn't know the difference between an entrance and an exit wound."

Who made the decision that these three physicians would be the ones to perform possibly the most important autopsy in history? We still don't know the precise direction the shots were fired from and how many shots were fired. An autopsy typically provides these answers.

The Findings at Bethesda

Foremost is the finding made by Humes, who described a massive wound (six inches or thirteen centimeters), chiefly involving the right fronto-parietal bone, but extending into both the occipital and temporal bones. This defect was devoid of scalp and skull and was located toward the top of the head and forward.

This wound was at least two to three times as large as the wound described at Parkland, which was located more toward the right posterior aspect of the skull.

An exit wound located in the anterior aspect of the skull would indicate an entry from behind whereas an exit wound located in the posterior aspect of the skull would indicate an entry from the front—two completely opposing views.

- The pathologists claimed the fatal shot to the head had been fired from the rear, had blown away two-thirds of the right cerebrum, and had been fired by a high velocity rifle. It must be remembered that the

Mannlicher-Carcano, the rifle said to be the one used by the assassin, was a bolt-action rifle and would certainly not be considered high velocity.

The next discrepancy involves the anterior and posterior neck wounds.

- The autopsy pathologists describe a rather large wound in the anterior aspect of the president's neck, therefore believing that this wound was one of exit. It wasn't until the following morning when Dr. Humes talked to experts in Dallas that he found out this neck wound was the site used for the emergency tracheotomy done in an attempt to save the president's life. He was told that a small oval wound was present initially (said to be a wound of entry), and this had to be expanded in size for the tracheotomy. There should have been an effort by Dr. Humes to consult with the Parkland physicians on the eve of the autopsy (rather than the following morning) to obtain all of the original findings and learn about procedures done on the president that could have influenced the autopsy findings. I would assume he would want to know what was seen and reported by the physicians at Parkland prior to the arrival of the president's body in Washington. How could he even perform an autopsy without knowing if any of the original anatomy had been altered at Parkland?

Was It Incompetence?

The posterior neck wound also became a puzzle for the pathologists. Initially, Humes described a low back wound (about five inches below the collar line) but he was unable to find the bullet or its exit track. Humes made the statement at this time that "dissecting the neck was totally unnecessary and would have been criminal." He stated that the second bullet (meaning that which pierced the neck) was not of overriding importance.

Speaking as a physician, I am totally shocked by these statements but have to consider that he was inexperienced and unqualified in cases of this type. These statements point to the incompetence of the pathologist.

- When Humes learned that the tracheotomy site was also the site of a bullet, he assumed (*or was told to assume*) that the posterior back wound had to become a transit wound, and that bullet had to have made its exit through the area of the tracheotomy. For this to occur (back to front direction), and to get the proper trajectory, the originally placed low back wound was moved up six inches and had now become a high neck wound. This is an example of the pathologist changing his report to accommodate a theory (*or to oblige someone who told him what to say*). In addition, by making this back wound come out through the front of the neck, he was also totally ignoring what the Parkland physicians told him—that they determined the anterior neck wound was a wound of entry and that its large size was a direct result of the tracheotomy.

Ignoring Evidence

It's easy to arrive at a particular conclusion if you totally ignore testimony that is contrary to your position. Being selective about which evidence was relevant was standard operating procedure throughout the entire investigation of Kennedy's assassination.

Humes submitted an amended autopsy report and this eventually became the basis for the single bullet theory, which was completely endorsed later by the Warren Commission. It was necessary for the back wound to be moved up in order to account for the proper trajectory Oswald needed in order to have fired the fatal shot from the sixth floor of the Texas School Book Depository. There is some difference of opinion as to who actually did move the posterior neck wound in an upward direction. Some say it was Dr. Humes, whereas others say it was reported by a member of the Warren Commission; possibly Gerald Ford, a future president himself and who recently died on December 27, 2006. The Parkland group never mentioned seeing a bullet entry wound in the posterior neck.

How could there be such a discrepancy between the direct and immediate observations of the Parkland staff and the results of the most important autopsy in history?

Notes Destroyed

There are many other aspects of the autopsy that are suspicious. The initial notes and the first draft of the autopsy done by Dr Humes were destroyed (burned) and the final report was obtained from his memory. What was he trying to hide and why would he burn the original documentations of what he himself had seen? His explanation was that the notes were stained with the president's blood, and he did not want the public to view this if the notes ever went on display.

- He made a second copy of the autopsy notes, strictly from his memory. This obviously could affect his graphs and measurements. It could never be as accurate as the original. Did Humes destroy his original autopsy notes because he felt they would disprove the idea of a lone gunman firing from behind? Did he want to keep certain observations secret so that the truth about the medical evidence would never be revealed? I personally suspect this was the case. However, it is probably something we will never know with certainty since James Humes died of lung cancer in 1999 at the age of seventy-four.

Artist's Rendition

The artist's interpretation of the actual location of the wounds was drawn based upon information supplied by Dr. Humes. The medical illustrator did not see any photographs, and he could not be sure if his drawings matched exactly the original autopsy report. However, the drawings did place the bullet high enough in the neck to accommodate a downward incline and trajectory so that it could exit low in the throat.

- What was not considered at that time was the true location of the bullet holes in the president's shirt and jacket. The rents in the clothing were located low in the back, about five to six inches below the top of the collar. This was virtually the exact spot that Humes initially placed the posterior back wound before he learned of the bullet wound in the anterior throat.

- In fact, Hume's original conclusion as to the location of the back wound was substantiated by the death certificate signed by Dr. George Burkley, the personal physician to President Kennedy. He placed the back wound at the level of the third thoracic vertebrae, which would be about six inches below the base of the neck.

This would have been too low for a bullet fired from the sixth floor of the Texas School Book Depository to have secondarily inflicted a wound in the low anterior neck. Was Humes truly conducting an impartial investigation or did he know ahead of time what he would avow at the autopsy?

Chaos Reigns

The autopsy was not done in a quiet room that would be conducive to allowing the pathologists to perform their job, probably the most important job they ever performed.

- The room was filled with people, and it's probably safe to assume they did not behave in a quiet, organized manner. Among the people in the autopsy room were physicians, technicians, radiologists, photographers, Admiral Burkley, the president's personal physician, and several people from the Federal Bureau of Investigation, Secret Service, air force, navy, and army.

- In addition it was reported there was direct communication with both Jackie and Bobbie Kennedy, the president's brother, who were located in rooms several floors above.

- The pathologists were outranked by many of the military personnel in the room and because of this one must wonder who really was conducting the autopsy. Who was giving the orders?

Elementary but Omitted

Valuable information can always be obtained by dissecting wounds during an autopsy to try to trace actual bullet tracts. This often gives vital details as to where the bullets came from and where they went. *This was never done by the pathologists at Bethesda.*

- From the onset, the autopsy seemed to show bias. It began with a description of the circumstances of the assassination based on information from newspaper or television reports. These all indicated that three shots were fired from the upper floor of the Texas School Book Depository. These events should play no role in a postmortem exam and yet these reports put out by the Dallas police and quickly interpreted by the media did seem to influence the final autopsy conclusions.

- Apparently, powerful people wanted to promote the single crazed gunman explanation. One man killed the president and no one else was involved. The end!

- By this time, everyone knew that Oswald was located behind the presidential motorcade at the Texas School Book Depository at the time of the shooting. If the autopsy could state that the fatal bullet had struck the president from behind, then by reasonable deduction, the killer also had to be behind the president. Since, by this time, the name Oswald was becoming familiar to nearly everyone in our country, the obvious deduction would be that President John F. Kennedy had been shot by Lee Harvey Oswald.

X-rays Surface

What happened to the autopsy X-rays and photographs, items that should have been considered vital to the medical evidence? Postmortem photographs are generally the most valuable documentary evidence in cases of violent death. They can give perspective to various points of reference, something that is impossible to verbally communicate. They were certainly taken during the autopsy, as they should have been. Or were they?

- The autopsy photographs and X-rays, first seen by the pathologists in 1966 (three years after the actual autopsy) and by the Parkland physicians in 1983 (twenty years after the assassination) displayed significant variation from both the Parkland testimony and the autopsy itself. The pathologists felt the photographs did not show things as they remembered.

- The X-rays illustrated a large head wound on the right forward side of the head, which did not extend to the rear. There is a significant amount of missing bone in this area. There was a large loss of skull and brain in the right parietal and frontal regions. It was estimated that two-thirds of the right side of the brain was gone. The occipital area (back of the head) was intact.

- This was in direct contrast to the Parkland observations (large defect in the right occipital parietal area) and, in fact, also disagreed with the autopsy findings where the wound was said to also involve the occiput.

A Fraud?

Multiple skull fractures were seen on the X-rays, and the right side of the face and right eye were missing.

- The latter was certainly not seen on the photographs (shows no damage to the face or back of the head) and was never mentioned in testimony by either those involved at Parkland or at Bethesda. This large defect would certainly not have been missed.

- In addition, the X-rays revealed a 6.5-millimeter fragment at the base of the skull with smaller metallic fragments coming from it going into the frontal lobe. This supposedly matched the bullet fired from the Mannlicher-Carcano rifle. This was also never reported at the autopsy.

- It's intriguing how bullet fragments can be seen in the frontal lobe if this lobe is indeed missing—a virtual impossible feat. It was later proved by Dr. David Mantik, a specialist in optical densitometry, that this object was not a bullet fragment but instead was placed over the X-ray film, virtually proving that it was a forgery.

Suspicious Photographs

The photographs also show marked differences from the observations made at Parkland and Bethesda in addition to differing from what was seen on the X-rays. The photographs were said to be of poor quality and clarity and had no documentation on them such as a case number, name, place, or date.

- They would never have been admissible in court. Of course, this case never came to trial, because the alleged assassin, Lee Harvey Oswald, was assassinated.

- Of great importance is the fact that the photographs reveal the head and posterior scalp with its attached hair to be completely intact. Nothing is seen missing from the back of the head or occiput. Well over forty eyewitnesses, both at Parkland as well as at Bethesda, said that there was a large defect in the back of the head. This area was not intact as depicted in the photographs. The photographs do not show the back of the head missing. Everything appears intact.

- After reviewing the photographs, the Parkland group said that what the photographs depicted was not what they observed when they first saw the president following the shooting. They said these photographs were inaccurate. Could these photographs have been taken of a different head and not President Kennedy's? Or could the photographs have been tampered with to conceal the existence of other bullet wounds and therefore other shooters and to change the direction of where the shots came from?

- Even Humes and his colleagues admitted that the skull and brain damage had extended down to the occiput. The photographs also showed a small bullet entry wound, located four inches above the external occipital protuberance, near the top of the head. This was never seen at Parkland or by any of the eyewitnesses at Bethesda. Humes, on the other hand, placed this bullet wound in the back of the head at the level of the external occipital protuberance, certainly lower than what the photographs or X-rays apparently showed.

- In large part, therefore, the photographs and X-rays did not agree with the autopsy findings and were certainly contrary to what was seen and reported at Parkland. It is almost as if the photographs and X-rays were of someone else and not President Kennedy. Some, in fact, have concluded that these brain photographs are not images of the brain of John F Kennedy and may actually be someone else's brain. In this way, the true nature of the president's head wounds would be suppressed.

- A substitute brain could be used to support the notion of a gunshot wound from the rear and to eliminate the possibility of a frontal shot. This has obviously never been proved but is certainly an interesting speculation.

There are many who feel that the autopsy photographs and X-rays have been altered to prove a back-to-front trajectory. Dr. John Ebersole, a radiologist present at the autopsy, said that a large fragment of bone was missing from the rear of the president's skull and was found on Elm Street in Dallas and was brought to Bethesda that night.

- This was photographed and was found to be proof of occipital bone that was blown out from the back of the skull. This should be proof of a shot from the front. That this was occipital bone was substantiated by Dr. Boswell, the prime assistant to Dr. Humes, although he contends that the occipital fragments were a point of entry. This was never revealed in the official autopsy report and was never reviewed by the Warren Commission. It should also be remembered that Jackie Kennedy is seen climbing on the back of the limousine, probably to retrieve part of her husband's skull; this is also obviously occipital bone that had to be going in a backward direction because of a frontal shot.

- In addition, one of the motorcycle policemen riding behind and to the left of the president was splattered with blood; this again could only be accomplished with a frontal shot.

- Dr. David Mantik, a highly regarded radiation oncologist and physicist, after studying the photographs and X-rays at the National Archives, concluded that it was not possible for a bullet to go straight from the back to the throat (as concluded by the Warren Commission) without causing significant and extensive damage to the spine, lungs, and bony structures of the neck. None of this was depicted by the X-rays.

- Actually, the photographs mysteriously disappeared for a time (supposedly given either to the Secret Service or Federal Bureau of Investigation) and were not even made part of the investigation conducted by the Warren Commission in 1964. It wasn't until 1977 (fourteen years after the assassination) that the members of the House Select Committee on Assassinations were able to review both the X-rays and photographs for the first time.

- It is also believed that many of the photographs taken at the autopsy are missing.

Why the Discrepancy?

What could have caused the marked divergence of opinion between two groups of physicians?

- The Parkland physicians said that the president was shot from in front and not from behind. This seemed to be substantiated by multiple witnesses along the motorcade route who believed that the shots came from the area of the Grassy Knoll.

- This is in contrast to the statements of the Bethesda pathologists who said that Kennedy was shot from behind, meaning the area of the Texas School Book Depository. This was later advocated by the Warren Commission and, in essence, helped frame the case against Oswald.

- The Warren Commission never conducted its own investigation and, in fact, relied on the data supplied to it by the FBI. In addition, it ignored or suppressed the testimonies of any eyewitness who might be considered in favor of a possible conspiracy.

- There are two possible explanations for this difference among the two groups of physicians. One is that they were completely wrong in their observations or that they lied about what they saw.

- There is no doubt in my mind that the Parkland physicians reported what they saw. They were experienced and familiar in dealing with cases of this type.

- On the other hand, the pathologists performing the autopsy at Bethesda were not. They conducted or were told to conduct a pathological autopsy strictly to determine the cause of death.

- These physicians did not conduct (and may have been told not to conduct) a forensic autopsy that would include sectioning of the brain, tracking the bullet paths for the proper trajectory, determining the exact points of bullet entrance, and so on.

- They made a major blunder by not consulting with the Parkland physicians prior to doing the autopsy to determine the original condition of the body when first seen following the shooting. Whenever I treat a patient, it is imperative that I obtain a past medical history. In the case of this autopsy, it was also imperative to know exactly where the president's wounds were and if they had been changed (as the anterior neck wound obviously was due to the tracheotomy incision).

- I believe that the Bethesda physicians were under extreme pressure in regard to reporting what they saw. The autopsy room was in chaos and people throughout the room were shouting out orders. Many of them outranked the navy physicians. The pathologists were not qualified to handle a case of this magnitude; only a forensic pathologist would be.

- It is probable the pathologists did the best they could, considering the circumstances. It is doubtful that they were part of a conspiracy cover-up, at least not knowingly.

Another Possibility

There is one other possible explanation for the divergence of observations and ultimate conclusions among the physicians. It is possible each group (Parkland and Bethesda) did report what they saw at the time. In other words, they were both right.

- This would mean that somewhere between Dallas and Washington, or in one of these cities, there was an alteration of the body of John F. Kennedy. This could explain the differences in what was seen at Parkland Memorial Hospital and Bethesda Naval Hospital. This theory may seem far-fetched, but it is certainly not any more unrealistic than quickly blaming Lee Harvey Oswald for the murder or in accepting the lone-assassin magic bullet theory and the pristine condition of the bullet.

- If we conclude that Kennedy was killed by a "lone nut" (Oswald), then we must also conclude that Oswald was killed by a second "lone nut" (Ruby). We must accept the premise that there was no conspiracy in either case. This is what the Warren Report says and what government officials want us to accept.

- Those of us who have always believed in a conspiracy resulting in the death of John F. Kennedy were partially vindicated in 1979 when the House Select Committee on Assassinations concluded that the president was probably killed as a result of a conspiracy but otherwise agreed with the Warren Commission.

David Lifton, a noted Kennedy assassination researcher, wrote a book entitled *Best Evidence* in which he espouses the possibility of body alteration. First of all, why would anyone want to or have to alter the body after the president was assassinated? The answer is really quite simple. It would have to be done to alter the facts about the shooting and to suppress and discount the Parkland testimony stating that the shots came from the front.

- If the Parkland observations were correct, then this would automatically indicate that more than one shooter was involved, because Oswald was located in the depository behind the president. This would, therefore, indicate a conspiracy. Altering the body (meaning surgically changing the location of the wounds to indicate a back-to-front direction) would conceal the true location of the shooters.

- In addition, altering the body would allow for the removal of bullet fragments from the body so that the actual weapon(s) used to murder the president could not be traced.

- Changing the wounds would also mean enlarging an entry wound so that it would be made to look like an exit wound. Finally, an alteration of the body would allow for the introduction of a "patsy" (Oswald) so that all further investigation and evidence would be focused on him. It would negate any reason to consider a political or international conspiracy. If the public could accept a single "demented" individual as the sole assassin, then they would not look further to discover the truth. If this theory is feasible (and nobody can say that it is not), then where was the alteration done?

Surgery around the Head

The answer has to be either Dallas or Washington or somewhere in between, meaning on Air Force One. The entire trip from Dallas to Andrews Air Force Base in Maryland covers 1,500 miles.

- There are other clues, which do point to the possibility of body alteration. The FBI had reported there had been surgery (preautopsy) around the head area. The FBI was dependent on the information they were furnished by the pathologists conducting the autopsy. This is something that Humes had mentioned verbally as he was doing the autopsy. One of his questions to the other pathologists involved in the autopsy was, "Where did this surgery around the head come from?"

- It certainly was not done at Parkland. Other than the tracheotomy, there was no surgery performed at Parkland. In addition, the report from Dallas was that the body of the late president was transported in an expensive bronze casket. The report from Bethesda, however, was that they received the body wrapped in sheets in a body bag.

- Finally, Commander Humes reported that there were many parasagittal lacerations in the brain. These would not have resulted from bullet wounds but from knife wounds, such as those used to remove bullet fragments, and would be much more likely.

- If the body was altered as has been suggested, the question remains as to where or how this was accomplished. However, if it is true, then we are dealing with a very sophisticated, complex, and well thought-out plan to assassinate the president of the United States. Several people had to be involved.

The Argument Against

The biggest argument against the body having been altered was that Jackie Kennedy was in very close proximity to her husband's casket throughout the entire trip back to Washington and, as a result, nobody could have gotten close enough to even consider changing the evidence in this way. Of course, we are assuming there was a body in this casket. What if the casket was empty? It seems as if there still are too many unknowns that continue to make this case virtually impossible to solve.

- The reality of the situation is that an autopsy was done, a report was written, and a conclusion was reached. All of the controversy occurred after the report was released to the American public. The official autopsy report declared that there were three bullets fired, all from behind the president. The Warren Report a few months later would agree. The first bullet completely missed the limousine. (This will be explained in a later chapter). The second bullet hit the president in the back of the neck, passed forward through Governor Connelly, then exited and was later found on a stretcher in a purely pristine condition (so-called magic bullet). The third bullet was the fatal shot that hit President Kennedy in the back of his head.

- Both reports mention three bullets as having been fired because this number had to match the number of shell casings found on the sixth floor of the Texas School Book Depository. Any number greater than three would have destroyed the single gunman theory.

Another Story

There is another version of the autopsy given by the FBI. There were at least two members of the FBI present during the actual autopsy, and what they heard obviously had to be told to them by Commander Humes. The FBI version agrees that there were three shots but differs by stating they all hit their target.

- The first shot hit JFK in the lower back, but an exit tract could not be found. It was considered a nontransit shot and was supposedly found on a stretcher at Parkland, possibly dislodged during the attempt at resuscitation.

- The second shot caused the fatal head wound to the president, and the third shot struck Governor Connelly, causing all his wounds. This version based on what the FBI agents heard during the autopsy would obviously preclude one shot passing through the president and hitting the governor and would, therefore, negate the single gunman theory.

- In fact, this version may have been compatible with the original autopsy findings until Humes learned about the bullet wound in the anterior neck and erroneously made it the exit wound for a shot also capable of hitting the governor.

Magic Bullet Theory

The magic bullet theory was offered by Arlen Specter a counsel for the Warren Commission and more recently a senator from the state of Pennsylvania. I believe this theory is a hoax. Unfortunately, the public accepted it, and it became the "nail" that sealed the case for the Warren Commission. The pathologists in essence assisted with the creation of the lone gunman theory and the magic bullet theory.

Humes originally spoke of the back wound as a nontransit wound with a depth of only 1 inch. He located it in the upper back six inches below the collar but could not find an exit for it.

- He did not thoroughly attempt to track this wound and assumed that the bullet had merely fallen out during resuscitative measures conducted at Parkland. When he finally spoke to Dr. Malcolm Perry at Parkland the following morning and learned of a bullet wound in the front of the neck, he assumed that the two wounds were related, changed his original observation, and made the back wound a transit wound with its exit in the front of the throat.

- He did this despite being told by Parkland representatives that medical personnel there felt the throat wound was an entrance wound, not an exit wound. Humes seemed determined to make all the entrance wounds come from behind. Was he following orders?

- In any event, the Warren Commission eventually used this conclusion to formulate its own version of the magic bullet theory. As you will discover in a later chapter, the single bullet theory was necessary to prove there was a lone gunman.

It is my belief that Lee Harvey Oswald never fired a shot at the president. However someone had to make it appear that he was the shooter.

What Do They Know?

The Warren Commission would later say that the Parkland physicians were simply mistaken. Where did these members of the government, chosen to investigate the assassination, get the audacity to question the medical expertise the Parkland contingent possessed? This is almost laughable but unfortunately it worked for many years and concealed the truth behind the assassination of President John F. Kennedy.

The *JAMA* Caper

In 1992 (nearly thirty years after the assassination) and in response to the pro-conspiracy feelings created by Oliver Stone's movie *JFK*, the *Journal of the American Medical Association (JAMA)* printed a series of papers whereby it tried to show that the autopsy conducted by Humes, Boswell, and Finck was representative of the true findings of the assassination.

- In other words, that the president was shot from behind by a single killer and the autopsy photographs were legitimate and proved the conclusions that were drawn by the three nonforensic pathologists at

Bethesda. This actually contradicted the statements made by Humes and Boswell in 1978 when they were interviewed by the House Select Committee on Assassinations. When shown the autopsy photographs and X-rays at that time, they said the wounds were not in the right place. The head and back wounds had moved.

- By this time, there had been numerous books written that had repudiated the autopsy photographs, the autopsy conclusions, and the findings of the Warren Commission Report. Foremost among these books is *Conspiracy of Silence* written by Dr. Charles Crenshaw, one of the Parkland physicians, who cared for JFK on that tragic day.

- *JAMA* also attacked Dr. Crenshaw personally by stating that he was not present during the autopsy. This was not true! The public was finally starting to question all these reports. Almost every poll taken around this time showed that the overwhelming majority of citizens believed President Kennedy had been murdered as part of a conspiracy and not by a single lone gunman.

- Why would *JAMA* take a stand on this controversial subject? It is a medical journal intended to inform physicians of recent advances in medicine related to treatment or diagnosis. It is not supposed to be a political journal. Yet by attacking the conspiracy theorists and upholding the official autopsy report, it was thrust into the middle of a very delicate situation.

- *JAMA* writers stated there was new evidence to present that would prove the official autopsy report to be accurate. There wasn't any new information! Humes simply said what he had said back in 1963.

In 1992, I attended a conference in Chicago in which the guest speakers were Dr Humes and Dr. Charles Lundberg, who at that time was the editor in chief of *JAMA*. I approached Dr. Lundberg and told him that I disagreed with his reports and that he certainly did not represent the majority of physicians who make up the American Medical Association. He didn't really seem to care what my thoughts were on this subject.

- His personal discussion at this meeting in trying to validate the conclusions of the autopsy as well as to substantiate the single assassin theory met with considerable disagreement and disfavor. In fact, I suspect that Dr. Lundberg and his associates wished they had not attended this meeting.

- Lundberg admitted that he knew very little about the assassination itself. He felt that his role was that of a journalist, and he was concerned only with those bullets that hit the president.

  Why would *JAMA* go out on a limb and publish these articles, which by this time would create more negative than positive feedback? Was it to attract readers to the journal or was there a more sinister reason?

- Was this part of a cover-up? The *JAMA* articles came out after the release of the movie *JFK* by Oliver Stone.

- Why did it take Humes and Boswell over thirty years to finally publicly state their case? Was this strictly in retaliation for the negative comments and provocative notions the movie presented regarding the autopsy?

- Were the *JAMA* articles timed to counteract the information presented by Oliver Stone in his historic movie? More importantly, whose idea was it originally to get *JAMA* and the pathologists together in order to refute what was said? I am certain it was not Dr. Lundberg's idea.

- I seriously doubt that Drs. Humes and Boswell would want to stir things up again on their own after remaining in the background for so many years. The answer probably rests with a few very powerful individuals (in the so-called military-industrial complex or the power elite) who did not want the controversy about the assassination rekindled. The movie had already done this, and new generations of Americans had been aroused and were already making troubling statements about a government cover-up.

I believe that a small group of individuals directly tied to the military- industrial complex was intimately connected with the conspiracy to assassinate the president. It was soon after the *JAMA* articles that Dr. Lundberg resigned his position as editor in chief of the journal. It probably would have been better if the articles were never published. They certainly did not vindicate the pathologists and probably made things worse. The concept of a conspiracy was becoming further ingrained in the minds of the general public.

Television Reporting

We know that all the physicians and nurses at Parkland who observed the body on November 22, 1963, were in agreement. They all held their own hands up to the occipital-parietal area and said this part of the skull was missing. This observation was indirectly corroborated by the televised report of Chet Huntley, a well-known television news anchor man, who was on the air at the time of the president's death. In trying to keep the nation informed, Mr. Huntley stated that "President Kennedy was shot through the right temple through his head." He credited this statement to Dr. Burkley, the president's personal physician.

Not Your Usual Murder

This was the gruesome assassination of the most important man in our country, the president of the United States. This was the man who was loved by the average citizen in our country. Part of our hearts and spirits were taken away from us when he died. We had the right to know why and by whom!

The "Botched" Autopsy

Why was the most important autopsy in history not done properly?

- The true bullet trajectories were never determined, because the bullet tracts were not dissected. In fact, Dr. Pierre Finck, the one pathologist experienced in forensic medicine, said that the autopsy team was "ordered by a general or admiral not to dissect the back wound."

- The brain was never sectioned to determine the path of the bullet. Without these results it was impossible to determine where the bullets came from or how many were fired.

- According to the *JAMA* articles, Humes said that two-thirds of the right cerebral hemisphere was missing. This difference could have been resolved by a thorough examination of the brain. (It's nothing short of *criminal* to have omitted this procedure.)

- The brain weighed 1,500 grams (normal weight about 1,350 grams for an adult male age forty to forty-nine). How is it possible for the brain to weigh this much when large portions were supposed to have been missing?

- Could the brain examined in the autopsy have belonged to someone other than President Kennedy?

- Two weeks after the assassination, a supplementary report was submitted and eventually given to the Warren Commission. It's believed (at least by those who suspect a conspiracy) that there were two separate examinations of Kennedy's brain. The first examination took place a couple of days after the assassination and showed findings thought to be consistent with a shot from the front.

- This would completely negate the single gunman from behind theory and would support a second gunman shooting from in front of the limousine. This would be contrary to the government version. This first examination was done by Humes and Boswell.

- About two weeks later, a second examination was done, this time attended by Humes, Boswell, and Finck. Why did a second examination of the brain even need to be done, unless it was to change the findings found during the first exam?

Because the evidence pointed to a shot from behind, the conclusion must be that a second brain was substituted for the first. In addition, the autopsy X-rays showed the cerebellum to be intact, whereas all witnesses said there was extrusion of the cerebellum from the occipital-parietal wound. Was there a second brain used in the investigation? Another Person's Brain:

- Multiple deep linear lacerations of the brain tissue were found (from the occipital to the frontal lobes). Humes stated he didn't make them. Who did? The linear lacerations didn't match what a bullet wound would do. They were compatible with what a knife could achieve. Lacerations could also be made to extract bullets from the brain and thus conceal the real bullets fired.

- The brain was easily removed from the cranial vault, and, in fact, the autopsy physicians were able to lift it out. It was as if the supporting structures had previously been cut. This could only be done if the brainstem had been surgically cut. By whom? It was certainly not done by the autopsy physicians.

- Following the autopsy, the photographs, X-rays, and physical evidence including tissue slides, bone fragments, and the president's brain (preserved with formaldehyde) were transferred from the Bethesda Naval Hospital to the custody of the Secret Service, where they were stored in a locked cabinet under the control of Admiral George Burkley, President Kennedy's personal White House physician.

- These items remained there (either forgotten or ignored) until April 1965, more than a year after the Warren Commission had issued its final report. At that time, Robert Kennedy, then a senator from New York, instructed Dr. Burkley to transfer this material to another location, under the care of Evelyn Lincoln, President Kennedy's personal secretary.

- Later the material was transferred to the National Archives. In October 1965 an inventory was made of these items, and it was discovered that all the physical specimens, including the brain, were missing. The most crucial evidence in the assassination case had disappeared.

- Photographs that turned up later were said to be printed on paper that was different than paper used in 1963.

- In 1966 under the influence of the Justice Department, as well as President Johnson himself, there were two affidavits signed by the autopsy surgeons stating that the photographic file was complete and that it substantiated the autopsy conclusions given to the Warren Commission.

- These pathologists had changed their testimony and now contradicted themselves. Were they coerced by a higher authority to sign the affidavits?

- It must be remembered the investigative arm of the Justice Department is the FBI. Who was really in charge of the autopsy? And, who was in charge of the cover-up?!

Could They All Be Correct?

The medical evidence is fraught with contradictions and opposing views. One says that the president was shot from the front; the other says that he was shot from behind. Who is telling the truth? I contend that each is accurate!

On November 22, 1963, John F Kennedy was assassinated and was shot from both the front and the back. In other words, he was assassinated as the result of a conspiracy. This theory of multiple gunmen far outweighs the theory of the lone gunman.

Zapruder's Final Straw

There is one more vital piece to the puzzle of the medical evidence: the Zapruder film. Abraham Zapruder, a Dallas-based dress manufacturer, wanted to film the president riding in the motorcade. He stationed himself on a small pedestal on the western section of Dealey Plaza with his new Bell and Howell 8-millimeter movie camera. At the time of the murder, he had just left his office at the Dal-Tex building (virtually across the street from the Texas School Book Depository) and was facing south toward Elm Street. He had the perfect vantage point to film the motorcade.

- He was located just 185 feet from the southwest corner of the Texas School Book Depository and was only 65 feet from the center of Elm Street. He was able to film the entire motorcade essentially in one continuous shot from its sharp turn down Elm Street (off Houston Street) all the way to the triple-tunnel underpass.

- As Zapruder awaited the presidential car, his camera was recording. When the limousine approached, shots rang out. Zapruder didn't realize the president's assassination was in progress, and he was filming it.

- This was by far the most important eyewitness account of the events in Dealey Plaza on that fateful day.

- The Zapruder film was the one eyewitness that the Warren Commission could not ignore. Yet, the agent in charge of the Dallas FBI office made the comment that he doubted whether the Zapruder film had any evidentiary value. He said this before he personally had viewed the film.

- He was demeaning a real-time, visual account of the assassination, which to most people would be considered the most crucial piece of evidence available.

- What was the FBI (or at least this agent of the FBI) afraid of? Was there something on the film that they did not want the public to see? Could this be considered a cover-up?

- The film itself lasted only twenty-six seconds and encompassed 486 frames. It captured events at 18.3 frames per second. People have analyzed this film frame by frame and were even able to determine the timing of the shots.

- The proponents of the film say that it refutes the Warren Commission single bullet and lone gunman theories. They say that more than three shots were fired from more than one direction and this by itself should define a conspiracy.

- It was determined that 2.3 seconds was the minimum time that two shots could be fired from the Mannlicher-Carcano rifle, the alleged rifle of the alleged assassin Lee Harvey Oswald.

- An analysis of the Zapruder frames shows that Kennedy and Connelly each reacted to being shot in less than 2.3 seconds. This was obviously less than the time needed to have fired the rifle on two separate occasions. A single gunman could not have fired two shots that quickly and therefore, there had to be two separate shooters firing nearly simultaneously. This meant a conspiracy.

- This in turn led Arlen Specter, at that time a junior counsel member of the Warren Commission, to come up with the magic bullet theory. This basically said that one bullet went through the president to cause all the injuries to the governor. The bullet was recovered off the governor's stretcher in an unscathed pristine condition.

- Although many individuals (including some of those on the Warren Commission) questioned the feasibility of this theory and knew there was no definite proof to substantiate it, it was nevertheless accepted as plausible considering the circumstances and rumors (most unfounded) behind the assassination.

What Happened to the Film?

Abraham Zapruder sold the original film to the *Life* magazine empire the day after the assassination for $150,000. (This is equivalent to approximately one million dollars in today's economy.) *Life* magazine executives didn't make immediate use of the film.   They kept it under wraps for over ten years, although they did release a few isolated frames in 1964. Obviously, they didn't recoup investment dollars. *Why?*

Did the publisher conceal the film because it was connected with certain individuals who may have been associated with the assassination? The publisher retained all rights to the Zapruder film, although it did furnish copies to the Secret Service, the FBI, and the Warren Commission.

This represents a corporate ownership of a vital part of our history, probably the most important piece of evidence concerning the assassination. By keeping the film from the public, it hindered nongovernment investigations of the assassination. In any event, the public was not able to view the film for about twelve years after the assassination.

Too Gruesome?

Earl Warren, the appointed head of the Warren Commission, saw the film but indicated it was too gruesome to show to the public. The film was not available to be viewed by the general public until 1975.

There are those who say the Zapruder film has been altered. It's not surprising that those who argue against the legitimacy of the Zapruder film are the same people who argue against the possibility of a conspiracy.

The assassination of John F. Kennedy was captured on film as it was happening. The truth is (or was) there for all to see.

One, Two, Three

Here's why Zapruder's film shoots down the lone gunman theory:

1. All the shots were fired within 42 frames of the Zapruder film at a speed of 18.3 frames per second. This meant the minimal firing time between shots was 2.3 seconds. The amount of time needed to operate the bolt action of the Mannlicher-Carcano rifle (load, cock, aim, fire, and reload) was more than 2.3 seconds and therefore could not account for the shots fired. (A former sharpshooter telephoned me to

say he was one of those asked to see if he could reproduce the speed of firing of the Mannlicher-Carcano rifle as Oswald supposedly did. He told me, "No expert marksman was able to reproduce these results even at a stationary target.") By the way, Oswald was never considered a good marksman, especially by United States Marine's standards.

2.   The Warren Commission accepted the explanation that the bullet hit the president in his back, exited through his neck, and hit the governor, thereby causing all his wounds (i.e., the magic bullet theory). In the Zapruder film, it's easy to see President Kennedy reacted to being shot at a distinctly different time than Governor Connelly. The president raised his elbows when he was hit. At that moment, the governor was still looking ahead and then had time to turn around to view the president. Governor Connelly always maintained that he was not hit by the same bullet that wounded President Kennedy. He did not believe the single gunman theory. At the time he was hit, he yelled out "My God, they're going to kill us all."

A bullet was allegedly found on the governor's stretcher at Parkland in pristine condition. It supposedly penetrated multiple layers of skin and fabric and resulted in the fracture of at least two bones (Kennedy's ribs and Connelly's right wrist).

Now You See It, Now You Don't

There should have been a marked deformity of the bullet if all this was accomplished. The bullet left behind more fragments in Connelly's wrist than were missing from the bullet. In addition, there was no blood or fabric seen on this bullet. Finally, for this bullet to have been fired from the sixth floor of the Texas School Book Depository on a downward trajectory, hit the president's neck, exit from his anterior neck, hit Connelly's back, exit from the axilla, fracture his right wrist, and then finally imbed in his left anterior thigh, the bullet would have had to go in a zigzag course, change directions in midair, and truly defy the laws of gravity!

•   The most important piece of medical evidence favoring a conspiracy and brought out by the Zapruder film dealt with the infamous "head snap." This was seen at Zapruder frame 313 and designates the fatal head shot. The film shows the president lifting his arms as he reacts to the first wound and a few seconds later, his skull explodes into a red burst. He is thrown backward and to the left as he spins off into his wife's lap. This backward thrust could not possibly have occurred from a bullet fired from above and behind.

The impact of a bullet shot from a high-powered rifle will force the object that is hit to move violently away from the source of the shot. A backward deflection of the head would indicate a shot from the front.

Some people contend there was a small forward thrust of his head prior to the backward deflection. Others say that the president's reaction was a neuromuscular reaction. Some even believe that the Zapruder film has been altered and spliced and therefore isn't reliable.

Without the Zapruder film, the case against Lee Harvey Oswald and the lone assassin theory would have been more difficult to refute. It cannot be ignored as a prime piece of medical evidence.

Who Do We Believe?

- Do we trust the experience of those doctors at Parkland who were in the best position to see the president's wounds right after the shooting?

- Do we rely on the forensic inexperience of the government pathologists who tried to conduct an autopsy under extremely chaotic conditions? They were novices who changed their original conclusions, burned notes, and ignored the tracheotomy site. They concluded it was the site of an exit wound.

- Do we believe autopsy photographs and autopsy X-rays (seen several years after the assassination) that contradict the testimonies of both the Parkland and Bethesda medical personnel?

- Do we believe the size of the president's brain was virtually the size of a normal brain considering the fact that all eyewitnesses (physicians included) stated that much brain tissue was missing?

- Do we believe that the president's brain is now missing or has possibly been stolen?

- Do we believe that a single bullet, shot from a very old and cheap rifle, could hit both men simultaneously, run in a zigzag course through the air, and be found in a pristine condition, especially after it had penetrated several bony structures?

No!

The president of the United States of America
was assassinated as the result of a conspiracy.

A Step Back in Time: JFK — Pre-Presidency Years

John Fitzgerald Kennedy was born May 29, 1917, to Irish Catholic parents. He was one of eight children and the second oldest son. The Kennedy family was extremely wealthy. Joseph Kennedy Sr., the father and patriarch of the family, was considered one of the richest men in the world at that time. He was a Harvard graduate who made his fortune through several ventures: banking, investing, stocks and bond manipulation on Wall Street, the movie industry, and bootlegging during the Prohibition era.

Joe, Sr. was outspoken on many issues. He stated that "money was the key to everything." It meant power and flexibility and commanded respect. He made no secret of his feelings that the poor and underprivileged were not capable of changing their circumstances. "They will always be underdogs because that's what they want to be."

On the other hand, and in direct contrast to his father, JFK was sympathetic to the underprivileged. He had a great deal of compassion toward them and realized how fortunate he was to be wealthy. He felt he owed his victory in the 1960 election to those who were less fortunate, and he would never forget the "common" man.

Joseph Kennedy Sr. wanted to be president. While he served as U.S. ambassador to England (1938–1939), he began issuing statements that were anti-Semitic and pro Nazi Germany. He espoused an isolationist policy for America in the upcoming war against Germany and, as a result, showed his lack of concern for England. This tirade on the part of the senior Kennedy soon brought an end to his ambitious political career. Franklin Delano Roosevelt, the sitting president, was enraged by Kennedy's remarks and appointed another ambassador to England. This ended any political aspirations the elder Kennedy harbored.

The dream of the father then turned to his four sons; one of them could be president of the United States. He reasoned that he could do whatever was needed to accomplish the goal. He had both money and connections to influence decisions. He was convinced that people of wealth were obliged to serve their country, and he wanted his sons to reach the peak of American political life.

He initially focused on his eldest son, Joseph Kennedy Jr., as a potential future president of the United States. Joseph Jr. tragically lost his life while flying a dangerous bombing mission over the English Channel in August 1944. Trying to compensate for the loss of his eldest son, Joseph Sr. responded by saying, "We must carry on like everyone else. We must continue our regular work and take care of the living because there is a lot of work to be done." This eventually became the Kennedy motto through all their times of misfortune and tragedy.

The next son in line to fulfill his father's dream was John F. Kennedy, the second oldest, and now the one to be touted as a future president. The future of the Kennedy sons seemed to depend on the will and desires of their father. Few fathers did as much for his sons as Joe Sr. did for his; yet few fathers demanded more of his children. He once said, "We don't want any losers around here. In this family we want winners. We would never accept second place." Ted Sorensen, President Kennedy's chief domestic aid, advisor, and writer, once referred to Joe Sr. and his involvement during the 1960 campaign as "someone who was never present, but whose presence was never absent."

John F. Kennedy was a very sickly and fragile child and faced death on more than one occasion. His childhood illnesses were not unusual and consisted of scarlet fever, measles, mumps, and chicken pox. There were no vaccines available for these illnesses at that time, and he seemed very susceptible to infection. Colitis, cystitis, hepatitis, and urethritis complicated his later years. As an adolescent, he had many confinements at the Mayo and Lahey Clinics for fever and various pains, generally undiagnosed. His most serious incapacity, however, was chronic debilitating lower back pain. This was caused by a congenital deformity of the spine that was complicated by osteoporosis and several post-traumatic events including an injury sustained while rescuing his crew during the *PT-109* incident.

During World War II, John F. Kennedy had joined the navy and was the commander of an American Patrol Torpedo boat (*PT-109*) in the Solomon Islands. On August 2, 1943, a Japanese destroyer rammed his boat and virtually sliced it in half. Lieutenant Kennedy valiantly saved the lives of his crew (ten men in all) by leading the wounded survivors through the water (requiring a three-mile swim) to a small island where they were eventually rescued. Kennedy risked his own life for his crew and became a wartime hero. He had established true leadership and this became a vital attribute in his future political endeavors. However, he paid the price of reinjuring his already weakened back. Kennedy experienced constant back pain throughout his life. He wore a back brace and even had difficulty lifting his own children. During the years 1954–55, Kennedy had three operations on his back that were considered life threatening. By the age of forty, he had been given last rites on four separate occasions. It was while convalescing from these near fatal events that John F. Kennedy wrote *Profiles in Courage.* This dealt with the stories of eight United States senators who fought for their beliefs despite very powerful opposition that threatened their political careers. It showed the pressures they experienced and the grace with which they endured them—the risk to their careers, the unpopularity of their courses, the defamation of their characters, and the vindication of their reputations and their principles. This book won a Pulitzer Prize and became a bestseller, though some feel this was accomplished through the work and influence of his father who manipulated the media into excessive coverage and major promotions.

The worst affliction, however, affecting the future president, which nearly did cost him his life and which remained undiagnosed for several years, was Addison's disease. This is a primary failure of the adrenal glands (two small glands situated on top of the kidneys) to function. By secreting certain hormones called corticosteroids into our system, the adrenal glands play a critical role in our ability to maintain our psychological and physical health by regulating metabolism, maintaining sexual characteristics, preventing infection, and handling stress and injury. Many of JFK's prior hospitalizations were in fact related to the Addison's disease that had not previously been diagnosed. Fortunately for the president, the hormone cortisone was discovered in 1947, and this proved to be the definitive and life-saving treatment for him. Not only did it keep him alive, but it also enabled him to eventually function as the president of the United States. Without cortisone, the disease is fatal. The Kennedy family, as well as JFK himself, always minimized the seriousness of his illnesses to the public, and in fact, denied the reports of his Addison's disease. They felt the public would be hesitant about a potential president who was not well, and therefore, his chance of election in 1960 would be severely hampered. Despite the fact that he was on many medications, including painkillers, no one ever doubted the ability of the president to make the proper decisions. These medications did not affect his ability to function as president. In the public eye, JFK appeared as the perfect example of youth, vitality, and good health. His main goal (unknown to the public) was to simply get through the day and appear vibrant and active. Mentally, he remained extremely sharp, especially in regard to his sense of detail and fact. These were essential traits for a president. Despite his many illnesses and treatments, Kennedy seemed to function without difficulty. He made his decisions rationally and with utmost thought and consideration for the safety of the people.

John F. Kennedy was a Harvard graduate. He initially did not show much interest in politics but eventually majored in international relations. His first true interest was journalism and writing. In 1940 his senior thesis was published as a book entitled *Why England Slept*. It was an appraisal of the events leading to World War II and dealt primarily with England's lack of preparation for the war. He believed England had ignored the warnings of Hitler and did not feel it would ever become involved in this war. He showed the shortcomings of democracy when confronted by a dictatorial government. John Kennedy had earlier spent much time in London, so he was able to see for himself the workings of the British government. He knew about the psychology of its people and its philosophy of appeasement, pacifism, and disarmament. Kennedy believed in taking the initiative and yet having your defense ready. He believed in being aggressive and at the same time being prepared. This philosophy would eventually carry over into his presidency, which would occur twenty years later.

Following his graduation from Harvard, Kennedy worked as a journalist and, in fact, covered the opening of the United Nations. His life took an abrupt change in 1944 after his older brother Joseph was killed in the war while flying an exceedingly dangerous mission. John Fitzgerald Kennedy found himself destined for the political arena. JFK had always been in the shadow of his oldest brother, Joseph, throughout his life—whether concerning their education and choice of schools (Choates or Harvard) or trying to compete in sports. Joseph was the natural athlete, whereas Jack was not. Jack was always trying to find his own identity. This rivalry even persisted after his brother's death, tragic as it was. Jack could not escape his brother's memory as their father now urged Jack to go into politics, virtually as a replacement for Joe Jr. Jack did not feel he had the right to refuse, even to pursue his own life, wherever that path would lead him. Under the influence and tutelage of his father as well as the influence of his maternal grandfather (Honey Fitz, himself a former mayor of Boston), JFK decided to fulfill his father's dream: the quest to become the first Catholic president of the United States. Was this also Jack's dream? This is something we will never know.

JFK was first elected to the House of Representatives from the state of Massachusetts in 1946 at the age of twenty-nine. He served in the House for six years, although he did not feel excessively challenged or stimulated by this position. In 1952 he was elected to Senate by defeating a very formidable opponent named Henry Cabot Lodge. In preparation for his campaign against Lodge, he personally traveled to both Europe and Asia so that he could learn for himself what was happening throughout the world. He had already established himself as a literary scholar (*Why England Slept* and *Profiles in Courage*) as well as a wartime hero (*PT-109*). Kennedy had a tremendous thirst for knowledge. This was his guiding force in making his decisions. Kennedy remained a United States senator for the next eight years and then ran for the presidency in 1960. JFK never lost an election during his political career. On January 2, 1961, at the age of forty-three, John F. Kennedy was inaugurated as the thirty-fifth president of the United States.

In 1953 Jack Kennedy married Jacqueline Bouvier. Jackie added dignity to the office of the presidency and eventually became the most popular first lady our country has ever had. She was widely respected by the foreign dignitaries with whom she made contact and was adored by all in our country. Jackie was a perfect complement to her husband. We all remember the heroism and courage she displayed at the time of the assassination. This was translated to her later years when her number one concern was her children. She never wanted her children to be in the limelight and did her best in helping them lead as normal a life as possible considering the circumstances. Jackie herself never enjoyed the political arena. She did not enjoy going on the campaign trail and, in fact, was advised by her doctors not to accompany the president on his Dallas trip. Nonetheless, at the request of her husband, she did agree to travel with him on this last infamous journey. Jackie was nearly as popular as the president himself and certainly added to his public persona.

JFK was a fatalist, something he most likely learned from experiencing the death of his older brother Joseph, the death of his sister Kathleen also in a plane crash, the death of a son Patrick only a few days after his birth, and his own potentially fatal Addison's disease. He believed in living for the present and regarding each day as if it might be his last. The mystique of the entire Kennedy family was to live and work for the present. What has happened has already happened, and the past cannot be undone. Do not grieve for any extended period of time. I suspect this is a very healthy philosophy though one which is very difficult to attain. Yet this is the motto that the Kennedys kept referring to when they have faced their numerous tragedies. This is the belief that has kept them so resilient despite all the adversity they have encountered.

In 1956 Adlai Stevenson was the Democratic nominee for the presidency, and JFK was nearly his running mate. In retrospect, it was probably advantageous for Kennedy not to have been the vice presidential candidate at that time. Because Stevenson lost the election in 1956, Kennedy probably also would have been considered a loser and might not have been able to reacquire public support for a potential presidential run in 1960. However, Kennedy aroused public interest and enthusiasm by giving a very powerful and moving speech in support of Stevenson and the Democratic Party. He had planted the seeds in the public's eye for a future candidacy, which he decided, would be in 1960. This is exactly what did happen. In 1960 Kennedy announced his candidacy for the president of the United States. His campaign slogan was "High Hopes" for the country and a new sense of optimism for the future. Kennedy considered the Eisenhower years as appealing to those people over the age of forty. He thought those years to be conservative and mediocre, with nothing special being accomplished and with nothing specific to look forward to. On the other hand, he wanted the Kennedy years to be the time where the emphasis would be placed on the youth. During his tenure, he wanted the young to play the prominent role in our society. JFK drew large crowds no matter where he spoke, and those who responded the most were the young people. Students hung on to every word he said. JFK was speaking for the youth of the 1960s and was truly their peer. I was a senior at the University of Illinois when I first heard JFK speak. He was charismatic, mesmerizing, tantalizing, and commanded respect. I felt he was speaking for me and was giving me hope for the future. This was his message for all the young people of that era.

However, his quest for the presidency would bring many obstacles. First of all, he was very young, actually the youngest candidate for president that the people ever had to decide upon. Secondly, he was Catholic and no Roman Catholic had ever been elected to such a high office. Even as a college student at Harvard, Kennedy faced difficulties that he attributed to his religion. He was not allowed into certain clubs and found himself associating with friends who were also Irish Catholic or at least sympathetic to their cause. Wealth did not seem to matter. Ethnicity and religion were something he was forced to overcome. The Catholic religion was in a marked minority and, in fact, not held in high esteem or regard by the majority Protestant religion. It was feared by some that Kennedy's Catholicism would become a liability in presidential politics. However, JFK met this issue head-on and actually used it to his own advantage. During one of his campaign speeches, he said, "Nobody asked me if I was a Catholic when I joined the United States Navy. Nobody asked my brother if he was a Catholic or a Protestant before he climbed into an American bomber plane to fly his last mission." Kennedy was trying to show the public that one's religion should not be the deciding factor when attempting to elect their future president and leader. He was succeeding in his appeal to the populace. In another one of his most famous quotations, he declared that he was not a Catholic candidate but instead, was the Democratic candidate for the presidency who just happened to be Catholic. JFK ran a very enthusiastic and energetic campaign and was victorious. He would be nominated as the Democratic candidate for the office of the presidency of the United States. Through his nomination, he would defeat Lyndon Baines Johnson, later to be selected as his vice president and only two and one-half years after that, to be the successor as president, following the assassination of JFK.

In the pre-1960s people were primarily involved with their own lives and not that concerned with the world around them. The expectations were not high, and it was felt that each succeeding day would be like the one before it. There seemed to be a general feeling of apathy in our country in regard to the past as well as the present and certainly in respect to the future. The average family income at that time was between $5,000 and $12,000 per year. Twenty per cent of American families during this period were classified as poor with earnings less than $3,100 a year. John F. Kennedy brought a new excitement to this time with a chance for prosperity and new hope. The country seemed to be looking for new avenues as well as challenges and JFK was the one to bring it to them.

In running for president, Kennedy's persona reflected courage, intelligence, and a voice for all people. His own personal wealth did not seem to be an issue even to the poor people. Kennedy was in the right place at the right time. The people needed someone they could look up to, and they needed someone who would look out for them. He was able to promise political and economic progress. He promised a space program superior to the Russians where the United States would be the first to set foot on the moon. He promised an end to poverty. Were these merely campaign promises heard at every election, to get the people to vote for him? Possibly so. Yet the people felt there was so much more. They were becoming entrapped in a state of euphoria. They believed in the excitement and glamour of John F. Kennedy and his New Frontier.

John Kennedy's opponent for the presidency was Richard Millhouse Nixon, the current vice president and a man of national experience. JFK had the charisma, but Nixon did not. The nation was ready for a new challenge, and they endorsed the young senator from Massachusetts who they felt could lead them to the New Frontier, certainly the pledge Kennedy had delivered in his vigorous campaign. John F. Kennedy took advantage of the most recent addition to the media: television. For the first time, the opponents in a presidential election would debate on national television in full view of the entire country. The issues were debated, but it was the appearance and personalities of the two individuals that would eventually determine who would come out on top. Kennedy was vibrant, enthusiastic, charismatic, well versed, and extremely capable of captivating his audience. His good looks and picture of health had a great influence on the viewers. JFK possessed a sense of humor that added to his appeal. On the other hand, Richard Nixon was overly serious, dry, less enthusiastic, and lacked the charisma that was bubbling over in his opponent. Nixon presented a "five o'clock shadow," a feature that diminished his appeal to the public. He certainly had knowledge of the basic issues, but it was obvious the public wanted a personality more than they wanted someone who seemed too rhetorical. In any event, it was clear that Kennedy fared much better than Nixon in these debates.

On November 9, 1960, John Fitzgerald Kennedy was elected the first Roman Catholic and the youngest man ever to be elected to the office of the presidency of the United States; he was only forty-three years of age. Yet this turned out to be the closest election ever held, up until the election of 2000. Kennedy won by a popular vote margin of only 112,881 votes. This was out of a total of 69 million voters and essentially comprised only one-tenth of 1 percent difference. On January 20, 1961, on a cold blustery day in Washington D.C., John Kennedy was give the oath of office by Earl Warren, the Chief Justice of the Supreme Court. This is the same Earl Warren who only three years later would head a commission to investigate the assassination of our thirty-fifth president.

During his inauguration speech, President Kennedy attempted to rekindle America's sense of idealism in order to tackle the challenge of a new era. He was known for his magic with words. Of the many famous quotations attributed to JFK that people of my generation long remember, I believe that the three most significant and meaningful were the following:

1. "Let the word go forth from this time and place, to friend and foe alike, that the torch has been passed to a new generation of Americans."

2. "Let every nation know that we shall pay any price, bear any burden, meet any hardship, support any friend, oppose any foe to assure the survival and the success of liberty."

3. "And so, my fellow Americans: ask not what your country can do for you but ask what you can do for your country." The new president had succeeded in stirring up the emotions and raising the hopes of his constituents. For the first time in a long time, the people were excited about their government and the direction JFK would lead them to. Nobody realized at the time that their newly elected president would have only a thousand days before he would be struck down by an array of assassin's bullets.

Section Two

ENEMIES AND POSSIBLE MOTIVES

III

Moving Right Along:
The Bay of Pigs and the CIA

By the time John F. Kennedy became president, World War II was in the history books. Two superpowers had emerged: the United States and the Soviet Union. A new struggle, known as the cold war, ensued. This struggle did not involve physical warfare but instead involved intense economic and diplomatic conflict. Both sides (the United States and the Union of Soviet Socialist Republics) developed atomic weapons in competition with each other, and this competition was known as the arms race. For the next several decades, it was a matter of East versus West, dictatorship versus democracy, and communism versus capitalism. (Great Britain and France had been allied with the United States during World War II, and a close liaison continued.)

Ninety Miles Off Shore

During the arms race, Fidel Castro assumed control of Cuba. Castro, who was wealthy and well educated, initially offered hope to the Cuban people who lived under Batista's oppression before Castro ousted him. However, Castro's dictatorship resulted in even greater impoverishment and persecution, and many Cubans fled their country and became exiles in the United States.

When I was practicing medicine in Arizona, I had the privilege of caring for two Cuban citizens, both physicians, who had been very prominent in their home country. They had fled Cuba because they were no longer allowed to practice medicine there.

The Line Forms Here

Castro's activities served as a thorn in the side to many including:

- President Kennedy and Attorney General Robert Kennedy
- The Central Intelligence Agency
- The Mafia (i.e., the well-established criminal element in the United States)
- Anti-Castro exiles
- All would certainly benefit if Castro were removed from power.
- The CIA was geared to stamping out communism everywhere.
- The Cuban exiles wanted their country back.
- Organized crime had a large financial interest in Cuba because it controlled all the resorts and casinos there.

In addition:

- Many United States corporations ran the sugar plantations in Cuba and did not want to lose control of them.

During Dwight Eisenhower's and Richard Nixon's terms of office, a program to invade Cuba and remove Castro from power was hatched. The Central Intelligence Agency was heavily involved in the project.

What's This?

The CIA, originally established in 1947 and formerly known as the Office of Strategic Services (OSS) had been chartered "to gather information so leaders of the government of the United States could make appropriate decisions based on national security." The agency was to collect and analyze information for the president about international events, which posed a potential threat to the safety of our country. The agency's mission was clear and concise.

We're the Good Guys

We would never undermine other governments, invade other countries with secret armies, spread lies, or plot to kill men in foreign countries who were against our form of government. Our history always placed an emphasis on political morality. This was the belief that the American people held onto so deeply.

However, the functions, purposes, and actions of the CIA began to change. The agency began to deal in overt actions such as sending paramilitary teams behind enemy lines to conduct sabotage and support and train guerilla forces. It was also dealing with covert and clandestine operations. These very secret and concealed operations were known only to the CIA. In the late 1940s, and during the Eisenhower administration, the CIA was especially powerful and feared. It had become an aggressive, proactive, clandestine warfare center, which was operated like an alternative government of the United States. The CIA furthered its scope of action to the overthrow of governments, assassination plots, paramilitary operations, and espionage operations. Among the foreign countries affected by the CIA were Iran, Guatemala, the Philippines, El Salvador, Nicaragua, and the Congo.

The CIA was supposed to be under the direction of the president. While conducting covert operations, it had to make sure that no responsibility was linked to the president, his staff or, other government officials. This was known as *plausible denial.* Since there could be no proof of government involvement or responsibility, written orders were never generated. Even though the CIA was said to be under the watchful eye of the president, it is my feeling that many of its operations were unknown in detail, even to the president. Examples would be the Bay of Pigs affair and President Kennedy's knowledge (or lack of knowledge) of its details and the assassination of foreign leaders. It took an executive order by President Ford, in 1976, to put an end to this outrage.

Ten different presidents left the agency to perform its own functions as long as they felt assured these dealt with anticommunism. It's worth noting the only president who did not act in unison with his predecessors and who wanted to disband the CIA, following the Bay of Pigs incident, was President John F. Kennedy. He did not live long enough to see this accomplished. And, as this chapter unfolds, you'll note many people felt threatened by Kennedy's intentions and actions.

A Legacy

John F. Kennedy was faced with his first major challenge as president only four months after being sworn in (April 1961). Beginning in January 1960, and with the full approval of the Eisenhower-Nixon administration, there were already definite CIA covert and overt operations being set up to get rid of Castro and rescue the small country of Cuba from communist control. This was the mission that became known as the Bay of Pigs.

Cuban exiles were trained under the direction of the CIA in Miami, New Orleans, and Guatemala to lead the invasion. The original plan called for an infiltration of Cuba by anti-Castro Cuban exiles in the United States along with Cuban dissidents still residing in their own country. This was predicted to result in an internal revolt against Castro, a successful takeover of government, and Castro's likely death. The CIA believed the Cuban exiles had enough support to overtake Castro and his forces.

As far back as August 1960, President Eisenhower had specified no U.S. personnel would be used as combat units in CIA operations. President Kennedy adopted the same position.

The director of the CIA at that time was Allen Dulles, later to serve on the Warren Commission in the investigation of the assassination of the president. The chief of operations of the CIA during this time, largely responsible for the planning of the Bay of Pigs invasion, was Richard Bissell.

The success of the Bay of Pigs invasion depended on multiple factors:

- A spontaneous uprising of the unarmed population of Cuba in conjunction with an amphibious landing on the Cuban coast by the anti-Castro rebels. This meant guerilla warfare, which had a poor track record because communication between cooperating parties was faulty, at best.

- The quality and impact of the political response within Cuba. The attack was estimated to include 3,000 people supported by 20,000 sympathizers, possibly 25 percent of the entire Cuban population. Yet, this group was to oppose a Cuban militia of over 200,000 men.

The CIA underestimated Castro's popularity and did not believe he could mount an effective counterinsurgency operation. They were wrong!

Neglected to Mention

With the information JFK received from intelligence agencies and advisors, he determined the operation could be carried out without overt American participation. It was never made clear to him that the CIA knew that a larger invasion to include U.S. air support would be necessary.

- It was assumed by the responsible parties in the CIA, as well as organized crime and the anti-Castro exiles, that the new president would go along with this invasion and not do anything to prevent its implementation and eventual success.

- This assumption proved to be wrong and devastating both to the Cuban exiles and the CIA and *possibly to President Kennedy himself.*

- The Bay of Pigs operation failed when the CIA went ahead with the planned invasion despite the fact that JFK refused to authorize the much needed air support.

Why Didn't JFK Support this Mission?

He said both publicly and privately that the United States would not intervene militarily in Cuba. He had insisted on plausible denial. Nothing could be traced back to the government. The operation must appear as if it was being organized from within Cuba. These were the guidelines the new president had advocated, and he did not intend to back down. In addition, Adlai Stevenson, then our ambassador to the United Nations, had also claimed we would not invade Cuba.

President Kennedy found himself in a dilemma. If he did not agree to the invasion, he would be accused of being a coward and soft on communism. This would not be the best way to begin his presidency, especially because during the election campaign, he had ridiculed Vice President Nixon for not standing up to Castro. If he did support the Bay of Pigs invasion, he feared there would be many repercussions. He had no love for Castro, yet he felt he did not want to involve our country in an assassination plot against another world leader.

Another major unfavorable consequence of a direct United States invasion of Cuba would be that world opinion (i.e., the United Nations, and the Latin American countries) would turn against us. It would not sit well with the rest of the world to see the mighty United States attack the small defense-less island of Cuba.

Attacking Cuba could also create a problem with West Berlin, our most valuable outpost behind communist territory. After World War II, Berlin was divided into an eastern section under Soviet control and a western section under the control of the United States. Each day, thousands of workers, many highly skilled and educated, would cross from East Berlin to West Berlin in the hopes of turning away from communism and acquiring a better life. The United States had to keep access to this west sector. JFK could not let the communists drive us out of Berlin. He had a commitment to all free people and, as a result, began building up our military spending, personnel, and civil defense. Kennedy was preparing for war. At the same time, Kennedy feared that our going into Cuba would be deleterious to our position regarding Berlin.

I remember this period vividly when many families built underground air-raid shelters in the event of a nuclear war. In addition, the air-raid siren would sound every week (in the Midwest, it was at 11 AM every Tuesday) so that Americans would know what to do in case the warning signal ever became a reality. This was a potentially devastating period because both countries were equipped for nuclear war.

This threat ended in August 1961 with the construction of the Berlin Wall that separated East from West Berlin. It blocked the migration of people from east to west but most importantly, it ended the potential for a major war—at least at that time.

JFK showed courage by not giving in. By not authorizing our involvement in the Bay of Pigs Affair, President Kennedy inadvertently was able to avoid any potential conflict over Berlin and possibly a nuclear catastrophe.

I don't believe that JFK was ever given enough positive credit for his action. Instead, he was given the blame for an operation that would probably not have been successful from the start.

The Bay of Pigs invasion was a disaster. The Castro army completely overpowered the anti-Castro contingent. The exiles were either captured or killed, and Castro was victorious. The powers behind this invasion were devastated. The CIA, Mafia, and Cuban exiles all felt betrayed by President Kennedy. They blamed JFK solely for the failure of this exposition. Kennedy assumed responsibility for the failure of the Bay of Pigs, although he blamed his advisors as well as the intelligence units for not fully informing him about the potential consequences of this mission.

The United States received international condemnation for defending the rebels against the lawful government of Cuba. Castro was now strengthened and had the full support of the Soviet Union. Our relations with the Soviets took a turn for the worse. JFK felt personally responsible for what the more than 1,300 rebels suffered—1,189 captured and in Cuban prisons and 140 killed.

There was a lack of trust in JFK's leadership abilities. Yet, despite this being the lowest point of his administration, the American people gave him an 82 percent approval rating, a true test of his immense popularity even at that time.

JFK felt betrayed by the CIA. He realized the CIA had acquired the power to do whatever it wanted, whenever it wanted. The president believed he had to prove the CIA served the presidency. After the failed attempt at the Bay of Pigs, Kennedy took steps to disband the CIA, and he fired its Chief, Allen Dulles.

Cuba and Castro, personally, were supported by the communist regime in the United Soviet Socialist Republics, headed by Premier Nikita Krushchev. If Kennedy had authorized the air support and Castro had been overthrown, what would have prevented the Russians from retaliating and starting another world war somewhere else? The fear at that time was that a third world war would be synonymous with all-out nuclear war. This was also the potential danger of the West Berlin crisis.

Hindsight Can Be 20/20

Was President Kennedy wrong in not wanting to chance a severe conflict with the Russians? Personally, I don't think so. He thought he was acting in the best interest of our nation, but he alienated the CIA. The CIA had become a much-feared organization and, in fact, had engaged in assassinating foreign leaders.

Who is to say the CIA could not turn against a group or single citizen of the United States if CIA operatives thought the security of the country was being threatened—even against its own president?

Assassination Attempt

In the fall of 1960, the CIA made a binding contract with the Mafia. A CIA-Mafia coalition to kill Fidel Castro continued until the middle of 1963. Prior to Castro's regime, the mob controlled Havana's casinos, bootlegging, prostitution, and drug trafficking. They had become very wealthy on this small island of Cuba, and they wanted it back.

- Those names affiliated with organized crime that are repeatedly mentioned in the Castro assassination plot are mobsters: Santos Trafficante from Miami, Florida; Carlos Marcello, from New Orleans; Sam Giancana, from Chicago; Johnny Roselli, from Las Vegas; Guy Bannister, a former FBI agent, from Chicago; and David Ferrie, an expert pilot and eccentric individual who had ties with Carlos Marcello. All of these people had a definite stake in the Bay of Pigs and felt deceived and betrayed by the failure of the president to support this mission.

- There is another individual who most certainly had ties to the various intelligence agencies as well as organized crime and his name was Lee Harvey Oswald. Oswald had handed out leaflets for the Fair Play for Cuba Committee (FPCC), supposedly making him pro-Castro and yet had been seen conversing and socializing with anti-Castro individuals, making it difficult to determine exactly what side he really stood on. Maybe he was being used by several factions and indeed was a patsy, as he so desperately claimed when accused of being the assassin of our president.

Decades Later

We're still close to the coast of Cuba. Cuba remains under the control of Castro, though due to recent health problems, Fidel Castro has turned over the operations of the country to his brother Raul. I suspect, however, that Fidel still holds the iron hand. I don't believe we have ever felt threatened by Cuba other than during the time of the Cuban Missile Crisis.

Today, as we piece together events leading up to Kennedy's assassination, it's important to reach back in time and remember The Bay of Pigs fiasco. The CIA, the Mafia, and the anti-Castro exiles were the three primary groups that felt betrayed by President Kennedy's failure to fully support the overthrow of Fidel Castro.

In addition, the leaders of the military-industrial complex, a group of extremely wealthy and powerful individuals, could not have been satisfied by Kennedy's decision that ultimately allowed Castro to remain in power. There was no shortage of enemies or motives for JFK's demise.

IV

The Cuban Missile Crisis

While the Bay of Pigs invasion has been declared to be Kennedy's biggest failure, the Cuban missile crisis has been judged to be Kennedy's greatest success.

On October 14, 1962, United States intelligence (through U-2 reconnaissance photographs) detected a missile buildup in Cuba. This constituted a grave danger to national security. These missiles were both long- and intermediate-range ballistic missiles, capable of carrying nuclear warheads. Our government considered these missiles offensive weapons and feared they would be used for an attack on the United States. (Remember, Cuba is situated only ninety miles off the coast of Florida.)

The Union of the Soviet Socialist Republics and Cuba, both under communist rule, shared mutual interests. The president of the USSR, Nikita Krushchev, claimed these weapons (supplied by the USSR) were to be used solely to defend Cuba against a possible invasion from the United States. Not only were the missiles to enhance Castro's defense capabilities, they clearly demonstrated the Soviet's intention to retaliate in the event of an attack.

Friends and Foes

Why would Russia fear an attack upon Cuba by the United States?

- Even though the Bay of Pigs was a failed mission, it had demonstrated a willingness to overthrow Fidel Castro's government and to assassinate Castro.

- Since the failure of that mission, concerns about Cuba remained a top priority within the United States. Robert Kennedy, the United States attorney general and brother to the president, openly displayed the same antagonistic passion toward Cuba that he displayed against organized crime and Jimmy Hoffa in particular.

American foreign policy was influenced by concerns about Castro and the perceived danger he and communism presented to Latin America.

Operation Mongoose: Strange Bedfellows

The failure of the Bay of Pigs did not dampen the enthusiasm to get rid of Castro. In fact, it probably enhanced it.

- The quest against Castro led to Operation Mongoose, a program of covert and overt operations against the Cuban dictator. The aim and goal was to kill Castro.

- Operation Mongoose was a joint cooperative effort of the Central Intelligence Agency and organized crime, better known as the Mafia.

- These two organizations, on opposite sides of the law, now worked together. Their goal was the assassination of the leader of a foreign country. (Did President Kennedy know of this liaison between the CIA and the Mafia? We don't know the answer.)

Missiles Proliferate

The Soviets knew the United States government had placed Jupiter missiles in Turkey and Italy, aimed toward the Russian border.

Even though these missiles were primitive (and probably militarily inept if they had been fired) and even though JFK had unsuccessfully tried to get these missiles pulled out of Turkey, they were there.

Initially, the Soviets denied there were any missiles in Cuba. After much perseverance and determination on the part of President Kennedy and his administration, it was finally admitted that there had been a buildup of weapons in Cuba essentially in line with our borders on the coast of Florida. We faced the potential disaster of nuclear war.

Kennedy's advisors and military personnel engaged in heated discussions regarding what our response should be to this potential threat to our National Security.

Concepts and Controversy

The military advisors, especially the Joint Chiefs of Staff, were virtually all in favor of attacking Cuba to show our military superiority. They proposed either a limited attack on the missile bases or a direct invasion of Cuba.

President Kennedy was diplomatic but forceful and determined. He expressed his fears, yet attempted to exert pressure. He assumed the Soviet leader would not "deliberately plunge the world into war which no country could win and which could only result in catastrophic consequences to the whole world." Kennedy learned from his experience during the Bay of Pigs and never acted in haste. He knew his decision had to be one that would result in a favorable outcome for the United States. He could not afford to make the wrong decision when the threat to the United States was so serious.

He listened to all options and opinions and paid careful attention to those who thought differently than he did. Kennedy did not believe in military intervention and had a profound distrust for the military and its potential rule of the country. He felt he had been coerced by both the military and the CIA before. He focused squarely on the people he served and based his decisions on how they would be affected. He was especially concerned with how his decisions would affect the children of the world.

Greatest Fear

Kennedy feared nuclear confrontation and potential devastation of the world. He attempted to persuade his advisors to accept his way of thinking. But he anticipated reprisals and disagreements with his decisions.

The primary theme that seemed prevalent during President Kennedy's short term in office was to promote peace and avoid war, no matter how much criticism he received.

The Cuban missile crisis became a confrontation between Kennedy and Krushchev. Krushchev was an older more experienced adversary. Kennedy showed his maturity by making every effort to maintain peace while giving Krushchev his own time to reflect and consider his options. He knew that war would occur if he misjudged his opponent. Kennedy did not want to humiliate Krushchev or make the Russians act out of desperation. Kennedy needed to keep the respect of both his own people as well as those in other countries around the globe.

The Berlin Factor

Berlin played a role in the president's assessments during the Cuban missile crisis; in fact, it acted as a significant constraint. Kennedy feared an attack on Cuba would open the flood gates to a reciprocal attack on Berlin. At the same time, inaction by the United States would also give the Soviets provocation to move on Berlin.

The Soviets had always wanted to occupy West Berlin and in 1961, in conjunction with East Germany, it built a wall around West Berlin. The intent was to halt the exodus of East Germans, especially those with technical skills and professional expertise, to the Western sector. The Soviets were fearful that the East Germany economy would collapse and expected other Soviet strongholds, including Eastern Europe, would follow.

Kennedy felt an obligation to protect West Berlin but knew the only way this could be done would be by using nuclear weapons.

The Berlin Wall lasted twenty-seven years, but at least nuclear war was averted.

Years Later

Theodore Sorensen, one of Kennedy's closest advisors and friends asked, "What, if any, circumstance or justification gives this government or any government the moral right to bring its people close to destruction?" Even though these words were uttered in 1967, four years after the assassination, the question had to be going through the president's mind when he faced this challenge.

Contrary to the advice of many of his cabinet members as well as most of the military, Kennedy decided to take a conservative path and not directly confront Cuba and the USSR.

A Different Direction

He opted for an embargo that basically meant that all ships heading for Cuba would be stopped and searched by personnel from our ships. Ships that might pose a danger to our security were not permitted to proceed. Kennedy imposed a naval quarantine with the threat of further military action (i.e., air strikes) to prevent additional ships and weapons from being delivered to Cuba.

The scene was extremely tense, and many thought we were close to another world war. No one at that time had any idea how the Soviets would respond.

Kennedy believed this strategy could save the nation and the world from total disaster and allow us to save face so that our allies and enemies would not say the United States backed down in the face of political pressure.

The quarantine worked. On October 24, 1962, a Soviet ship refused to challenge the American naval quarantine; changed its course and turned back.

A Firm Stance

It was Kennedy versus Krushchev. Each attempted to keep the upper hand while not forcing the other into something too drastic. Both found themselves pulled by their own advisors in opposite directions, some advocating limited action for defensive purposes while others stressed aggressive action.

Finally, after thirteen long tedious days of negotiation, a mutual agreement was reached between the United States and the USSR. The Soviets would withdraw their missiles from Cuba if we would agree not to attack Cuba. In addition, we had to stop the quarantine. Kennedy could not approve of any operation against Cuba, even those supported by elements within the CIA.

Fallout

This predictably resulted in hard and bitter feelings toward the president by some Cuban exiles, members of our own intelligence agencies, and certain elements of organized crime.

A later concession to this agreement, which the government tried to keep secret, was that the United States would remove missiles that were in Turkey facing the Russian border. Removal of these missiles was not part of the original agreement, at least as told to most of Kennedy's advisors as well as to the public.

JFK had attempted to remove these missiles well before the Soviets had their own missiles in Cuba. However, this was never accomplished due to the objections of the Turkish government. Kennedy feared the reactions of Turkey and the rest of the NATO alliance if it became known that the trading of the Cuban missiles for the Jupiter missiles was tied to solving the Cuban missile crisis.

Kennedy would be perceived as the president who was willing to sacrifice Europe for the sake of preserving the security of the United States. He couldn't let this happen. It was his intent to appear strong and forceful in dealing with the Soviets. During this period he reinforced our country's military superiority and nuclear capability so that no one would question our purpose and intent.

The Bad News

Kennedy's pledge to never invade Cuba met with disfavor in many quarters. People feared there would be a permanent hold on Cuba (and perhaps other Latin American countries) by Castro and his communist dictatorship. The top military brass, much of the CIA and Pentagon, and the national security establishment had all advocated an invasion of Cuba. Now, the opposite was done. If they had known, they certainly would not have agreed to the trade of the missiles in Turkey for the missiles in Cuba. When the Jupiter missiles were finally disbanded and withdrawn from Turkey, most people did not consider it a part of the agreement to end the Cuban missile crisis.

A Tortuous Test

President Kennedy stood up to his adversary, Premier Krushchev, and a war had been avoided.

The attorney general, Robert Kennedy, was with the president continuously during the thirteen days it took for the final resolution of the Cuban missile crisis. He was able to directly observe the president's modus operandi during this time when the world was so close to nuclear disaster. Robert said about his brother, "It was as if no one else was there, and he was no longer the president. I thought of when he was ill and almost died, when he lost his child, when he heard that our oldest brother had been killed."

- John Kennedy had again been tested and passed the test.

- Nuclear war was avoided.

- Kennedy stood up to the Russians and reversed the humiliation he suffered both at the Bay of Pigs and during a summit meeting he had with Krushchev in Vienna in June 1961. (It was during this confrontation in Vienna with the head of our arch rival of the cold war that JFK felt humbled and inferior to the Soviet commander. He had hoped to achieve some resemblance of a peaceful negotiation with Krushchev and possibly even discuss a nuclear test ban commitment. Instead, Krushchev castigated the young president and even talked of war on the matter of Berlin. At the end of this meeting, JFK said, "So, he beat the hell out of me.")

- Both Kennedy and Krushchev realized there had to be a way to control these nuclear weapons. They finally had to rely on each other's trust and have both sides comply.

- This was the mandate for closer communication between the two countries. It wasn't too long after this (August 1963) that the Nuclear Test Ban Treaty was signed between the United States and Soviets. Its effect was to ban both atmospheric and underwater nuclear testing.

- This proved to be a milestone, assuring that the forty-five-year-old cold war struggle would not turn into an international conflict that could destroy mankind.

- It also served as a warning to communist China and other countries not to develop a nuclear arsenal.

- The average citizen applauded the president for these two extremely important and vital events in the quest for peace. Following this latest altercation with the Soviet Union, President Kennedy's popularity and approval rating went up to 75 percent.

- Strength and nonnegotiable demands became the hallmark for President Kennedy and later became the mode of operation for future presidents in their negotiations with other countries.

Pockets of Discontent

There was a small group of individuals that thought we were getting too soft, especially when it came to dealing with our arch enemy of the cold war.

The Cuban missile crisis in essence resulted in a pledge by JFK to Krushchev never to attack Cuba. In addition, all covert operations around this small island of Cuba were to be brought to a halt. There was a crackdown on all guerilla bases and commando raids. This was a devastating blow to the hundreds of thousands of Cubans who were preparing to liberate their homeland from communist control. It was a blow to all of the anti-Castro Cuban exiles; the same group of individuals who felt deeply betrayed during the Bay of Pigs again felt let down by the president. Cuba would remain under the leadership of Fidel Castro, and there was apparently nothing JFK would do about it.

John F. Kennedy had become a hero but in the process, made more enemies. It was apparent to them that the philosophy of President Kennedy was diametrically opposed to their own beliefs.

Could a small select number of members of one or more of these various groups (i.e., military-industrial complex, anti-Castro factions, and organized crime) organize, orchestrate, carry out, and then cover up the greatest unsolved murder of the twentieth century—the assassination of President John F. Kennedy?

To a great extent, I'm basing my affirmative answer to this question on powers of deduction. Still, it's difficult to ignore that all roads appear to lead in this direction.

V

Vietnam

In this chapter, I concentrate on events leading up to our country's involvement in and subsequent withdrawal from Vietnam. I do so because these events point to probable motives for the assassination of John Fitzgerald Kennedy.

Five American presidents gave the affirmative nod to military involvement in Vietnam. President Kennedy vowed to pull troops out of the country.

On September 2, 1963, Kennedy, during a television interview with renowned newscaster, Walter Cronkite, made the following statement:

> It is their war. They are the ones who have to win it or lose it. We can help by sending equipment or our men there to act as advisors. In the final analysis, it is their people and their government who have to win or lose this struggle.

Toward the end of 1963, JFK officially announced a withdrawal of one thousand U.S. military personnel. He pledged to completely withdraw from Vietnam within the following year.

Leaders of companies getting rich on sales of weapons and military supplies and individuals getting rich on rampant drug trafficking in Vietnam had to be alarmed by his intentions.

Strong feelings about our country's Vietnam involvement persist today.

In the interest of full disclosure, you should know that I served in Vietnam. I was already a physician and held the rank of captain.

For readers who need a quick history, it is provided below. Others may wish to move ahead and read this chapter beginning with the subtitle "Diplomatic Philosophy."

A Little History

Vietnam is a small country in Southeast Asia. It was, for a long time, a primitive land dominated by dense jungle and rice paddies.

- The French ruled Indochina (consisting of Vietnam, Thailand, Laos, and Cambodia) for well over one hundred years.

- During World War II, Japan attempted to occupy Vietnam.

- In 1940 Ho Chi Minh, a Soviet sympathizer, organized his people in a fight for independence against France and Japan. His organization, known as the Vietminh, set up a government in Hanoi and declared independence as the government of North Vietnam.

- In 1945, France tried to reclaim Vietnam as its colony. Ho Chi Minh asked the United States for assistance to maintain independence.

- The United States refused. In fact, the United States helped finance the French operation in Vietnam. (It's likely that U.S. government leaders wanted to win favor with French leaders, anticipating their cooperation in thwarting communist expansion in Europe.)

- The French were ultimately defeated in the battle at Dien Ben Phu.

- Following the Geneva Convention (1954), the victorious Vietminh agreed to a temporary partition of Vietnam at the 17th parallel. This resulted in dividing the country into North Vietnam and South Vietnam.

- Because of strong communist ties Ho Chi Minh maintained with both the USSR and China, leaders in the United States wanted to prevent the reunification of Vietnam. They calculated the southern sector would remain Communist free.

- John F. Kennedy, who at that time was U.S. Senator Kennedy, spoke out against U.S. intervention in Indochina. "I am frankly of the belief that no amount of American military assistance in Indochina can conquer an enemy which is everywhere and at the same time nowhere, an enemy of the people, which has the sympathy and covert support of the people."

- President Eisenhower helped Ngo Dinh Diem become the first leader of South Vietnam. It was during Eisenhower's tenure as president that the war switched from being labeled a colonial war to a war between communism and the free world.

- The "domino theory" was embraced, and dire consequences were predicted. *If Vietnam fell to the communists, so would all of Southeast Asia.*

- Communism (Russia as represented by North Vietnam and the Viet Cong), versus democracy (the United States as represented by South Vietnam) were opposing forces in the struggle.

- When John F. Kennedy became president, he again vowed he would not send combat troops to participate in the war effort. He increased the number of advisors in Vietnam.

- On November 2, 1963, the president of South Vietnam, Ngo Dinh Diem and his brother were assassinated in a coup d'état. This was only three weeks prior to the assassination of JFK, and because of this close proximity, the question has been asked whether there was a direct connection. Did President Kennedy know in advance about this coup, and did he give his approval? If so, could there have been retaliation by the Vietnamese? These questions cannot be definitely answered, although some feel that Kennedy had heard about the possibility of a coup and that he was unable to prevent it. It is doubtful that the generals (comprising the new government of South Vietnam) would have gone through with the coup if they had not received some American support.

Diplomatic Philosophy

In both Cuba and Vietnam, Kennedy emphasized diplomacy over aggression. Avoiding war was a greater priority than making war.

- Similar to his approach to the Bay of Pigs, Cuban missile crisis, and the Berlin crisis, President John F. Kennedy took one step at a time even when advisors wanted him to move aggressively and without delay.

- It was understood *we were trying to save a country not making an effort to save itself.* This made our job of logistical support and the training of the South Vietnamese Army difficult, at best.

- Kennedy's primary concern was to avoid nuclear war. He feared that sending American troops into Vietnam would lead to intervention by both the Russians and the Chinese.

The Road to Defeat

Kennedy's death led to our defeat in Vietnam.

- The fourth president forced to deal with the situation in Vietnam was Lyndon Baines Johnson, who succeeded President Kennedy following Kennedy's assassination.

- Our total involvement and commitment in Vietnam occurred in August 1964 after the Gulf of Tonkin incident. This was reported to be an unprovoked attack against U.S. warships in international waters off the coast of North Vietnam.

- In 1965, President Johnson ordered the bombing of North Vietnam and the dispatch of combat troops to the south.

- Later it was rumored that the U.S. military, with the approval of President Johnson and the Pentagon, contrived the Gulf of Tonkin incident to make the American people think the United States was fighting a war of self-defense against an extremely aggressive communist enemy. No North Vietnamese attack vessels were in the area at the time of the so-called Gulf of Tonkin incident. This information didn't become public knowledge until many years later.

- The Congress overwhelmingly approved a resolution stating that the president of the United States had the authority to take any necessary measures to repel attacks against the United States and to prevent further aggression.

- This led to bombing North Vietnam.

- Over 50,000 U.S. deaths and over 2 million Vietnamese deaths are attributed to the war in Vietnam.

- Emotions were raw on the home front and strong dissension was the order of the day. The image of the United States at home and abroad was gravely damaged.

The Finale

- The fifth and final president to become involved in Vietnam was Richard Nixon, the man John F. Kennedy defeated for the presidency in 1960. In 1973, President Nixon ordered the final withdrawal of U.S. troops from Vietnam. *He allowed the North Vietnamese to remain in South Vietnam.* Two years later, the Saigon government of South Vietnam collapsed. The war was over. Vietnam became a communist country.

Why Did We Fail?

In June 1962 while giving a talk at West Point Academy, President Kennedy described the unique challenge.

> This is another type of war—war by guerillas, subversives, insurgents, assassins; war by ambush instead of combat, by infiltration instead of aggression, seeking victory by exhausting the enemy instead of engaging him. It seeks to undermine the efforts of new and poor countries to maintain their freedom. It preys on economic unrest and ethnic conflicts.

The government of South Vietnam was weak and corrupt. It was soon obvious they were incapable of carrying on the struggle alone.

One of the primary obstacles to the success of the United States in the Vietnam War was Ngo Dinh Diem, the self-appointed president of South Vietnam. Diem did not have the backing of his military or the support of his people. He antagonized everyone who made contact with him, especially the Buddhist majority in Vietnam.

A Bad Marriage and the Result

Was Diem really helpful to our cause or was he more of a hindrance?

- The United States supported Diem because of his anti-communist views.

- Diem believed the United States was there for the long haul and would never abandon him or his interests.

- He believed our number one priority was to stamp out communist aggression.

- But the South Vietnamese people could not depend on their own government and started to look away to the other side for reinforcement-the communist side.President Kennedy, and several of his advisors, questioned our role in this country located 10,000 miles way from our own shores.

- Kennedy began to realize the United States could not continue to support the status quo in Vietnam. He believed he had four alternatives:

  1. He could increase our own direct military involvement to fight the communists. Many of his political and military advisors advocated this action.

  2. There could be a replacement for Diem (via a coup) with the establishment of a military government that could win the support of the people. A new government would, perhaps, fight the war without relying totally on American support.

  3. He could gradually withdraw U.S. troops from Vietnam as a scare tactic with the hope that South Vietnam would begin to defend itself.

  4. He could gradually withdraw U.S. personnel from Vietnam with the realization that this war was hopeless and we could not get involved in a war that was not ours to begin with.

- JFK's advisors (i.e., military leaders and various intelligence sources) were certain we would win the war.

- During President Kennedy's one thousand days in office, there were about 17,000 men from the United States actively employed in Vietnam. They were there in an advisory and supportive capacity and not for direct ground combat.

- By 1969, or six years after the assassination, there were 550,000 U.S. troops in this small foreign country.

- There were one hundred American soldiers coming home in body bags each week. Our involvement truly escalated after the assassination.

- Vietnam was probably the only war the United States has actually lost. Of course, our powers would never admit that we lost this war. (In fact, Congress never declared our involvement in Vietnam a war.)

- The government does admit we had nearly 58,000 casualties, young men and women who were called upon to protect the interests of our country.

- The final actual death count was 57,939 Americans. This is nearly fifteen times the number of troops killed in Iraq, to date.

- The death toll began in 1965, when we first sent combat troops to Vietnam, two years after the assassination of President John F. Kennedy.

- The Vietnam War became a catastrophe for the United States.

- Of the 3 million Americans who were eventually sent to Vietnam, over 800,000 were either killed or injured.

- Over 2,500 soldiers were classified as "missing in action" and are presumed dead.

- Nearly $200 billion was expended in the war effort.

- After the war, the death rate of Vietnam veterans was nearly twice as high as those veterans who never served in Vietnam. This is blamed on the use of different toxic chemicals and defoliants such as Agent Orange.

- Finally, the suicide rate among Vietnam veterans was much higher than expected.

- There were over 4 million Vietnamese either killed or wounded during the war. This figure represented 10 percent of the total population of the country.

- Vietnam was a no-win situation from the beginning. It had a long history of struggles for its independence against the Chinese, Japanese, and French.

- We should have taken a lesson from history. We did not.

Being There

I spent one year in Vietnam serving as a physician. I attended daily meetings with other officers and the top brass to learn what progress had been made during the past twenty-four hours.

- Our success was determined to be largely dependent on the body count: the number of enemy soldiers killed in battle. If there were more enemy Vietnamese bodies than U.S. casualties found that day, we were successful. If the reverse was true, the day was not considered a success.

- This was the crude and primitive method (devised by our government) of determining whether the United States was "winning." It must be remembered that there were infinitely more Viet Cong and North Vietnamese in the country than Americans and, therefore, more Vietnamese deaths than Americans were to be expected.

- Using this criterion, the government attempted to make a case for the Americans winning the war. Yet this perception is not accurate. Our success or lack of success could not be dependent on a casualty count.

- The truth is we were never winning. The military became obsessed with measurements such as enemy casualties, weapons seized, and prisoners taken. This was the information they sent to President Kennedy.

Antiwar Protests

As time went by, the average person in the United States did not support our commitment to this war. Many turned against the actual soldier in Vietnam fighting the war. I found this response to be reprehensible, especially because military personnel were not setting policy and were not there of their own volition.

- The media was negative about our war effort and reported that we were engaging in combat before such activity was sanctioned. The media spoke out against the Diem government and reported on the corruption.

- Kennedy found the media reports to be markedly different from the official advice he was receiving.

- The Vietnam War was unconventional. Leaders in Hanoi (capital of North Vietnam) dictated the war by organizing the Vietcong in the south and infiltrating North Vietnamese Army units into the south (i.e., guerilla warfare).

- President Kennedy was on record with the following observation:

    We can prevent one nation's army from moving across the border of another nation. We are probably strong enough to prevent one nation from unleashing nuclear weapons on another. But we can't prevent infiltration, assassination, sabotage, bribery, any of the weapons of guerilla warfare. One guerilla can pin down twelve conventional soldiers, and we've got nothing equivalent.

Untenable Conditions

The conditions in Vietnam under which we were fighting were impossible.

- We were fighting in a dense jungle. There were no front lines, and the enemy often wore civilian clothes. As a physician in Vietnam (1969–70), I took care of North and South Vietnamese as well as Viet Cong. Other than the enemy being guarded with drawn rifles by our troops, there was no good way of differentiating between them. There was nothing distinguishing about the enemies' appearance.

- Many South Vietnamese disliked us. I believe the Vietnamese people just wanted to be left alone. They wanted all foreign intervention to end and wanted their country back.

- Unfortunately, their own government let them down. Many Vietnamese felt the United States let them down. They turned against our government because we were supporting President Diem.

- As a result, the only place the people could turn was to the enemy; the Viet Cong.

- Just because the Viet Cong were our enemy did not mean the people of Vietnam considered this communist group their enemy. Democracy is not the answer for every country, and perhaps in Vietnam this was proven.

The Role of the Green Berets

The Green Berets, whose specialty was counterinsurgency training, arrived in South Vietnam in May 1961 and actually represented an expansion of the American commitment in Vietnam. This happened in spite of the fact that President Kennedy believed the South Vietnamese should assume the ultimate responsibility for success (or failure).

Instead of the enemy being an external aggressive force, the enemy was now an internal local group (Viet Cong, also known as the communist South Vietnamese) probably equipped from the outside (North Vietnamese). Backed by the Soviet Union, they were suppressing segments of their own population that were economically and culturally deprived. The Viet Cong were the insurgents, and to combat this, the United States had to institute a counterinsurgency program.

※ ※ ※ ※ ※ ※

The president was not told about the lack of aggressive leadership on the part of the Diem government.

- He was not told about the poor morale in South Vietnam and the lack of trust between peasant and soldier.

- He was not told that one of the primary obstacles we faced in Vietnam was President Diem! Diem's military was poorly prepared and poorly motivated and were not supported by the people.

- In addition, suppression of the Buddhists was looked upon with enormous disfavor. Diem had an extremely oppressive policy against the

Buddhists, which made up the majority (70 percent) of the populace of South Vietnam. He favored the Catholics over the Buddhists in virtually every activity.

- Buddhists committed suicide (immolation) in full view of the television cameras in protest against Diem. People could not understand how Kennedy, a true leader of democracy, could support someone who flagrantly supported repression and sanctioned brutality.

- In October 1961, the Joint Chiefs of Staff concluded that the Viet Cong threat as well as the North Vietnamese intervention could be easily dealt with by sending U.S. combat troops to the area.

- Kennedy continued to hold out against sending combat ground troops. It is my personal feeling that if JFK had not been assassinated, the history of the war would have been altered.

Differing Assessments

Secretary of Defense Robert McNamara and General Maxwell Taylor both urged the deployment of U.S. forces into Vietnam. In May 1962 McNamara, after a return from a trip to Vietnam, stated we were winning the war.

A few months later (December 1962), Senate Majority Leader Mike Mansfield went to Vietnam to see for himself how we were faring. In his report to the president, he refused to make any optimistic comments on the progress of the war. He felt we weren't accomplishing anything positive and put the blame on Diem and the South Vietnamese government.

Kennedy was initially upset with Mansfield, because this was the first time he had been informed about the true nature of the war. The president felt deceived and betrayed, similar to his feelings about the CIA during the Bay of Pigs operation.

This deception, whether intentional or not, eventually trickled back to the average citizen who was kept informed of events by the media. The media initially praised the success of the United States in Vietnam. After all, they were also told by the government and military that we were winning the war.

The Role of the Media

The media is in a position to formulate and shape public opinion, mood, and perception. Journalists and broadcasters rarely question official statements that deal with issues of our national security. It wasn't until 1971 (eight years after the assassination) that the Pentagon Papers were released, describing the true nature and history of the United States involvement in Vietnam. This was a top-secret study of the U.S. decision-making process from 1945–68. It concluded the military had been lying about the war. We were in a no-win situation. The increased skepticism and suspicion that followed created new and renewed feelings that the assassination of JFK might be a government cover-up.

If the government, or powers-that-be, could deceive the people about Vietnam, why couldn't they have deceived the people about the JFK assassination? There was widespread distrust, and new questions arose.

The Drug Connection

Drugs were a major commodity in Southeast Asia. President Diem was assisted by his brother, Ngo Dinh Nhu, who was head of the security forces and was in charge of the Vietnamese heroin network.

I learned of this during my stint in Vietnam. Several corpsmen working for me told me of their drug habits. Heroin was cheap, very pure, and easy to obtain.

Vietnam was a major supplier of opium, which was sent to France for purifying and conversion to heroin and then to the United States for distribution. Kennedy's threatened withdrawal from Vietnam would disrupt this drug network. Surely, many people had to be making fortunes in this drug trade.

In addition, the Kennedy's anti-Mafia campaign (spearheaded by U.S. Attorney General Robert Kennedy) would also affect this drug traffic. Besides organized crime and its tie to the drug market in Vietnam, there was another organization that would also stand to lose if we left Vietnam.

The CIA was involved with international drug trafficking (sale and transportation of illegal drugs such as cocaine and heroin) as a method of moving money from one country to another. This money was needed to promote revolutions and coups in certain countries in order to dissuade them from communist rule. Those countries included

Panama, Iran, Laos, and Vietnam.

Election Time Just Ahead

The pressure at home to bring our troops back became insurmountable.

- Kennedy was soon to face a possible reelection and knew if he were to serve a second term as the president, he somehow had to end our commitment to this war.

- He was promising all the fathers, mothers, husbands, and wives that there was to be no further bloodshed of American troops in this conflict.

From My Side

How did I see Vietnam based on my own personal experience?

- I spent my year in Vietnam six years after the assassination of JFK. I was in the war at the time we were most involved. It had become our war, and I personally saw the devastation inflicted on our troops. In retrospect, I have to admire President Kennedy for having the insight not to want to commit our combat troops to this area. He knew what could happen, and I saw what did happen.

- Shortly after the assassination, our new President, Lyndon Johnson adopted a policy, which, in essence, was opposite to the policy that President Kennedy had agreed to carry out. There were two official U.S. State Department documents or National Security Action Memoranda (NSAMs) declared after the assassination in very close proximity to each other and which differed markedly regarding our commitment to the Republic of Vietnam.

- The first (NSAM 263) was the beginning of a pledge by JFK to begin troop withdrawal (one thousand U.S. advisors by the end of 1963 and possibly total withdrawal by 1965). This was drafted by national security advisor for the president, McGeorge Bundy, just after the November conference in Honolulu. We will never know the true intent of President Kennedy in this regard. However, I do believe that he was sincere in wanting to remove our troops no matter what his reason was. I also firmly believe that this would have been accomplished if it wasn't for the events of November 22, 1963.

- After President Johnson assumed control of the country, (November 22), there was a revised version of the memorandum (NSAM 273), again prepared by Bundy. Johnson intended to win the war and, as a result, he approved this new version on November 26, 1963. It took Johnson only four days after JFK's death to completely change our foreign policy towards Vietnam. This document called for an acceleration of U.S. military presence in Vietnam. As a reaction to the assassination of Diem, this appeared to be a reinforcement of the pledge to assist the people and government of South Vietnam to continue the fight against communism. It is highly doubtful that President Kennedy (had he lived) would have completely changed his position on Vietnam in such a short time.

- It would not be beyond the realm of possibility that the new president, Lyndon Johnson, would change our foreign policy regarding Vietnam. *It took the assassination of a president to have our policy toward Vietnam completely reversed.* Even Johnson had to admit we were entering an endeavor for which we had little chance of success. Johnson said: I don't think that we can fight them 10,000 miles away from home. I don't think it's worth fighting for, and I don't think that we can get out. It's just the biggest damned mess that I ever saw.

- The Vietnam War officially ended on January 27, 1973, as a cease-fire agreement was signed by the United States as well as representatives of North Vietnam, South Vietnam, and the Viet Cong. This was nearly ten years after John F. Kennedy was assassinated. It has now been over forty years since South Vietnam fell to communist forces. The city of Saigon is now known as Ho Chi Minh City.

- What was our intrigue in being in Vietnam? Was it strictly to try to contain communistic influence from spreading across the world? Did we really think that we could stop the Asian countries from turning away from our own values toward the communist values? Did we really believe that the average Vietnamese peasants who virtually spent their entire life working in the rice paddies would live a better life if they knew we were on their side?

- Or was there a more practical reason rather than an idealistic answer?

It is well known that wars cost money. Someone has to build the equipment: planes, tanks, barracks, supplies, helicopters, and so on. It can become a very lucrative financial and business venture. Ending the conflict would have cost many companies, let alone individuals, to lose a substantial amount of money. This in turn had to create many hostile feelings toward the president. The military-industrial complex wanted the Vietnam War to continue purely from a financial aspect. At this time, we were in a war-based economy.

- In addition, there was a very lucrative drug traffic situation (especially heroin) in Vietnam that was essentially controlled by the CIA and distributed by organized crime. Both organizations acted as partners in this drug trafficking. It was a multibillion dollar operation, which, if ended, would impoverish certain individuals.

- Much to President Johnson's dismay, the Vietnam War is what caused Johnson not to seek reelection in 1968. He finally realized his policy of further U.S. intervention and aggression into this small Asian country had been wrong and had backfired. We were defeated, and so was he.

VI

Organized Crime

Keep your eye on the players. These powerful members of organized crime, referred to as the Mafia, were linked to the assassination of the president.

Their names are Trafficante, Marcello, Roselli, Giancana, and then, there's Hoffa.

- Santos Trafficante was the head of the mob's business in the Havana casinos and boss of the Florida underworld.

- Carlos Marcello was the boss of the underworld in Mississippi, Louisiana, and Texas.

- Johnny Roselli was the Mafia's link to the CIA.

- Sam Giancana was the mob boss in Chicago.

- James Hoffa was the head of the Teamsters Union, which essentially controlled organized labor.

Organized crime had basically been left alone by government authorities until JFK came into power.

In fact, J. Edgar Hoover, director of the FBI, initially didn't acknowledge the existence of the Mafia. Hoover had enormous pride in the FBI and avoided anything that might tarnish its reputation. This carried over when Hoover later denied the FBI had any connection to Lee Harvey Oswald.

This was a lie. The FBI had an extensive file on Oswald dating back to the time that Oswald reentered the United States after his defection to Russia. The FBI also knew that Oswald was working at the Texas School Book Depository when Kennedy made his trip to Dallas. Nothing about Oswald's whereabouts was ever reported to the Secret Service even though FBI officials knew the president's motorcade would be passing the depository.

Patriarch Kennedy and the Mob

Joseph Kennedy Sr. established ties to organized crime early in the course of attaining his enormous wealth, in part from bootlegging, during the days of Prohibition. As a result, he was well-known to the mobsters.

The Mafia was exceedingly powerful and had ties to many diverse business ventures and business people. It was difficult to exclude mob involvement when it came to lucrative financial dealings.

In 1960, Joseph Kennedy Sr. turned to the Mafia for assistance when his son John was running for president. He reasoned that JFK needed all the help he could get. His son was young, Catholic, and relatively inexperienced—all factors that didn't enhance his candidacy. Could the mob deliver certain key votes to JFK and insure his election? History provides the answer.

JFK was elected president by a very slim margin. In essence, the state of Illinois secured the election for Kennedy. Sam Giancana was considered the boss of the Chicago mob and the "Windy City" was the seat of the Democratic machine. Great sums of money were spent to get the voters of Chicago out for JFK.

The mob expected favorable treatment in return for this *favor*. But this president of the United States did not deliver!

Nothing New

In 1959 Robert Kennedy had been chief counsel for the McClellan Senate Racketeering Committee and John served on the committee. The committee investigated organized crime and corruption in the labor unions. Robert Kennedy seemed to have a vendetta against organized crime and especially against Jimmy Hoffa, the head of the Teamsters Union. Organized crime figures felt betrayed by the constant harassment they received from the Kennedy brothers.

One of the reasons that Giancana had agreed to help elect JFK was the stipulation that neither he nor other mob leaders would be bothered anymore. They wanted to be left alone to conduct their business. This was the promise the Mafia received from Joseph Kennedy Sr. What they didn't realize was that an agreement with the elder Kennedy did not represent a contract with his sons. In fact, it's doubtful that either Robert or John knew about their father's dealings with the mob. Organized crime figures were embarrassed by this betrayal and very resentful.

After the election, JFK appointed Robert Kennedy attorney general. "Bobbie" continued his unrelenting attack against organized crime. Hoover had to finally acknowledge the Mafia's existence, because Robert Kennedy asked for and received help from the FBI.

Carlos Marcello, the Mafia chieftain in New Orleans, was arrested and deported to Guatemala by the Justice Department. This action, five months before the assassination, was spearheaded by Robert Kennedy. Marcello was one of the most sought-after mobsters because of his connections in Texas as well as Mississippi and Louisiana. Marcello would eventually return to the United States with the assistance of David Ferrie. Ferrie was a key player with the CIA, Cuban exiles, and the Mafia. Ferrie was also well acquainted with one—Lee Harvey Oswald.

Santos Trafficante, head of the Florida mob, was another individual targeted for drug trafficking by the Justice Department. Very few of the Mafia leaders would escape the government's scrutiny and the wrath of Attorney General Robert Kennedy.

Not only did this give organized crime kingpins a motive for assassination, but Marcello and Trafficante also felt betrayed by the failure of the Bay of Pigs.

The Mafia had been very influential in Cuba before Fidel Castro's rise. The Mafia controlled virtually all the casinos in Havana. Money poured into Mafia coffers from Cuba, which is located only ninety miles off the coast of Florida. Trafficante and Marcello controlled mob operations in Cuba, and Giancana had high stakes in Cuba, too.

The Rules Change

The former leader, Fulgencio Batista was mob-friendly, but Castro closed the casinos. The mobsters stood to lose up to $100 million per year. Organized crime had to find a way to get back into this small country and recover assets.

Strange alliances were formed as the CIA teamed up with the Mafia in an attempt to overthrow Castro and take over Cuba. The CIA reached out, and a former FBI agent, Robert Matheu, contacted Sam Giancana and Johnny Roselli who decided to make Santos Trafficante the head of the Cuban operation.

This partnership was launched in the Eisenhower era and was inherited by Kennedy. The CIA and the mob assumed the new president would approve of this alliance and the plan to retake Cuba, which had become a Communist stronghold.

They Were Wrong!

President Kennedy would never condone this partnership even if he knew about it in advance. The Central Intelligence Agency was supposed to uphold the laws of our country and not do anything in opposition to our general well-being. The Mafia, on the other hand, was a separate section of our society and operated for its own benefit, without consideration for the welfare of the population at large.

Following World War II, the CIA was considered a covert government agency whose purpose was to counter Soviet operations throughout the world. The CIA under Eisenhower devised a plan to secretly train Cuban exiles in Guatemala. Their goal was to infiltrate these exiles into Cuba and begin guerilla warfare. It was hoped there would be enough local support and others would join in to defeat Castro's army.

The CIA was primarily responsible for the orchestration of the Bay of Pigs affair. When this failed, in part because of President Kennedy's unwillingness to supply air support for the invasion, the CIA continued its mission of "saving Cuba and ridding the world of a Communist Dictator."

The CIA had previously been in the business of promoting high level government coups and assassinations.

- In 1954 the CIA assisted in the overthrow of the democratically elected government of Guatemala. There was concern that Guatemala was becoming sympathetic to the Soviet Union.

- Two other assassinations of foreign leaders for which the CIA was believed to be directly involved were the murders of Rafael Trujillo from the Dominican Republic and Patrice Lumumba, the Congolese premier from Africa. The rationale of the CIA at that time was that both leaders were becoming too friendly with our arch rival in the cold war, the Soviet Union.

- There was another assassination that occurred during Kennedy's tenure, although it's highly unlikely Kennedy realized assassination would be the result. That was the murder of Ngo Dinh Diem, the premier of South Vietnam and our ally in the fight against communist aggression in Southeast Asia. Diem was hampering our efforts in Vietnam and becoming more disliked by his own people and military. A coup was carried out (exactly three weeks before Kennedy's assassination), and the CIA was said to be involved in its operation. This has never been denied by anyone in government.

The CIA had decided the best way to fight the spread of communism was to cause revolutions in countries that leaned toward a communist way of life. It didn't matter to the CIA if leaders were assassinated. The CIA acquired a level of superiority and ultimate power and didn't feel the laws of the land pertained to them. This perception was eventually challenged by JFK when he threatened to completely disband the CIA following the Bay of Pigs encounter.

- The merger of the CIA and the Mafia focused on the assassination of Fidel Castro. Each group stood to gain: the CIA would get rid of a communist dictator and allow the Cubans to take control of their country. Organized crime would again regain its financial sources and power.

- Richard Bissell from the CIA and Johnny Roselli from the Mafia were key figures in establishing this relationship. Obviously, many more individuals were involved.

We know the intelligence agencies originated this alliance, but who else in government knew about this unorthodox relationship remains unknown. If the president knew something, what did he know and when did he know it?

The plan to get rid of Castro through the Bay of Pigs operation was known to President Kennedy although the groundwork had been completed during the Eisenhower Administration. It's my belief that John F. Kennedy would never have sanctioned any assassination plot if he knew organized crime was a direct participant.

In any event, the Bay of Pigs turned out to be a big fiasco from the standpoints of our government, the CIA, the Mafia, and the Cuban exiles. Castro remained in power and the Mafia remained impotent. It was decided by the CIA that the Castro assassination attempts would be continued. This was with the agreement of Robert Kennedy who stressed that Castro remained a definite detriment to our country. The plan was to be carried out under the name of Operation Mongoose. This would involve select members of the CIA, Pentagon chiefs, and certain officials in Kennedy's administration. The Mafia and CIA alliance continued.

Operation Mongoose, whose sole purpose was to get rid of Castro, became the largest program conducted within the CIA. Since Cuba is surrounded by water, it was very difficult to perpetrate a covert operation. There was constant disagreement between the CIA and Mafia as to how this could be accomplished. Neither side was able to come up with a plan for Castro's overthrow other than via an overt American invasion. The failure of Operation Mongoose ended the CIA's assassination plots against Fidel Castro.

One of the pledges, made by President Kennedy, that helped put an end to the Cuban Missile Crisis, was that the United States would never invade Cuba. This by itself should have ended any attempts by the CIA to assassinate Castro. The CIA carried on with its plans as if it were not under anyone's jurisdiction—not even the president of the United States.

As the whole world knows, Fidel Castro was not assassinated. He continues to be the dictator of Cuba. It has been suggested by some that JFK was killed in retaliation for the attempts on Castro's life. However, this defies logic. It was because of Kennedy's decisions during both the Bay of Pigs as well as the Cuban missile crisis, that Cuba was never attacked. If it had been up to the president's advisors as well as the Pentagon officials, the opposite would have occurred. Cuba would have been invaded and Castro might have been killed. In addition, toward the end of 1963, JFK was working on a peaceful accommodation with both Castro and the Soviets.

Difficult to Refute

It was this idea of a lasting peaceful coexistence between the cold war antagonists that probably cost JFK his life.

By not attacking Cuba and by supposedly giving in to Russia, Kennedy was determined, by a small select group of "assassins," to be too condescending and forgiving. Russia was our archenemy, not our friend. This group pegged Kennedy as a traitor. His beliefs and actions were contrary to what they determined to be in the best interests of our country, let alone their own best interests.

Kennedy wanted Castro out of Cuba, but he did not want the United States to be an active participant. When JFK didn't cooperate, it meant the failure of the Bay of Pigs mission. It also meant death for well over hundreds of anti-Castro Cubans, true disaster for the other Cuban exiles who strongly supported this mission, and finally it was a harsh blow to the masterminds of these events; the Central Intelligence Agency and organized crime.

Threats and More

President Kennedy felt betrayed by the CIA and threatened to disband it. He fired CIA Chief, Allen Dulles, who a few years later would be appointed to the Warren Commission to find the "truth" behind the JFK assassination. (Does the Allen Dulles appointment strike you the way it strikes me: the fox being sent to guard the henhouse?)

Kennedy also replaced former CIA members, General Charles Cabell, the brother of the mayor of Dallas, and Richard Bissell, the mastermind behind the Bay of Pigs and the chief of the CIA Clandestine Services.

Remember, organized crime, especially Trafficante, Marcello, Giancana, Roselli, and union leader Hoffa had been besieged by the Senate Intelligence Committee and in particular by Robert Kennedy. In 1962–63 there were over 1,000 indictments and 400 convictions. This contrasts dramatically with the last year of President Eisenhower's administration (1959), when there were only 49 indictments against suspected mobsters. These cases were generally for income tax evasion, though there was also proof of interstate racketeering, trafficking, and travel to engage in illegal business enterprises.

Can It Get Worse?

Also occurring at that time was the release of the Valachi papers, which threatened to expose more of the illegal dealings of the Mafia. Joe Valachi was a New York mobster who became a star witness for Robert Kennedy and the Senate Investigating Committee, and who broke the code of silence when he spoke out about Mafia dealings and secrets. He had no misgivings in talking about specific individuals in the Mafia, and he discussed events related to murder and violence. Organized crime began to get extremely concerned, and they felt something had to be done.

There are several reports of threats against the Kennedy brothers by Hoffa, Roselli, Trafficante, Marcello, and Giancana.

- One report claimed that the CIA-Mafia coalition that was set up to assassinate Castro instead assassinated the president because of his failure at the Bay of Pigs as well as his threat and eventual action to disband the CIA.

- Other reports claimed that Carlos Marcello (who had earlier been deported to Guatemala by Robert Kennedy) took out a contract on JFK as a means of getting Bobbie and stopping his anticrime crusade. The pilot who brought Marcello back to the states following the deportation was none other than David Ferrie. Ferrie will be discussed in more detail later.

- After the assassination of his brother, Robert Kennedy ended his personal involvement with the Justice Department in fighting crime. He even blamed himself for the death of his brother. He knew he had pressured the CIA into getting rid of Castro, and he realized he had exerted undue pressure against the Mafia and Jimmy Hoffa in particular. He feared that if one or both of these groups were involved in the assassination (and Castro could not be disregarded) then he, too, must share some of the blame.

Confessions to Murder

There have been a few people actually confessing to the murder of JFK. However, despite these revelations, the government remains firm in its convictions and the people have not clamored for a new investigation. Have so many years gone by where the public just doesn't seem to care or are we still afraid to find and admit the truth?

- In September 1987, Santos Trafficante, on his deathbed, confessed to his personal lawyer, Frank Ragano, that he and Carlos Marcello were involved in the Kennedy assassination. It was believed Marcello had a relationship with Lee Harvey Oswald, the president's alleged assassin and with Jack Ruby, the Dallas night-club owner who assassinated Oswald.

- There is another mobster who has been incriminated in the assassination and that is Johnny Roselli. Roselli was the go-between for the CIA and the Mafia. Roselli was working for Sam Giancana of Chicago fame. (Giancana is the man who helped JFK get elected in 1960.) Johnny Roselli supposedly confessed that he shot and killed JFK from his position in a storm drain located in Dealey Plaza. This was the location many people believed was the site of a shot from the front and therefore could not have been fired by Lee Harvey Oswald.

- There are many reports stating the Mafia was involved in the assassination of JFK. The most recent report revolves around a man named James Files, currently a prisoner in Joliet, Illinois. He emphatically states that he was the assassin who shot JFK from the front and that Charles Nicoletti shot Kennedy from behind. Both are known mafia hit men. Yet the government never made any effort to either verify or disprove these statements. Did powerful government officials fear organized crime? Could they themselves be implicated in planning the assassination or the cover-up?

- The official version of the government never wavers from the "assassin" Oswald and the single gunman theory.

I believe organized crime was involved in the assassination in some way, possibly supplying one of the shooters. I do not believe the Mafia orchestrated and planned the assassination alone. There are too many aspects of this case, especially the discrepancies in the medical evidence, the Mafia could not possibly have controlled. It had the motive, but it did not have the means to get involved in the motorcade route or manipulate the medical findings or make sure the windows in the upper floors of the depository were left open. The

Mafia could not have gathered all the information on Lee Harvey Oswald by itself (and made him a patsy as I sincerely believe he was) without the assistance of the intelligence agencies. This was a very complex and detailed conspiracy, one that required much thought, planning, money, and power. It was not the hit-and-run type of murder that had been characteristic of the Mafia.

What Was the Role of the FBI?

It's claimed the FBI had been notified through informants of the death threats made by Marcello and Trafficante. However, J. Edgar Hoover never informed either the Kennedy brothers or the Secret Service of these threats. As mentioned earlier, the Secret Service was not informed of the presence of Oswald at the book depository at the time the motorcade route was determined. Security risks are kept in separate Secret Service files (know as the Secret Service Protective Research Section), but Oswald's name was not included. Was this an omission or was it part of the cover-up? Hoover disliked the Kennedy brothers for several reasons. He didn't approve of the flamboyant and glamorous life style of the president. He even had his own file on some of Kennedy's female companions, which he threatened to use for blackmail purposes if necessary. Hoover also feared he would be forced to retire from the FBI under the Mandatory Retirement Act if Kennedy were reelected. He wouldn't have this fear if Lyndon Johnson were president. Finally, Hoover's boss was Robert Kennedy, the attorney general. There was certainly no love lost between these men. Each had a sincere disdain and distrust for the other. So, John F. Kennedy acquired more enemies (i.e., the mob and Hoover) along with the CIA and Cuban exiles during his short tenure in office. And, the enemy list multiplied quickly, because the mob infiltrated unions, police departments, various corporations, law offices, and various governmental agencies.

The Kennedy brothers threatened the continuance of the Mafia dealings both within the United States as well as across the ocean in Cuba.

After Kennedy's Assassination

A few years after the assassination, other names tied either to the CIA or the mob became known. In 1966 an investigation led by James Garrison, district attorney for the city of New Orleans, was widely publicized, especially by the people who questioned the findings of the Warren Commission.

- Garrison was dismayed that Lee Harvey Oswald had been in New Orleans shortly before the assassination. Garrison set out to prove or disprove the rumors that New Orleans was the site of dealings among certain people that could have led to the assassination. If true, this would favor the idea of a conspiracy and would contradict the Warren Commission's conclusion of Oswald being the lone assassin.

- Garrison heard about a call to a lawyer from a man named Clay Bertrand (aka Clay Shaw) asking the lawyer to defend Lee Harvey Oswald. This occurred soon after Oswald's arrest in Dallas and aroused Garrison's curiosity.

- Garrison became very interested in David Ferrie, a man of many trades, including a definite connection with organized crime through the Mafia chieftain, Carlos Marcello, as well as a possible connection with Lee Harvey Oswald. It appeared that Ferrie once served as Oswald's instructor in the Civil Air Patrol in Louisiana.

- After the Bay of Pigs, Ferrie harbored strong anti-Kennedy sentiments and joined the Cuban anti-Castro revolutionary front.

- Garrison learned of a David Ferrie, Lee Harvey Oswald, and Clay Bertrand meeting and a conversation at this meeting stating that JFK had to be killed and that a cross-fire method would be used.

- This meant that there would be simultaneous shots, coming from in front and from behind. This, of course, meant at least two shooters. This was the scenario embraced by all the critics of the Warren Commission.

This prompted Garrison to look into the possibility of a conspiracy being responsible for the death of the president. His timing was good. By now many people doubted the lone gunman theory and were skeptical and suspicious of the Warren Commission Report. Garrison hired a large staff and became obsessed with the idea of proving that President Kennedy was assassinated as the result of a conspiracy. Not long after Garrison started his investigation, David Ferrie, his initial prime suspect, suddenly died, supposedly of a cerebral hemorrhage. Two suicide notes were found, but these were apparently discounted by the New Orleans Police. The cause of death was listed as "natural." Strange—suicide notes are not found when someone dies of natural causes.

Oswald had been murdered prior to this investigation, and this left Clay Bertrand, whom Garrison equated with a man named Clay Shaw, as the only man left of the three who had supposedly plotted, at a meeting in New Orleans, to kill the president.

Clay Shaw was a respected man in New Orleans and the director of the New Orleans International Trade Fair. Garrison's goal was to prosecute and indict Clay Shaw for conspiracy in the murder of John F. Kennedy. Garrison was able to garner much publicity. He thought both Shaw and David Ferrie were connected to the CIA. Of course, this simply fueled the fire and propelled Garrison even further in his quest to prove a conspiracy. Suddenly, Garrison found himself under attack. There was a multitude of people including fellow lawyers, both locally (New Orleans) as well as nationally (Washington D.C.) whose purpose was to smear Garrison and obstruct his investigation. There were informants in his inner group. Witnesses were harassed and subpoenas weren't delivered. Garrison was apparently in the process of uncovering something very big that certain people wanted kept secret. Garrison became the "bad guy" as he began to question our government's possible role in the assassination. This scenario has a ring of familiarity to it. *If the truth had come out, I would not be writing this book and you would not be reading it.*

- Clay Shaw did eventually come to trial, but he was exonerated and freed. Garrison did not have enough evidence to convince the jury that he was part of a conspiracy plot to kill JFK. However, this did not necessarily mean that Shaw was innocent of any involvement in the assassination. At the time of the trial, there was no definite evidence that Shaw was working for the CIA. This came out a few years later when it was learned that Shaw was a director for a company called Permindex, which was a company suspected of being a CIA front involved in laundering money for organized crime as well as funding political assassinations.

- Would the verdict have been different if the connection between Shaw and the CIA were known? This is something we will never know for sure, though *I suspect the verdict would have been different.*

The Garrison Assessment in a Nutshell

Garrison believed people with CIA connections (either former or current employees) were responsible for the assassination of JFK. He believed they acted independently as a small selective group. He believed the federal government (at least a small contingent within it) conspired to keep the facts from the public and the CIA kept vital evidence from the Warren Commission. The principal outcome of Garrison's investigation was that for the first time, someone had the courage to blame others for the assassination of John F. Kennedy.

- The jury said Shaw was "not guilty," owing to a lack of damaging evidence. There was enough evidence, however, to indicate a conspiracy to assassinate JFK and that more than one shooter was involved.

- This was prior to anyone knowing about the CIA-Mafia link to kill Castro. This critical fact had been withheld by the intelligence agencies from the Warren Commission.

- Garrison believed Lyndon Johnson profited the most from the assassination. It was well-known that Johnson had always wanted to be president of the United States, and he became the president on November 22, 1963.

- The mob contributed excessively to Johnson's campaign to run in the primary against JFK in 1960. The mob also contributed to his Senate campaign in exchange for his cooperation in ending antiracketeering legislation. Finally, as president, Johnson ordered all FBI "bugging" of the Mafia to stop. Crime-fighting agencies were severely hindered.

Additional Nutshell Observations

- President Johnson stated he had evidence about the assassination that he planned to keep secret for seventy-five years, the full lifetime of most Americans. The unknown truth about the assassination would continue and would only resurface if the next generation of Americans reopened the case with enough enthusiasm to finally discover the truth.

- This declaration by LBJ suggests he had information about the assassination that was too dangerous to disclose. It suggests he also had extreme doubts and skepticism about the findings and conclusions of the Warren Commission.

- President Lyndon Baines Johnson did not believe the Warren Report even though it was the product of his appointed committee—all highly knowledgeable members, all with definite government connections. *This is my personal conjecture, but I defy anyone to disprove it.*

- Garrison believed the CIA comprised an invisible government with unlimited power and unlimited resources. He knew it acted in secrecy and reported to no other entity or individual. This was not only Garrison's view. *I believe many people including President Kennedy felt the same way.*

- Garrison felt the media suppressed news about the assassination and, therefore, suppressed the truth. *I agree with this, in part.* The media suppressed the truth by continuously agreeing with the government's version of what happened.

- In the 1960s the media would never disagree with the government. Today, the media, in general, is not afraid to express its own view.

While being a guest on the popular Johnny Carson television show, Garrison came right out and said that an element of the Central Intelligence Agency killed the president and that the present administration was concealing this fact. It wanted to perpetuate, not end the cold war, he said. He saw the assassination plot as being instigated by a facet of the intelligence community, which prided itself on being staunch cold war advocates and anticommunists. They felt Kennedy was developing a peaceful coexistence policy with the Russians, and this was contrary to their wishes. Finally, Garrison said that there is a faction known as the power elite that has the ability to manipulate the mass media and is committed to leading the war in Asia. This most likely would be equivalent to the military-industrial complex, the same group of individuals that President Eisenhower had warned the people about during his last speech prior to leaving office. Garrison, in essence, staged a campaign against government secrecy. Though he lost the Clay Shaw trial, I believe Jim Garrison was victorious in awakening the public's perception of a potential conspiracy in the assassination of JFK.

The movie *JFK* directed by Oliver Stone was a takeoff on the Garrison investigation. It was viciously attacked by the media several weeks before it was released. What were people afraid of? Who was conducting an "assassination smear" on a movie and why? What was there to hide, and finally, why shouldn't the people know the truth about the assassination of their president?

Oliver Stone's movie did not answer all these questions, but it created renewed interest in the assassination. It increased doubt about the validity of the Warren Report. It actually resulted in more questions that hopefully someday will be answered. It also seemed to unite people, as now the great majority of people believe JFK was the victim of a well-thought-out conspiracy and that the lone assassin theory was simply a ploy to deceive the people. This deception worked well for over forty years.

Credit and not discredit should be given both to Jim Garrison and to Oliver Stone and his superb movie.

* * * * * *

I saw Stone's movie on four occasions and had the pleasure of meeting Oliver Stone at a convention on the assassination in Dallas in 1993. The movie *JFK* was made on the basis of much research that I generally believe to be correct and is also found in many of the books written on the subject. I do not agree with all of its conclusions, but I do know this movie was not based on fantasy. It is more realistic than the Warren Commission findings. Garrison and Stone truly awoke the American people to the potential operatives who were in effect on November 22, 1963.

The Warren Commission attempted to have the public accept its conclusions and to dispel rumors about a conspiracy. The Warren Commission was dependent on the media and its total acceptance of the report. Who controlled the media at this time?

The answer might reveal who was ultimately responsible for the orchestration of the assassination of John F Kennedy. The movie *JFK* prompted individuals (both pre- and post-1963) to make up their own minds about the assassination and to raise questions and demand answers regarding the true events of November 22, 1963.

Section Three

A Shattering Shock and the Aftermath

VII

November 22, 1963

Election time was near. President Kennedy decided to seek another term and had to campaign for votes. In the 1960 election, Kennedy nearly lost the state of Texas to Richard Nixon, the Republican candidate. This happened even though Texas favorite son, Lyndon Johnson, was on the ballot with Kennedy as the vice presidential nominee. In the end, the majority of voters in Dallas gave their support to Nixon.

The major reason for Kennedy's trip to Texas in 1963 was because of a split in the Democratic Party. Liberal and conservative factions, spearheaded by Governor John Connelly and Senator Ralph Yarborough, were at odds. Kennedy wanted to resolve differences. He also needed to win support for his reelection, because having a Texan as a running mate didn't guarantee winning in Texas. He accepted Governor Connelly's invitation to visit Texas. Plans were made for Air Force One to fly Kennedy to San Antonio. He would travel to Houston, Fort Worth, and finally to Dallas where he was to make a speech at the Dallas Trade Mart.

Kennedy had been told by several advisors it would be a dangerous trip. He had misgivings about going.

"God, I wish you could think of some way of getting me out of going to Texas. Look how screwed up it's going to be. I just wish I didn't have to go. Can't you think of some emergency we could have?" Kennedy posed the question to George Smathers, a personal friend and a Senator from Georgia.

Kennedy knew Texas was populated with right-wing zealots who hated him. The general mood in Dallas was one of hostility. The anti-Catholic sentiment was entrenched in the deep South. Many of the older voters could not shake their stereotypes and biases. Kennedy was called a traitor. On the morning of his arrival, a prominent Dallas newspaper ran a full-page ad accusing the president of going soft on communism. This ad had a funeral black border similar to a death announcement. Placards stating that JFK was "wanted for treasonous activities against the United States" were distributed. Among those voicing displeasure was E. Howard Hunt, an extreme right-winger, who strongly believed Kennedy was running a communist government. Hunt had ties to the CIA and years later would resurface as one of Nixon's Watergate burglars. There are many who believe that Hunt was directly involved in the assassination.

Many radical groups, the most prominent being the John Birch Society, the Minutemen, and the Ku Klux Klan, considered Kennedy soft on communism. As far as they were concerned, his position during the Bay of Pigs, the Cuban missile crisis, and the Nuclear Test Ban Treaty confirmed it. All three operations concluded with a peaceful solution rather than a direct attack against Cuba and subsequently, the Soviet Union. These resolutions were also contrary to the desires of the CIA, organized crime, and Cuban exiles. Kennedy felt a peaceful solution was a sign of strength whereas his enemies felt it showed weakness.

The majority of the Democratic voters in Dallas in 1960 had supported Republican Richard M. Nixon because they didn't agree with JFK's support of civil rights issues. The president wanted the Negro population (not referred to as African Americans in the 1960s) to be guaranteed the right to vote and have equal opportunity when it came to employment. There was Southern resentment toward these policies. Certain people in Dallas were not afraid to vent their feelings and frustrations. Vice President Lyndon Johnson, even though he was a Texan, was frequently the subject of slander. The ambassador to the United States, Adlai Stevenson, had been hit by a picket sign in Dallas just a month prior to Kennedy's scheduled visit. No wonder this trip to Texas was considered dangerous.

From 1961 to 1962, thirty-four threats against Kennedy's life originated in the state of Texas, yet, the Secret Service did nothing to increase protection for the president. The FBI and the Dallas Police followed that lead. *Nothing!*

In fact, the Dallas police were informed they would not play an active role when the presidential party arrived. The Secret Service protection for the president's motorcade was not even up to standard. Previous presidential motorcades included police motorcycle escorts on both sides and in front of the presidential limousine to form a protective shield.

Security for the Dallas Trade Mart, where the president was scheduled to give a speech, was very tight. Why didn't these various law enforcement agencies increase security for the president everywhere in Dallas? We don't know.

We do know that John F. Kennedy was a fatalist.

He experienced the death of his oldest brother, Joseph, in the war; his sister Kathleen had died in 1948; he had lost his baby Patrick only a few days after Patrick's birth. JFK had several brushes with death when he had life-threatening operations for his chronic and severe back pain. He was also diagnosed with Addison's disease. It was potentially fatal (especially in the 1960s), and he accepted that reality.

He refused to have the bubble-top cover his car in the motorcade because he wanted the people to see him. It wasn't bulletproof. Still, if it had been secured over the limousine, it might have diverted the bullets' path(s).

Shortly after boarding the plane on the morning of his fateful trip, JFK told his wife, "If anyone really wanted to shoot the president, it was not a difficult job. All one had to do was to get on a high building with a telescopic rifle, and there was nothing anybody could do to defend against such an attempt." *Did the President have a premonition?*

Two years earlier, (December 1961), when he and Jackie took a trip to Latin America, their motorcade was scheduled to go through downtown Caracas, Venezuela. It was considered a very dangerous trip, and there were many warnings about possible attempts on the president's or the first lady's life. Despite the danger and concerns that everyone had, JFK decided to go because he wanted to show to all underdeveloped countries the commitment of the United States to democratic life. The security for this motorcade was immense. Two thousand troops were involved. It was estimated there was one armed soldier watching over him every ten feet for a total of thirty miles. There were police motorcycles on both sides of the presidential limousine with Secret Service men standing on the running boards.

It's inconceivable (and, in my opinion, inexcusable) that President Kennedy was not given excellent security precautions in his own country, whereas he was well protected in Venezuela (and, Venezuela was a poor country!). The

failings of the Secret Service, Dallas Police Department, and FBI in protecting the president during his final and fatal visit to Dallas will all be discussed
in a subsequent chapter.

The Eagle Has Landed

On November 22, 1963, Air Force One landed at Love Field in Dallas, Texas,
after a 13-minute flight from Fort Worth. The weather was pleasant, and
the reception was cordial. Jackie was seated next to the president in the limousine, and Governor and Mrs. Connelly were seated in front of them. Sitting in front of the Connellys were two Secret Service men; Roy Kellerman
and William Greer, the limousine driver. The lead car in the motorcade was
driven by the Dallas police chief and trailed by three motorcycles. Following
this was the presidential limousine, which in turn was followed by a convert-
ible carrying more Secret Service agents. I find it puzzling as to why there
was not more Secret Service protection in front of the presidential car. There
were over twenty cars in the motorcade as it began its ten mile trip from the
airport, down through the heart of Dallas bound for the Trade Mart where
the president was scheduled to speak.

The route was known to all, although the original plans had been changed.
The motorcade would travel down Main Street, turn right onto Houston Av-
enue, and proceed to Elm Street. It was necessary to make a sharp left turn
to enter Elm Street. The motorcade was to stay on Elm where it would pass
under the Stemmons Freeway and continue to the final destination.

As it traveled on Elm Street, it would pass a building known as the Texas
School Book Depository (TSBD). This motorcade route differed from the
original parade route and was illustrated on the front page of the *Dallas
Morning News* on the day prior to, as well as on the morning of, the assassination. The original route was to proceed straight down Main Street through
the center of Dealey Plaza as it headed towards Stemmons Freeway. In this
route, the turn onto Houston Street and then onto Elm Street would have
been diverted. However, for whatever reason, there was a sudden change in
the motorcade route to allow for a right turn onto Houston Street. Now it
would be necessary to make a very sharp 120-degree hairpin left turn onto
Elm Street where the limousine would have to dramatically slow down before
it proceeded to pass the TSBD and the area of the Grassy Knoll.

Rule-Breaking Pace

One Secret Service regulation was that the presidential car had to maintain a certain speed, usually twenty to thirty miles per hour. This pace was of great importance because it was determined that a slower-moving car would make anyone in the car an easy target for a potential sniper. On this new route, the limousine was required to slow to a speed of about ten miles per hour. This route was chosen under the direction of the Secret Service as well as the mayor of Dallas, Earle Cabell. It's worth noting that his honor the mayor was the brother of General Clark Cabell, the deputy director of the CIA, who was fired by JFK following the Bay of Pigs incident.

The people of Dallas turned out in great numbers (estimated at over 200 thousand people) to line the motorcade route. They appeared very enthusiastic and supportive of the president. The motorcade proceeded with its designated route, first down Main Street. It then made a ninety-degree turn onto Houston Street and was then heading north toward the TSBD.

I have viewed and walked this route and firmly believe this would have been the ideal time for an assassin to have fired at the president. The shot would have been unimpeded. Instead the assassin alleged to have been shooting from the sixth floor of the TSBD waited until the limousine turned onto Elm Street. At that point there was an obstruction, a group of trees, which would hinder accuracy. Either the assassin(s) was not very bright or there was no assassin firing from the TSBD. I personally favor the second theory.

After witnessing the jubilant and enthusiastic reception the people were giving the president, Nellie Connelly, the governor's wife, turned around to the president and said, "Mr. President, you can't say that Dallas does not love you."

The motorcade then made the severe and abrupt turn onto Elm Street. An instant later, after passing the TSBD (12:30 PM), shots were fired. The president (after just waving to the crowd) raised his hand to his throat as he was shot for the first time. He then slumped backward onto Jackie's lap as he received the fatal head shot. Governor Connelly heard the first shot and turned to view the president, but then he, too, was struck by a bullet.

Radio and Television Coverage

People were stunned. Initially, viewers and listeners did not know what happened and did not know the source or direction of the shots. People at the scene panicked and many hit the ground. Others ran toward an area known as the Grassy Knoll in Dealey Plaza. Some people ran toward the TSBD. We were told the limousine carrying our beloved president was speeding to Parkland Hospital where a team of doctors was waiting.

Miniseconds after the shots rang out, Jackie climbed onto the back of the limousine, in her blood-stained pink outfit, and reached out to retrieve something. It wasn't until much later that we learned Jackie was reaching out to bring back fragments of her husband's skull that had been blown out by the fatal shot.

I stood transfixed in front of a television set watching the people who had lined up to cheer the president. They looked dazed, and many were crying. From this point on, media coverage was extensive and radio and television commentators kept the entire world informed of the tragic events. For the next few minutes (which seemed like hours), we waited for news of our president's condition. *Was he alive or was he dead? Could this all have been a mistake?* None of us knew what was going on in the Emergency Room at Parkland. Finally, the news came.

President John F. Kennedy was dead. The time of death was 1:00 PM. I learned of this while listening to Walter Cronkite, one of the foremost newscasters of the day. As he was telling the nation these horrible facts, he was crying, and I too began to cry.

My personal hero, the president of the United States, John F. Kennedy had died, not by natural causes, not through an accident, but through the intentional act of an individual(s). The assassination occurred at 12:30 PM, CST on November 22, 1963, a day that would forever be ingrained in our memories.

It seemed the world came to a standstill—not just our country; but the world! We saw documentaries of our late president, and each one brought additional tears to our eyes. Outside the White House, people were standing around, oblivious to the fact that it was raining and they were getting soaked. Some stood there for a few minutes, others for hours, barely moving and barely talking. They just wanted to be there; they seemed to be unaware of time passing. Many claimed they felt as though they lost a close family member or a personal friend. They wanted to be together, show their respect, and at the same time, share their grief.

Investigation and Allegations

Reporting continued round the clock. A rifle (initially described as a Mauser but later changed to a Mannlicher-Carcano) had been found on the sixth floor of the TSBD near an open window, and close to this were three spent cartridges, all apparently from the same rifle. Could this have been the murder weapon? There was a witness who thought he saw someone in the window holding a rifle just prior to the firing of the shots. An employee of the TSBD had mysteriously left the building shortly after the assassination and was nowhere to be found. He had earlier been seen on the second floor of this building, calmly drinking a Coke, soon after the shots were fired. This was confirmed by several witnesses including a Dallas policeman who rushed into the building immediately after hearing the shots. The man in question was Lee Harvey Oswald. He didn't appear to be anxious or rattled in any way. He did not fit the description of someone who just shot the president from the sixth floor of the TSBD and had to race down four flights of stairs. The amount of information known about Oswald, almost immediately after the assassination and before he was even arrested and charged, was nothing short of amazing.

Finally, word came that a policeman named Tippit had been gunned down in an area somewhat remote from Dealey Plaza, located about 0.9 mile away. The time was 1:16 PM, CST. There supposedly were eyewitnesses to this murder, and the description seemed to match that of Lee Harvey Oswald. However, many of these so-called eyewitnesses gave vastly different testimony. It was even suggested the police officer was killed by more than one assassin. Eyewitnesses could not positively identify Oswald as the shooter of Officer Tippit even in a police lineup. Yet, as we shall see later, this did not seem to bother members of the Warren Commission who, in subsequent months, would rely upon a single witness, Helen Markham, to incriminate Oswald as the prime suspect. In retrospect, she may have been the most unreliable of all the "witnesses" in the Tippit assassination.

The police then conveniently received a tip that a suspicious-looking man had entered a theater without buying a ticket. They promptly responded and Lee Harvey Oswald was caught and arrested in the Texas Theatre and brought to jail. He was taken into custody for the possible murder of a Dallas police officer. The assassination of the president did not even come into play at this time—or did it? The time was 1:50 PM CST.

Oswald in Custody in Record Time

The total time interval between the assassination of the president and the final capture of Oswald was only one hour and twenty minutes. This was truly a remarkable piece of police work, certainly one that everyone should be proud of, fast and expedient. Or, could there be another reason why Oswald was in police custody so soon after the fatal shots to our president were fired?

- Had Oswald been set up for the murder and were the authorities (which would have to include some of the conspirators) really looking for him at the outset, even if he were not directly involved in the assassination?

- At the time of the announcement of the Tippit killing, there was a large exodus of law enforcement officers to the Oak Cliff area where Tippit was found. These officers had just been in the immediate vicinity of the TSBD and Dealey Plaza. Why was it so important for so many of them to suddenly leave the site of the assassination of the president of the United States to look for a man who theoretically was an unknown and had not been charged with anything?

- Could the answer be they knew Oswald was spotted in the Oak Cliff area and he was the man who was supposed to be blamed for the killing of the president? He had somehow managed to leave the TSBD unscathed.

- Was this contrary to the original plan? Was Oswald supposed to leave the TSBD alive? In addition, why was Tippit patrolling in the Oak Cliff area whereas the rest of the Dallas police department was at the site of the assassination in Dealey Plaza?

- There were some who felt that Officer Tippit was supposed to kill Oswald but that Oswald got him first. Tippit was killed a few blocks from the apartment of Jack Ruby.

- Was this strictly coincidental or is it possible that Oswald was on his way to meet Ruby when he was spotted by Tippit?

- The other possible scenario is that Tippit had just met with Ruby. Personally, I doubt if Officer Tippit was strictly an innocent bystander who just happened to get in the way.

- At this time there was absolutely no evidence that would directly tie Oswald to the assassination. Was somebody trying to get a predesignated patsy to blame for the assassination of the president?

- The FBI under the direction of J. Edgar Hoover also seemed to have a great interest in Oswald soon after the assassination. Within minutes after the arrest of Oswald for the shooting of Officer Tippit and less than twenty four hours after the assassination itself, Hoover telephoned Attorney General Robert Kennedy and informed him they had caught the man who had killed his brother, the president.

- This was strangely presumptuous since Oswald had not yet even been accused of the murder of the president. Hoover described Oswald as a "nut who was an ex-marine who had previously defected to Russia." Hoover was already stating that Oswald had pro-Castro feelings and that he was a communist sympathizer.

- Hoover had already made up his mind regarding his solution to this horrific murder and would never change it, no matter how much evidence might indicate otherwise. Yet, despite Hoover's claims, there was absolutely no evidence at this time to connect Oswald with the assassination. There were no witnesses to identify him as the shooter; there were no confessions; and there was no incriminating evidence whatsoever.

- Once Oswald was captured, there seemed to be a preoccupation and obsession to convince the public that the assassin of the president of the United States had been found.

The case against Oswald had been made even before he was charged with any crime. Whatever happened to the doctrine that we base our justice on: "innocent until proven guilty"? It did not apply here. In fact, after his arrest, there was no further investigation. The search for suspects was called off.

Who Were the Three Tramps?

Shortly after the assassination, three men were found hiding in a railroad car close to the Grassy Knoll. These men collectively known as the three tramps were taken across Dealey Plaza, photographed, and taken to the jail but were quickly released.

There are several researchers who believe the three vagrants may have been intimately involved in the assassination. They were all clean-cut and dressed very smartly, certainly not the type of men to hide in a railroad car. There is no official record of them being interrogated.

It has been suggested that two of these men may have been involved in the Watergate break-in during President Nixon's term of office. If true, there may be a connection between the assassination of JFK and the Watergate scandal. There's speculation that one reason Nixon destroyed some of the tapes was because he was afraid a tie to the Kennedy assassination might be found.

News Is Delivered in Rapid-Fire Succession

We learned that Governor Connelly was seriously wounded and was in surgery fighting for his life at Parkland Hospital. Jackie Kennedy was not hurt (physically), though we all vividly remember seeing pictures of Jackie with blood splattered over her pink suit. While multiple doctors and nurses at Parkland were working on the president in a vain attempt to save his life, Jackie remained at the hospital until her husband was officially declared dead.

Vice president Lyndon Baines Johnson initially went to Parkland but then was brought aboard Air Force One and sworn in as our thirty-sixth president. The law did not mandate that he be sworn in so quickly. Johnson wanted to take the oath of office prior to returning to the nation's capital. He wanted the world to know the Constitution of the United States is sacrosanct and government perseveres despite any emergency. Lyndon Johnson was sworn in at 2:39 PM by Federal Judge Sarah Hughes. Jackie Kennedy, now the former first lady, was in attendance at the swearing in event, though obviously she was extremely distraught. Johnson requested her presence to demonstrate to the American people that he intended to preserve the legacy of JFK.

The media now focused on Lee Harvey Oswald at the jail. Oswald had been arrested for the murder of Officer Tippit and shortly thereafter was charged with the murder of the president.

It's my contention that the powers that be knew people were dazed, grieving, and would welcome a quick fix. If a quick solution was not found, the public would ask many questions about who killed the president and why. This would make resolution of this horrific crime difficult and lengthy. Charging Lee Harvey Oswald with this murder was convenient. He was there, already under arrest, and the entire country, if not most of the world, was watching. If people could be made to believe that a single gunman had assassinated the president, the issue of a conspiracy would be quelled. The true assassins, fronting for the true conspirators, would accomplish their mission.

Oswald said that he was a patsy, meaning he was not responsible for the murder and was set up by others to take the blame. I personally believe he had no idea who orchestrated this assassination. I also suspect that he had no prior knowledge that President Kennedy was to be killed, at least not at the beginning. The idea of a patsy and therefore, a conspiracy, was just too much for the public to comprehend at the time. It was suggested that Oswald's motive for killing the president was to gain notoriety and a chance to be famous, something he would probably never have achieved otherwise. If this were true, it is highly unlikely that he would have declared himself a patsy. If he wanted fame for killing the president, he would have readily admitted he was the sole man responsible for his death.

Oswald was interrogated at the jail for over twenty-four hours. The Dallas Police Department, the Secret Service, and the Federal Bureau of Investigation conducted the interrogation. We had to rely strictly on what they reported to us. Oswald was not allowed to have a lawyer. He had absolutely no defense and was essentially tried and convicted upon his arrest. A few months later, this was sanctioned (unjustifiably in my opinion) by the Warren Commission. Oswald was murdered before the Warren Commission convened and any opportunity to plead not guilty died with him.

Divulged and Undivulged

At the time, average Americans did not know anything about what the doctors at Parkland had observed in trying to save the president's life. We did not know about Dealey Plaza and the fact that many observers believed shots were fired from that direction. We did know (or at least were told) that there was a rifle found on the sixth floor of the TSBD and that Oswald worked in this building. We certainly did not know about the Zapruder film at this time or its implications.

The American public remained in a state of shock for days. The unknowns were numerous. Why was the president killed? Did the assassination involve our communist enemies, namely Cuba and the USSR? How could our security forces—the Secret Service, FBI, and the Dallas Police Department—let this happen? Was our country in danger now that our president had been killed? What would happen next?

The next ordeal we faced was the funeral. The television sets went on again, if indeed, they were ever turned off, and we were told about the funeral procession and the various international foreign dignitaries who would attend the funeral.

We continued to be deluged by media reports about the events of November 22. We heard from eyewitnesses, people who had stationed themselves at Dealey Plaza to get a glimpse of the motorcade and see our young president. Many people along Elm Street, upon hearing the shots, raced up the Grassy Knoll to pursue the assassin(s). Some stated they saw smoke and gunfire coming from this area. Most of the witnesses in Dealey Plaza did not believe that shots came from the TSBD. They claimed shots were fired from in front of the presidential limousine high up on the Grassy Knoll in Dealey Plaza. Clearly, it was the opinion of many eyewitnesses that President Kennedy was shot and hit from the front. Upon arrival at the Grassy Knoll, many of these eyewitnesses stated they were turned away by men wearing Secret Service badges.

There was no known record of extra police protection in this area, and there were not any Secret Service personnel assigned to this area. Could these men with the Secret Service badges actually have been part of the assassination? Could they have been there to protect the shooters or could they have pulled the triggers themselves? Further discussion on the Secret Service and its ineptitude and lack of protection for the president as well as its possible association with the assassination will be found in a later chapter.

Within seconds after the shots were fired, the Dallas Police Chief, Jesse Curry, as well as Sheriff Bill Decker, both of whom were in the motorcade, radioed instructions to investigate the top of the Grassy Knoll. Did they believe this was the spot where gunfire originated? Other people entered the TSBD in response to a witness who stated that he thought he had seen a man on the sixth floor with a rifle. Within seconds after the shots were fired, Patrolman Marrion Baker entered the TSBD and found an employee on the second floor of the depository, drinking a Coke in the building's lunchroom.

We already know this was Lee Harvey Oswald. It's interesting to note, however, that not enough time had elapsed between the firing of the shots and the time it would take Oswald to race down from the sixth floor to the second floor. Further, the elevators in the building were still on the upper floors just after the assassination and, as a result, the stairs were the only way down. In addition, according to all witnesses who had observed him at this time, Oswald was calm and composed. Oswald left the building to go back to his boarding house. It is quite possible that at this point, Oswald had no knowledge the president had been shot.

Fourteen minutes after the shooting (12:44 PM CST) an all points bulletin was sent out describing the alleged assassin as an unknown white male, age approximately thirty, one-hundred and sixty five pounds, and with a slender build. This description fit Oswald, though certainly it could fit many other men as well. However, at this time, there were absolutely no suspects for the shooting, unless this was part of the preconceived plan to blame Oswald, who indeed was a real patsy. It appears someone already knew the description of the alleged assassin even before the assassination took place. The description that went out over the police radio was the one supposedly given by Howard Brennan, who became a witness for the government and who said that he saw someone standing on the sixth floor of the TSBD. Brennan was standing on the southwest corner of Houston and Elm Streets facing the TSBD when the shots rang out. His description was a "slender white male, five-foot, ten inches, and in his early thirties." Brennan then went on to say that this man appeared "unsmiling and calm. He didn't seem to feel one bit of excitement. His face was almost expressionless and he seemed preoccupied." One discrepancy is that Brennan could not have known how tall the would-be assassin was since the shooter would have to be kneeling to get a shot fired from the window, which was half closed. Brennan's eyesight was not the best, and even though he was said to have identified Oswald on the sixth floor of the TSBD, he could not identify Oswald in a police lineup. In addition, he failed a polygraph test. Despite all this, the Warren Commission considered him a reliable witness.

What Comes Next Is No Less Bizarre

The president was dead, and a man named Oswald was in custody as the alleged assassin. If everything stopped here and if Oswald had stood trial and was found guilty, then the public would probably have accepted this verdict. Johnson would be our new president, and our country would go on, for better or for worse. There would be no shouts of conspiracy, and we probably would have accepted the idea of a lone gunman. The evidence (which I contend has always pointed to more than one assassin even from the beginning) would not be thoroughly scrutinized. The skeptics would be few in number, and I would probably not have been one of them.

It was only after watching the movie *JFK* on four different occasions that I began to realize that what I believed for so many years could not be true. Oliver Stone's movie had been much maligned and ridiculed before it was ever released. It was seen by millions of people in this country as well as across the world. The public generally welcomed and accepted it even though the media did not. It was well researched and substantiated what many other researchers had been saying about the assassination for many years.

This movie led to my own research, which strengthened the theory that JFK was killed as the result of a conspiracy. I commend the foresight of those who came to this conclusion much sooner after the actual assassination. Unfortunately, the official government version as well as the media interpretation has not changed even after all these years. Despite the conclusion of the House Select Committee on Assassinations (1979) that there may have been a conspiracy, the standard answer to the question of who killed JFK is still Lee Harvey Oswald.

Jack Ruby Murders Oswald

The primary event, in my opinion, which led to the cry of conspiracy, occurred two days after the assassination of the president. On November 24, Lee Harvey Oswald was assassinated in front of millions of television viewers. Once Oswald was assassinated, doubt began to creep into the minds of most Americans as to whether he was responsible for Kennedy's murder and if he was, whether he acted alone. In other words, was there a conspiracy?

Following his arrest at the Texas Theatre, Oswald had been interrogated all day and all night by the Dallas police and other law enforcement officers. A press conference was arranged for midnight on November 23. Jack Ruby was not a member of the media or a law enforcement agency, but he attended the press conference.

Ruby was the owner of a Dallas strip club known as the Carousel Club. Ruby spoke out when the Dallas police chief wrongly said that Oswald had been a member of the "Free Cuba Committee." Ruby corrected him by stating the organization was called the "Fair Play for Cuba Committee." Purportedly Oswald was the only member of the Committee, so how did Ruby know this?

It was well-known that Ruby had ties to organized crime. He ran errands and did favors for those considered to be Mafia leaders. His name was often associated with Giancana and Roselli.

How Well Did Ruby Know Oswald?

The government version was that there was no connection between the two. Several people, however, maintained they saw Ruby together with Oswald at the Carousel Club on several occasions.

When Oswald was asked by a reporter if he killed Kennedy, he replied he had not been charged with the murder of the president and was being used as a patsy. Further, he had asked for legal assistance but did not receive it. It was later revealed that a lawyer had been contacted by a man named Clay Bertrand to defend Oswald. This man, also known as Clay Shaw, would serve as the impetus that District Attorney James Garrison of New Orleans would use to conduct his investigation into the assassination, trying to prove that there was a conspiracy.

How was Ruby allowed to go to the jail basement to view the transfer of Oswald? Ruby was probably admitted to the area by somebody associated with the Dallas Police Department. Ruby had ties with several of the Dallas police officers and was often seen entertaining many of them in his nightclub, the Carousel Club. In any event, Ruby was intermingling with others in the basement and was free to come into very close proximity with the prisoner. As television cameras operated, Jack Ruby shot and murdered Lee Harvey Oswald. Most Americans saw the assassination of Lee Harvey Oswald, since people were already placed in front of their television sets to watch the funeral of JFK.

Radio and television networks stayed on the air for seventy hours and twenty-seven minutes, all day and all night. There were no breaks and no commercials.

* * * * * *

Certain things come to mind when I reflect on the funeral. There was the frisky riderless black horse (Black Jack) with boots reversed in the stirrups, the symbol of the death of a leader. I remember the drum rolls accompanying the procession with the sound of bagpipes in the forefront. I remember Jackie leading the procession on foot to the gravesite, accompanied by the two Kennedy brothers, Robert and Ted. Walking behind them were many foreign dignitaries and heads of state, such as Charles de Gaulle of France.

I remember a three-year-old boy standing on the footsteps of the church and saluting as the casket carrying his father passed by. This, of course, was John F. Kennedy Jr. This scene would forever remain in our minds. It was rekindled on July 17, 1999, the day that this "three-year-old boy" (now grown into a mature adult like his father) was reported missing and finally found dead in a plane crash.

Finally, I remember the lighting of the eternal flame as President John F. Kennedy was put to rest. He was buried at Arlington National Cemetery in our nation's capital. Jackie chose this site rather than the Kennedy family plot in Massachusetts because as she so astutely said, "He belongs to the country."

There were two other burials on the same day as the president. One was Officer J. D. Tippit, and the other was Lee Harvey Oswald. Oswald was buried in Fort Worth, Texas. Attending his funeral were his wife, two children, mother, and brother. The pallbearers at Oswald's funeral happened to be reporters who were asked to participate.

The weekend ended. President John F. Kennedy had been buried. The so-called assassin Lee Harvey Oswald had also been assassinated and buried.

Someone once said "Events do not just happen. It is people that make them happen." I do not recall the source of the quote but it is appropriate. Unfortunately, many of the questions and answers related to these grizzly events have not been resolved even now some forty years later. Our governments' official position is still unchanged.

VIII

Lee Harvey Oswald

Soon after Oswald's arrest for the murder of Officer Tippit and the subsequent charge he had murdered the president of the United States, the public received an overwhelming amount of information about the alleged assassin.

Born October 18, 1939, (only one month after this author) in New Orleans, Louisiana, Lee Harvey Oswald spent his early years in Fort Worth, Texas, with his mother and a brother. His father died shortly before his birth.

Eventually the threesome adopted a nomadic way of life. Lee lived in multiple cities and attended many different schools. During this period, Lee was described as withdrawn, detached, and without friends. By age thirteen, he had undergone several psychological evaluations. He was depicted as emotionally disturbed, with passive-aggressive tendencies, and hostile to authority.

In fact, a psychiatrist who examined Oswald when he was a teenager stated in 1964 that he wasn't surprised when Oswald was arrested for the assassination. He had "all the qualifications of being a potential assassin." It's interesting to note in the 1950s this same psychiatrist wrote that Oswald gave no indication of psychotic mental changes, and there was no evidence of potential violence or homicidal potential. He was not considered a threat to society. Was the psychiatrist more objective in 1953 when he first examined Oswald? Did he become biased after the assassination?

The conspirators, and anyone promoting the validity of the Warren

Commission Report, no doubt welcomed the discovery of an unfavorable psychiatric profile in Oswald's early life. It served to influence public opinion that Oswald was the lone assassin.

A Crooked Path (1955–1963)

Even though Oswald didn't attend much high school, he was an avid reader. He read extensively about Marxism and socialism.

In 1955, he attended Civil Air Patrol meetings of a Louisiana-based student aviation group. David Ferrie, an expert pilot, was Lee's commander. (If the name is familiar to you, Ferrie was mentioned earlier in this book.) Ferrie was a staunch anti-communist who eventually became a key suspect in Jim Garrison's New Orleans investigation into the assassination of JFK.

In October 1956 at the age of seventeen, Oswald enlisted in the marines and was stationed in San Diego, California. He began to learn the Russian language. At the time, it was virtually unheard of that an active duty marine would voluntarily learn Russian. A more likely scenario was that he was told to learn the language. (Was he receiving intelligence training?)

In June 1957 Oswald was assigned to the Atsugi Naval Air Station in Japan where he worked in radio maintenance and operated electronic equipment for surveillance. He was trained in radar, map reading, and air traffic control. It was at that time the CIA was developing its U-2 program (i.e., spy planes that regularly flew over the Soviet Union from a base at Atsugi.) The U-2 program later became a very important and strategic event in our relationship with Russia. Many believe, including this author, that Lee Harvey Oswald was contracted by the CIA to work as a radar specialist, and while he was an intelligence trainee received additional technical training and further instruction in Russian.

He did not possess many skills when he first joined the marines. He was considered a below average marksman on the rifle range, and his mathematics and pattern analysis aptitude were below par. Yet he was granted high-security clearance—a necessity for his job. Surely Oswald was preparing (or being prepared by someone) for a life outside the marines.

In 1959 Oswald received a hardship release from the marines because his mother was sick. (Whether his mother was truly ill is doubtful.) In any event, he was awarded an honorable discharge.

Later, he threatened to disclose information he obtained as a marine to the Russians. His discharge was changed to a dishonorable discharge.

In October 1959 at the age of twenty, Lee Harvey Oswald obtained a visa with the intent of traveling to several countries including France, England, Germany, Cuba, and Russia. It appears that Oswald's true purpose in this trip was to defect to Russia and renounce his United States citizenship. Was this Oswald's idea or was he instructed to do this?

The reports of Oswald's activities in the Soviet Union are vague. In addition, it's difficult to corroborate information pertaining to his life in Russia. He applied for Soviet citizenship but was refused. He was disheartened and supposedly tried to commit suicide so that he could stay. Apparently his scheme worked, because he was allowed to remain in Russia. He was sent to Minsk where he was given a rent-free apartment and a good-paying job. Inexplicably his status had improved, and he was well treated.

In March 1961 Lee Harvey Oswald met Marina Nikolayevna Prusakova and within a very short time, they were married. Oswald abruptly decided he didn't like living in Russia, and he and Marina made plans to move to the United States.

In June 1961 Lee and Marina Oswald entered the United States without difficulty after the appropriate arrangements were made through the U.S. embassy in Moscow.

How was this possible? Who made it so easy for these two people—one an ex-marine who wanted to renounce his U.S. citizenship and who threatened to divulge military secrets to the Russian government and the other, his wife, who was a Russian citizen, to enter the United States?

This was the cold war era when relations between the two most powerful countries in the world were anything but friendly. It's almost incomprehensible that Oswald was not fully investigated by the Russians upon his entry into Russia and by the United States upon his return. He had retained his U.S. citizenship and seemed to be able to do as he pleased.

The Central Intelligence Agency opened a counterintelligence file on Oswald one year after his defection and prior to this simply placed him on a "watch list."

There was a Soviet Russia Division within the CIA, but it didn't seem concerned about him. Could it be the CIA had a hand in his defection and needed to lay back and not investigate him intensively?

Oswald made numerous notes about the economic conditions in the USSR, possibly at the request of the CIA. In any event, he eventually decided to return to this country (either because his mission had been completed or because he truly was disillusioned with his life in Russia). He wasn't treated as a traitor and, in fact, was greeted by members of the Federal Bureau of Investigation.

J. Edgar Hoover, FBI director, said the FBI had no knowledge of Oswald until after the assassination. In reality, the FBI began investigating Oswald in June 1962. The FBI was interested in finding out what his connections were to the Russians and whether he had been told to spy by the KGB (Soviet Intelligence Agency). Oswald was interviewed extensively on two occasions, but he would never admit to being a spy. He was arrogant and evasive and refused to answer questions about his Russian experiences.

Despite this, the FBI claimed Oswald was not a threat and closed its file on Lee Harvey Oswald. It wasn't until October 1962 that the FBI opened a file on Marina Oswald and reopened the file on her husband.

Both intelligence agencies denied having dealings with Oswald until after the assassination. Were they afraid that an earlier link to Oswald would cast doubts on them and precipitate unwanted questions?

Was Oswald a member of American intelligence (employed by the CIA or FBI or both) trying to obtain secrets in the USSR, or was he employed by Soviet intelligence (KGB) to disclose important secrets about our country?

One of the most famous Soviet defectors, at that time, was a man named Yuri Nosenko. Nosenko, a KGB officer and a ranking member of the counterintelligence department within the USSR, was personally in charge of Oswald's file during Oswald's stay in the Soviet Union. He told the CIA that the Russians paid very little attention to Oswald and, in reality, considered him insignificant and generally unstable (remember Oswald had reportedly attempted suicide). Oswald was never debriefed on his military background by Soviet intelligence and was never considered worthy of being an agent. When Oswald decided to return to the United States, Russia didn't offer opposition even though he was taking a Russian wife with him. Why wouldn't the Soviets have an interest in Oswald and want to learn about his marine background and U-2 knowledge? The CIA did not believe Nosenko's testimony and considered Oswald to be a possible agent of the USSR.

On May 1, 1960, a U-2 spy plane was shot down by Soviet missiles. This occurred two weeks prior to a proposed summit meeting between President Eisenhower and Soviet Prime Minister Krushchev. The incident destroyed any potential for peace at that time between the East and the West. The CIA wondered whether Oswald supplied information to the Russians based upon his experience at Atsugi.

The CIA (in specific, James Jesus Angleton, the agent in charge) did not believe Nosenko's testimony and worked to keep him in prison for several years, hoping he would change his story. He never did.

Now You See It, Now You Don't

If Nosenko was correct in stating the Russians had no real interest in Oswald, this would indicate the Russian KGB had no connection to the assassination of John F. Kennedy. Blame could not be placed on the Russians if there was no direct connection to Oswald. The Warren Commission Report does not even mention the Nosenko affair. This could be a very serious omission, especially if Nosenko's testimony was accurate.

Echoes of Denial

The official CIA position on Oswald had always been that there was no relationship of any kind between the agency and the alleged assassin.

In 1964 John McCone, the CIA director, told the Warren Commission that "Oswald was not an agent, employee, or informant for the Central Intelligence Agency." He went on to say there was no communication with Oswald, and the agency never interviewed him or solicited any information from him.

In 1978 the CIA said the same thing to the House Select Committee on Assassinations (HSCA): that there was no connection between the CIA and Lee Harvey Oswald. The Warren Commission never questioned these statements and never investigated further. The HSCA also accepted the CIA position but did say that because of the complexity of the CIA, it could not perform an adequate investigation.

We now know these statements by the CIA were false. The JFK Assassination Records Act of 1992 revealed multiple files from our intelligence agencies regarding Oswald. The CIA lied both to the Warren Commission and the House Select Committee on Assassinations. This does not necessarily mean that the entire organization, as differentiated from certain renegade members, had a hand in the assassination or cover-up.

FBI Agent James Hosty had an extensive file on Oswald as well as personal communication with him and Marina. Hosty knew that Oswald was working at the TSBD but never informed the Secret Service that Oswald might present a threat to the president on that fateful day of November 22, 1963.

Strange Bedfellows

Once back in the states, the Oswalds went to Dallas where they were befriended by members of the White Russian community, which had close ties to members of the American intelligence agencies. The most prominent of these members was a man named George DeMohrenschildt, who virtually took Oswald in and became his mentor. DeMohrenschildt had a very suspicious background; he was connected with the oil industry and had a background in intelligence. He was involved in the CIA training of exiles in Guatemala for the Bay of Pigs invasion. What is the reason that a man such as DeMohrenschildt would associate with Lee Harvey Oswald unless it was to watch him and possibly direct his activities? After all, Oswald at this time was virtually an unknown, at least to the general public (although not to the intelligence agencies, as we have seen).

After returning to the United States in June 1962, Oswald became more openly active. He lived in Dallas-Fort Worth until April 1963 when he went to New Orleans. In New Orleans he was seen passing out pro-Castro leaflets (Fair Play for Cuba Committee) in an area of town that was anti-Castro. He gained notoriety and even got involved in a fight with an anti-Castro exile. This led to the making of a television documentary where he had an opportunity to state his case. Lee Harvey Oswald was building a reputation or, it was being built for him. The name Oswald was becoming familiar to many.

The address 544 Camp Street was printed on the leaflets Oswald was distributing for the Fair Play for Cuba Committee. This was the address of a building that housed offices used by many anti-Castro enthusiasts.

First, there was Guy Bannister, a former FBI member from Chicago who was instrumental in the anti-Castro exile movement. In addition, there was David Ferrie who was intimately involved in training the Cuban exiles for the potential overthrow of Castro. Ferrie worked as a pilot for Carlos Marcello, the top mob figure in New Orleans, and he had a personal connection with Oswald, because he had been the young Oswald's commander in the Civil Air Patrol in Louisiana. (Both Bannister and Ferrie were prominent figures in Jim Garrison's investigation of the JFK assassination.) Lee Harvey Oswald was seen in the company of Bannister and Ferrie on several occasions. The "sighting" was probably contrived as part of the ongoing process to set up Oswald as a patsy. It should also be remembered these anti-Castro Cuban exiles were directly under the influence of the CIA with the chief liaison being E. Howard Hunt.

Oswald's activities and his associations established a pattern that would make him appear both pro-Castro and anti-Castro. The significant thing is that one way or another his name was linked with Castro.

In September 1963, he supposedly left New Orleans to go to Mexico City to try to get a visa so that he would be allowed to go to Cuba. Since there was a U.S. ban on travel to Cuba, imposed in January 1961, his visa was denied. Later the United States officially ended diplomatic relations with Cuba.

Pretenders on the Scene

If Oswald had received the visa and had gone to Cuba, he most likely would not have been in Dallas on the day that JFK was assassinated!

There's another interesting aspect to this trip to Mexico City. A photograph taken of "Oswald" leaving the embassy bore no resemblance to the Oswald who was arrested for the murders of the president and Officer Tippit. In addition, this man reportedly spoke "broken" Russian whereas the Oswald we know spoke fluent Russian (verified by both Marina as well as George DeMohrenschildt.) The "embassy Oswald" had to be an imposter.

The entire intelligence community based in New Orleans was housed within close proximity to the building on Camp Street. This included the FBI, the CIA, and the Office of Naval Intelligence.

Why would Lee Harvey Oswald spend so much time in this area if he were planning to assassinate the president? Of course, if Oswald was an agent, he would feel comfortable in these surroundings. To spectators, Oswald was an activist and Castro sympathizer and supporter while at the same time he associated with the anti-Castro underground.

There were many other examples of Lee Harvey Oswald becoming more public prior to the assassination. This required several people to impersonate him; the so-called Oswald imposters. They appeared at various spots often at the same time. One was seen at a rifle range, causing a commotion, and shouting his name so others would "remember" Oswald. Another brought in his Mannlicher-Carcano rifle to a gun shop to have a scope mounted when, in fact, the rifle already had a scope in place when it was purchased from a sporting goods store in Chicago. Another was seen buying and test driving a car when, in fact, it was thought the real Oswald didn't know how to drive. I have already mentioned the man seen at the Soviet embassy in Mexico City asking for a visa to Cuba. This imposter was later verified by the FBI. On the day after the assassination, J. Edgar Hoover notified President Johnson that someone had been impersonating Lee Harvey Oswald at the Soviet Embassy in Mexico City on September 28, 1963. There were many witnesses who claimed to have seen and talked to "Oswald." They saw different Oswalds in different places at about the same time. Lee Harvey Oswald could not have been in two places at the same time, not even by government standards. The description of these Oswald imposters differed as did the sounds of their voices. These incidents were undoubtedly staged to establish a link between Oswald and Castro. Unfortunately, our intelligence agencies chose to ignore the idea of the Oswald imposters just as they ignored the testimony of many valuable witnesses.

The Ever-Present Question: Why?

Why was it important for the name and face of Oswald to be heard and seen at so many different places? Why was it necessary for this name to become familiar to various governmental agencies as well as the media and the populace at large? I believe the answer to these questions is that Lee Harvey Oswald was being set up as a scapegoat for the murder of our president. He had to have ties (factual or factitious) to our enemies and especially to the enemies of JFK. A patsy was valuable if he could help create conditions for an assassination by taking the focus away from the true murderers and to dispel the possibility of a connection between the victim and the conspirators.

He also had to attract the attention of the media away from the true forensic evidence and ballistics. He needed to make himself the focus as the shooter, as the lone assassin. I believe that Lee Harvey Oswald was a perfect prototype for the patsy in the assassination of JFK. He was a drifter and essentially isolated from society. His past was questionable and suspicious, and he was portrayed as someone who could commit murder. This was accomplished by the assassination attempt on Major General Edwin A. Walker.

Trouble and More Trouble

Walker was a former U.S. Army commander in West Germany who once declared that our government was under communist control. He was considered an extremist and a radical and was strongly anti-Kennedy. He once stated, "Kennedy is a liability to the free world." Walker was a racist and a member of the John Birch Society. In April 1963 someone tried to shoot Walker at his home. The shooter missed. The person accused of this shooting was Lee Harvey Oswald, with most of the so-called incriminating evidence being given by Marina Oswald.

Marina's testimony after JFK's assassination is widely open to scrutiny; it must be remembered that she was very young (age twenty-two), had two small children, spoke very little English, had very little money, was from Russia, and was virtually kept in captivity and seclusion for an extended period by the Secret Service. She feared being deported back to the Soviet Union if she did not give the answers she thought they wanted. She was questioned for many hours, and I suspect she was coached regarding parts of her testimony. She may have been promised full immunity and protection if she testified. In any event, Marina's testimony in 1963–64 (which was accepted as truth by the Warren Commission) added fuel to the fire and gave the indication that Oswald could behave in a violent manner. The government jumped on this testimony to help make its case. Marina eventually retracted many of her original statements and implied she had been coerced into making them.

Place and Time

Lee Harvey Oswald got the job at the Texas School Book Depository in Dallas with the aid of an acquaintance named Ruth Paine several weeks before the assassination. Marina Oswald and her children lived in Mrs. Paine's home in Dallas for a time while Oswald was in Irving, Texas. At the time Oswald got the job at the TSBD, the trip by President Kennedy to Dallas was not a certainty. Therefore, Oswald could not have known the president's motorcade route would pass the depository. This too was apparently a last-minute decision. From Oswald's point of view, it was purely coincidental that the motorcade just happened to pass his place of work. From the conspirators view, however, this was an absolute necessity.

Approaching Destination

The specific route for the motorcade was printed in the *Dallas Morning News* on November 22. The final destination was the Trade Mart where JFK was scheduled to give a speech at a business luncheon. The original plan was to go straight down Main Street to Stemmons Freeway and then to the mart, therefore bypassing the turns onto both Houston Street and Elm Street. This would mean the motorcade would not pass the depository. At the last minute, the route was changed by the Secret Service. It called for the presidential limousine to leave Main Street and turn onto Houston and subsequently Elm Street to proceed past the depository.

How convenient that the motorcade would now pass the building where the patsy was located. The sharp turn onto Elm Street required a prohibited slowing of the presidential limousine and would create a perfect opportunity for someone to shoot the president from the front. The conspiracy to assassinate the president was in full force. The route was changed to bring the intended victim (President Kennedy) to the alleged assassin (Oswald).

Where Was Oswald?

What was Lee Harvey Oswald doing at the time of the assassination? First of all, Oswald carried an object into the depository that morning that he claimed were curtain rods. The government, however, (and the Warren Commission substantiated this) stated that this object was the Mannlicher-Carcano rifle that was supposedly used to shoot the president.

Oswald was carrying this object in his arm between his armpit and palm. It could not have been the rifle because the rifle was much longer and could not have been carried in this fashion even if it was disassembled.

Oswald was seen eating lunch on the second floor of the TSBD between 12:15 and 12:25 PM. The motorcade bringing the president was due to arrive in this area at 12:25 PM. His presence in the lunchroom at this time was verified by several witnesses. I do not recall the proponents of the lone assassin theory stating that the bullets were fired from the "second" floor lunch room of the TSBD. Oswald would not have had time to race up to the sixth floor, make all the necessary preparations such as arranging the boxes necessary for the sniper's nest, get this primitive rifle ready to shoot, and then fire three shots within a span of slightly over five seconds at a moving target and over some trees that were obstructing his view. To make the scenario even more unbelievable is the fact that these shots were accurate enough to hit their target on at least two occasions. Shortly after the shooting, Oswald was seen, still on the second floor, drinking a Coke. The time was 12:32 PM; JFK was shot only two minutes earlier at 12:30 PM. Oswald's presence on the second floor was verified by two other witnesses, M. L. Baker, a Dallas police officer, who raced into the depository a few seconds after the shots were fired, and Roy Truly, the superintendent in charge of the depository. If Oswald had fired from the sixth floor, as has been concluded by the Warren Commission, why would he not race out of the building in order to escape? Instead he stopped at a vending machine on the second floor to get a Coke. When seen by Baker and Truly, Oswald appeared relaxed, composed, and not at all short of breath. This would not be the description of a man who had just shot the president of the United States and raced down four flights of stairs. It seems that the elevators in the depository were not operational at the time. In fact, the elevators were still on the sixth floor. Once again, Oswald would not have had time to run from the sixth floor and arrive on the second floor prior to the arrival of Officer Baker and Superintendent Truly. I contend that Lee Harvey Oswald was not on the sixth floor of the TSBD at the time of the assassination.

Oswald then left the book depository through the front door (also surprising if he were the true assassin), boarded a bus, but then switched to a taxi because of the excessive traffic due to the shooting. While on the bus, he was seen by his former landlady, Mary Bledsoe. Her description of him at that time is very strange. She said the following: "Oswald boarded the bus. He looked like a maniac. His shirt was undone. His sleeve was out here (demonstrating). He was dirty. He looked so bad in his face. His face was so distorted."

Are we to believe this testimony made by this woman that directly contradicts what was seen a short time earlier in the TSBD? Oswald was described as calm and collected by Officer Baker and Superintendent Truly and certainly was not considered disheveled as she states. She made it sound as if Oswald had been in a fight between the time he left the TSBD and boarded the bus. We know this is not true, or at least there has never been any testimony to say so. Obviously, the Warren Commission cited her as a reliable witness because her description of Oswald on the bus would tend to make one believe that he had just been involved in something totally horrific.

This is the same approach that the author Gerald Posner made in his book *Case Closed* where he did everything possible to make the public believe that Oswald was the assassin. He used witness testimony that favored his argument and ignored those witnesses whose testimony would be opposite to his conclusions. He essentially reiterated the Warren Commission's conclusions, and even though his book was a bestseller, he failed to convince the public of its validity. (Mr. Posner and his book will be discussed in more detail in a later chapter.)

Oswald then arrived at his boarding home, took a revolver, and left at 1:04 PM. Why did Oswald need his revolver? Did he fear for his life? Was he beginning to suspect he had been set up?

One theory was that Oswald had been told of an anti-Castro operation to intimidate and threaten the president because of his recent cooperative ventures with the Russians. Oswald didn't realize this was a real assassination plot until it was too late.

Just before he left home, his landlady saw a police car stop in front of the boarding house. The driver honked twice (as if giving a signal), and the car departed. What was Oswald's connection to the men in the police car?

Oswald walked in the direction of the Texas Theatre. At 1:16 PM Officer J. D. Tippit was shot and allegedly murdered by Oswald in the Oak Cliff area (slightly less than a mile from his house and several miles from the TSBD). This was about forty-five minutes after the assassination of President Kennedy.

Was Tippit trying to arrest Oswald for the murder of JFK, and if so, how did he know that Oswald was even a suspect? Oswald was not officially charged with the murder of JFK for another ten hours.

Or could there be another scenario? Oswald probably realized he was being set up as the assassin. This would explain why Oswald picked up his revolver at his boarding house. Was Tippit part of the conspiracy team? He may have been told to silence Oswald so that he could not talk and tell what he might know about the assassination. No one ever proved what Tippit's role was on November 22. Was he an innocent bystander? (Not likely.)

Tippit was killed two blocks from the home of Jack Ruby. Did Tippit just return from meeting Jack Ruby or was Oswald on his way to meet Ruby? This is something we will never know.

The news of Officer Tippit's violent end caused an immediate exodus of law enforcement officers from the Dealey Plaza location (the site of the assassination of the president) to the Oak Cliff location, the site of Tippit's demise, a distance of several miles.

Why did these officers leave the major crime scene of Dealey Plaza and the Texas School Book Depository to investigate a police officer shooting at a distant location? The police, at this time, didn't have any idea of a possible connection between the two killings. Or did they? Could it be they knew Oswald would be there and that he was being set up for both murders?

Another question that has never been answered was why was Tippit patrolling in this area while the rest of the Dallas police were all at the JFK assassination site?

Oswald proceeded to the Texas Theatre, eight blocks from the Oak Cliff section of Dallas. It was as if he was going to the theater with a definite mission in mind. Was he to meet someone, exchange information, and get his assignment? Intelligence agents often meet in unremarkable places such as this one.

We don't know that Oswald actually killed Tippit. Some witnesses to the shooting say two men were involved. Empty cartridges, found at the murder scene, were fired from an automatic weapon and not from a revolver like the one Oswald carried. The various witnesses to the murder of Officer Tippit disagreed dramatically. One witness insisted Tippit was killed by two gunmen. Still, the Warren Commission was able to come up with a single report pointing to Oswald as the prime suspect.

If nothing else, the murder of Officer Tippit helped establish an image of Oswald as an assassin. It was easier to speculate that Oswald was a troubled man sufficiently violent to be capable of killing a police officer without provocation. As a result, he could also murder the president for no specific reason. In that case, Oswald would not have needed a motive to kill Kennedy.

One of the problems the lone gunman enthusiasts always had was they could never come up with a motive for the assassination. Oswald's apparent instability was motive enough. Remember, the potential violent nature of Oswald was also raised when he was accused of firing a shot at retired army General Edwin Walker. Oswald's so-called attempt on Walker's life was unsuccessful. I find it truly amazing the bullet missed a stationary target at close range and under ideal conditions. On the other hand, Oswald was thought to be able to hit a moving target on November 22 with a row of trees obstructing his view.

This discrepancy in Oswald's marksmanship ability defies logic and common sense. Of course, so does the entire government view of the assassination.

Oswald was arrested in the Texas Theatre at 1:50 PM CST. He most likely knew he was being set up for the murder of the president, especially since the arresting officers said that they got him on both counts, meaning the murders of Kennedy and Tippit. Oswald appeared extremely calm as he announced, "I am not resisting arrest." Either he was a tremendous actor or he was truly innocent. Another possible scenario is that he knew that he had accomplices and believed they would take care of him. Of course, he never realized how they would take care of him.

The Astonishing Omission of a Record

After his arrest, Oswald was interrogated by the Dallas chief of homicide, Will Fritz. Hours of interrogation ensued without benefit of any official recording, taping, or note taking. In short, no documented information was available to be used in a court of law.

Was it already known that Oswald would never stand trial? Would he be assassinated before this case ever got to court? Less than forty-eight hours after the assassination of John F. Kennedy, Lee Harvey Oswald was also assassinated in front of millions of television viewers.

He was being transferred from the city jail to the county jail when he was fatally shot by Jack Ruby. This ended Oswald's life, but in the eyes of the government, it certainly did not end his guilt in the assassination of John F. Kennedy.

Lee Harvey Oswald had been arrested, tried, and convicted by the press, Dallas police, and our government even though he had not been officially charged with a crime. The legal premise, which our country espouses, is that a person is "innocent until proven guilty." It did not hold true in this case.

In a Nutshell

The entire scenario is so preposterous it defies logic.

1. I believe that Lee Harvey Oswald was set up to take the blame for the assassination of JFK, but he was not part of the true conspiracy. He was a patsy. (See 4 and 5 below.)

2. It was the cold war era, and Oswald was considered to be a communist and a Castro sympathizer. Oswald received an honorable discharge from the marines, which was revoked, and he was issued a dishonorable discharge. Yet he had no trouble getting a passport and moving to Russia

3. While in the USSR, he renounced his U.S. citizenship and married a Russian girl, Marina. When he supposedly decided he no longer liked the way of life in Russia, he and Marina moved to the United States without difficulty.

4. A trap was laid to "use him." The only group that had the power, motive, and opportunity to set this trap was our intelligence agency, probably aided (at least financially) by the establishment or power Elite or military-industrial complex, whatever title you want to give this organization. Today, this could be called the trilateral commission. In essence, this is an organization composed of many powerful and extremely wealthy individuals from throughout the world. They come from the world of politics, business, academia, and the media. They view their prime purpose as to "help solve the many problems of the world."

5. Conspiracy theorists have a more sinister definition of this organization's purpose. I believe that Lee Harvey Oswald was an agent for either the CIA or FBI or both. He needed clearance and backup to accomplish all the feats that have been attributed to him. Someone had to pay his way, because his activities were costly and Oswald was anything but wealthy. In fact, upon his return to the United States, Oswald received a loan from the State Department. Somebody was directing his life for a future operation.

6. Upon his return to the United States, Oswald associated with people in New Orleans who had Mafia connections. They included Guy Bannister, former FBI chief in Chicago, and David Ferrie, a jack-of-all-trades, who worked for boss Carlos Marcello.

7. Oswald formed the Fair Play for Cuba Committee (he was the only member) and passed out pro-Castro leaflets. This was intriguing, because the address on the leaflets (544 Camp Street) was the same as Bannister's headquarters, which dealt with the anti-Castro exile movement and its attempt to get Castro removed from Cuba.

8. The attention Oswald generated (with the help of the Oswald imposters) grew in the year 1963. When the president was killed and Oswald was named the assassin, many people were primed to come forward and declare they had seen or heard of Lee Harvey Oswald.

9. Oswald was perceived as hostile and potentially violent. This perception was far from the truth. Even though he was a self-proclaimed Marxist, Oswald actually liked Kennedy and had a great deal of respect for him. He told his wife Marina this on several occasions.

10. Lee Harvey Oswald didn't have a motive to assassinate President Kennedy. This line of reasoning was acknowledged by the Dallas police and by the Warren Commission! Being a communist was not a sufficient motive to assassinate the president.

11. If Oswald acted as the lone gunman to gain notoriety or to show support for Castro and communism, would he have made the following statements to reporters at various times during his interrogation?

    *   "I'm just a patsy."

    *   "I didn't shoot anybody, no sir."

    *   "I don't know what kinds of dispatches you people (meaning the reporters) have .been given. I have committed no act of violence."

    Assassins who want notoriety are usually proud of their crimes and admit to them without hesitation. Oswald's statements are those belonging to someone trying to plead innocence. (Remember, too, Oswald didn't have legal representation. No one was admonishing him against self-incrimination.)

12. There were two pieces of evidence (both very superficial and circumstantial) that could be used against Oswald if this case had been brought to trial. First, Oswald was in the TSBD at the time of the

assassination. Nobody ever denied this, but the depository was full of people at that time. Most were probably viewing the motorcade. Multiple eyewitnesses said they had seen him on the second floor of the TSBD before and after the assassination. Next, Oswald owned (under the alias of A. J. Hidell) a Mannlicher-Carcano rifle, which was supposedly found on the sixth floor of the TSBD, and which was said to be the rifle used to kill the president.

13. The ballistics report apparently had the three shell casings found on the sixth floor of the depository match the rifle. However, how can we be absolutely sure that the casings weren't planted or for that matter, maybe the rifle was planted?

About the Rifle

When the rifle was first found and placed in evidence, it was identified as a German Mauser and not an Italian Mannlicher-Carcano.

This initial misidentification of the rifle was made by several law enforcement officials who were supposedly experts at recognizing different types of rifles.

It wasn't until twenty-four hours later that the rifle was identified as a Mannlicher-Carcano. This leaves open the possibility that there may have been a substitution of rifles or there may have been a second rifle found at the TSBD.

Oswald ordered a Mannlicher-Carcano rifle from Klein Sporting Goods in Chicago, Illinois, in March 1963. This rifle came with a telescopic sight already mounted. The Dallas police interviewed a rifle expert who stated that he was asked to mount a sight on the rifle by a man named Oswald. This most likely was one of the Oswald imposters.

The Mannlicher-Carcano rifle was a very old and outdated weapon. It had a bad reputation for reliability and workability. It was designed for short-range hits and was not a sniper's rifle. Ammunition for the rifle hadn't been manufactured since World War II. In fact, the rifle had been taken out of active service in 1918.

Expert riflemen examined the weapon and concluded it had many defects, including its bolt-action trigger, telescopic sight, and firing pin. These factors would reduce the rifle's accuracy especially for a shooter who had never fired it before.

Lee Harvey Oswald could have purchased a more accurate rifle, for the same price, by walking into a Dallas gun shop to do so. If he were the assassin, why would he buy via mail-order when the rifle could be traced back to him through his name, address, handwriting, or serial number? If he purchased the rifle at a local gun shop there would have been no records to identify him. Remember this was the 1960s, not the present time when criterion for purchasing a rifle is different.

The key point regarding the Mannlicher-Carcano rifle has to do with efficiency, or lack thereof. On the basis of the frames seen in the Zapruder film, there were at least three shots fired over a period of 5.6 seconds, at a moving target and through a group of trees that had to cause an initial obstruction in the line of fire. This would hamper the murderer's vision from the sixth floor of the TSBD, if indeed, this were where the shots were fired. To make matters more unbelievable, all the shots were said to have hit their targets; this was contradicted by the James Tague story, which declared that the first bullet completely missed its target.

It has been shown that in the hands of an expert marksman working the bolt-action Mannlicher-Carcano rifle, it could be fired no faster than once every 2.3 seconds, and this is without aiming. Yet the government wants us to believe this extraordinary feat was accomplished by an ex-marine who was considered a poor marksman during his tenure in the marines.

In the military, there were three categories to designate efficiency and accuracy in using a rifle. The lowest qualification was the "marksman." This was the category in which Oswald was placed as he had a score of 191 using a scale of 190–250. He was only one point above the minimum to qualify for the lowest of the three ratings. The average qualification was the "sharpshooter" and the highest most efficient class was called the "expert." Clearly Oswald was poorly rated at firing a rifle, and this was measured when the target was stationary. In addition, the bolt action of this rifle was very difficult to manipulate. Firing three shots in rapid succession with this rifle and with any kind of accuracy would be very difficult even for someone who was considered an "expert."

Mission Impossible

I don't believe it was possible for Oswald, himself a poor marksman, to have hit a moving target with this rifle with expert accuracy from a distance of over 160 feet (estimated to be the distance between the sixth floor window of the TSBD and the intended victim).

If the experts couldn't accomplish this, how can we believe that Oswald was able to do so? The answer is he couldn't and didn't. Yet the Warren Commission told us to believe that he had.

Another important point was the fact that the paraffin or nitrate test on Oswald's cheeks was negative. There were no powder marks on his chin. This would prove that he could not have fired a rifle recently. In addition, the FBI was unable to find a palm print on the rifle butt to match Oswald's. Mysteriously the Dallas police did claim that they had found a palm print. Could this have been transferred from his hand onto the rifle after Oswald had been assassinated?

What then was the police's case against Oswald?

Police found (or so they claimed) the Mannlicher-Carcano rifle that was believed to belong to Oswald (or at least an alias).

Police found three shell casings in the same area. Two bullet fragments were found in the limousine, and a whole "pristine" bullet was found on a stretcher in the emergency room at Parkland Memorial Hospital. There was a ballistics match of the bullets and fragments with the rifle. The rifle was considered the murder weapon.

It is my belief that the rifle and bullets were all planted in their respective areas to be used as evidence against Oswald. There is one interesting sidelight to the ballistic scenario that obviously is a very important part of the forensic evidence. The Warren Commission stated that only two bullets struck the occupants of the car, meaning President Kennedy and Governor Connelly.

It must be remembered that the single bullet theory, which will be discussed in a later chapter, was the sole basis for the Warren Report. However, later investigation using trace element evidence (examining recovered fragments of bullets for the trace elements of silver and antimony and determining their proportions in the fragments) revealed that more than two bullets were fired and hit these two occupants.

If this was true, there obviously had to be more than one shooter. All of the evidence against Oswald is circumstantial. In fact, former Chief of Police

Jesse Curry felt that Oswald did not act alone. He said, "We don't have any proof that Oswald fired a rifle and never did. Nobody's yet been able to put him in that building with a gun in his hand."

The FBI had a witness named Howard Brennan who stated that he saw Oswald standing at the sixth floor window of the TSBD when the shots were fired. However, later he was unable to pick Oswald out of a police lineup and identify him, thus making his testimony very doubtful and suspicious. In addition, if Oswald were the shooter, he would be kneeling in the sniper's nest to fire at the president; he would not be standing. I don't think that I could identify anyone who was kneeling and who was six floors above my head. I doubt if Mr. Brennan could either.

Was Lee Harvey Oswald a patsy as he claimed? This would indicate that he had an awareness that something was going to happen. Because of this, there would be movement very soon after the assassination of JFK to capture him (or to kill him.) This is exactly what happened. By declaring that he was a patsy, Oswald became a liability to the actual conspirators and assassins. A description of the proposed assassin did go out about fifteen minutes after the shooting of JFK. The perpetrator's description resembled Oswald though others could fit it, too. The investigation would have to be directed solely at Oswald, and any part of it that would swing away from Oswald (such as witnesses believing that the shots came from the direction of the Grassy Knoll) would be unnecessary and, in fact, unwanted. That is exactly what appears to have happened. After the arrest of Oswald, all prior reports, conflicting theories, and contrary witnesses seemed to disappear. Only those that incriminated Oswald were considered. The public would have to believe at a very early stage of the investigation that the "correct" assassin, namely Lee Harvey Oswald, was captured and in the custody of the officials, namely the Secret Service, FBI, and the Dallas Police Department.

And, so it came to be.

IX

Jack Ruby and the Assassination of the Assassin

Jacob Rubenstein, known to the public as Jack Ruby, grew up in Chicago where he became involved with organized crime. As a boy he worked for various mobsters including Al Capone. He eventually moved to Dallas where he became owner and operator of the infamous Carousel Club. It was at this club that many witnesses stated they saw Lee Harvey Oswald and Jack Ruby together. Others reported seeing Oswald and David Ferrie together on several occasions (especially in New Orleans). It seems that many of the players in the assassination scenario were not exactly strangers to one another.

At the time of the assassination, Ruby was living in the Oak Cliff section of Dallas. This was the same area where Officer J. D. Tippit was murdered, supposedly at the hands of Oswald.

Ruby's criminal activities expanded and eventually included encounters with many underworld leaders. A few months prior to the president's assassination, Ruby's contacts included associates of Marcello, Trafficante, and Hoffa. In addition, Jack Ruby was also thought to have ties to the intelligence agencies, especially the FBI. This was ultimately revealed in a letter sent by J. Edgar Hoover to the Warren Commission in June 1964 stating that Ruby was an informant for the FBI in 1959.

Silence Is Golden

It's highly likely that Lee Harvey Oswald was never supposed to leave the TSBD alive following the JFK assassination. Not only did he live through the assassination, but he also survived the Tippit killing and was "taken alive" when arrested at the Texas Theatre.

He was a threat to the true assassins and conspirators.

By stating he was a patsy, Oswald insinuated that other people or agencies or both were intimately involved in the assassination of the president. In addition, he was indirectly stating he knew who they were and that he was set up as the assassin. Even after his death, it had to be obvious to everyone that Oswald had ties to the CIA, FBI, and the Mafia. He could talk intelligently about the CIA-Mafia coalition and its attempts to assassinate Castro. The union of the two generally opposing organizations was not common knowledge at that time. If Oswald revealed the liaisons, men such as Carlos Marcello and Santos Trafficante Jr., as well as high-ranking CIA officials could be indicted. Multiple conspiracies were at risk of being exposed and many very powerful men were threatened. This risk was too great, and Oswald had to be eliminated.

Assassinating the assassin could put an end to the investigation. A dead assassin cannot defend himself. Jack Ruby, well-known to organized crime and the Dallas police, was chosen for the job.

How ironic that Oswald needed to be silenced to discourage talk of a conspiracy in the death of the president. Yet Oswald's murder captured public attention and planted seeds that gave birth to the conspiracy theory.

Following JFK's assassination, Jack Ruby began following Oswald. He was seen and photographed at Dallas police headquarters on the evening of November 22 at the same time that Oswald was being interrogated. It was during this session that Ruby corrected the district attorney who was questioning Oswald and said that Oswald belonged to the Fair Play for Cuba Committee, a pro-Castro group. How would Ruby even know this unless he had some definitive knowledge about Oswald well before the assassination?

Oswald was kept at police headquarters for two full nights, probably in an effort to convince the public that the assassin of our president had been found and was in custody. Then it was decided that Oswald should be transferred to the county jail the following morning by armored car (supposedly for security precautions).

Jack Ruby was well-known to all the people involved in the capture and questioning of Oswald. He loved to hang around with members of the media and the press. His face was familiar to many Dallas policemen. He was considered a friend and would often loan them money or entertain them at his club. As a result, his presence at the jail didn't seem unusual. He gained access to the basement of police headquarters where the transfer was to take place. He simply walked down the ramp (supposedly guarded by the police) unhampered.

He probably had help from an officer working at the facility, because Ruby had to be told exactly what time Oswald was to be transferred from the Dallas city jail to the county jail. The evening before, the police chief announced Oswald would be moved about 10 AM. As a result, many reporters were there at that time. Ruby, however, appeared an hour later. His timing was precise. Ruby arrived in the basement at 11:19 AM, and Oswald arrived in the city jail basement about one minute later.

At 11:21 AM, in front of millions of people who were watching on television, Ruby stepped through a crowd of reporters, television camera crews, and seventy police officers and shot Oswald in the abdomen at point-blank range.

Paradoxically, Oswald was taken to Parkland Hospital where President Kennedy had been declared dead just two days earlier. The alleged assassin had been assassinated.

Impact on History

If Ruby had not killed Oswald, there would have been a public trial, and I believe it is quite possible that Oswald would have been found not guilty.

The evidence would not have been any different, and yet the makeup of the case would have been drastically changed. There would not have been secret files, and there probably would not have been a Warren Commission. The thought of a conspiracy came into play when Oswald was murdered. This changed the course of history and, for the first time, caused the public to question its government.

Jack Ruby was immediately arrested and charged and eventually convicted (March 14, 1964) of the murder of Lee Harvey Oswald. He was sentenced to death. Seven months later, a Texas state court ruled that he was sane. He certainly could not deny his direct involvement because it was seen on nationwide television.

His personal defense was that he wanted to spare Jackie Kennedy the ordeal of having to return to Dallas for Oswald's trial. He felt he "owed this debt to our beloved president."

He did not want her to grieve any more than she already had—very noble but at the same time, extremely far-fetched. If Ruby was as devoted to the Kennedys as he professed, why wasn't he along the parade route watching the motorcade and the limousine carrying the president and the first lady? This would be an ideal way to show his support and devotion.

It appears unlikely that Ruby's reason for killing Oswald was based on his grief, stress, questionable emotional stability, and sense of patriotism. I contend that he was simply ordered by the conspirators to do away with Oswald as part of the original assassination plot.

Do As I Say

This is an opinion and a round-about way of saying that *Jack Ruby was just doing what he was told to do.*

An investigation of Ruby's telephone bills and calls weeks and hours prior to the assassination revealed multiple calls to various mob figures. It appears that this night club owner was certainly involved with the Mafia far more extensively than the government wanted us to believe. From his jail cell in Dallas, Ruby once told a journalist that the truth behind this "bizarre conspiracy regarding the assassination will eventually come out."

Ruby first appeared before the Warren Commission on June 7, 1964. At that time, Ruby was probably the most valuable source of information on the Kennedy assassination, and yet it appeared that nobody was eager to question him especially after he had been convicted of Oswald's murder. It was almost as if they did not want to stir up more controversy. In attendance for Ruby's appearance was Earl Warren, the chief justice of the supreme court, and head of the commission. Gerald Ford, senator from Michigan and, soon to be president of the United States, and Arlen Specter, the senator from Pennsylvania and head of the Judiciary Committee and the man who eventually espoused the single bullet theory were there, too.

In 1964 Specter was an assistant district attorney who served on the staff of the Warren Commission.

Similar to Oswald saying that he was a patsy, Ruby said he was being used as a scapegoat. His original explanation about why he killed Oswald had dramatically changed. Ruby had another story to tell but felt he could not disclose it while he was still in Dallas. He feared for his life. He made a plea to be moved from Dallas to Washington so that he could tell everything he knew. He felt the facts would never come out if he remained in Dallas. He said: "I want to tell the truth, and I can't tell it here," and "a whole new form of government is going to take over our country, and I know I won't live to see you another time" and "maybe certain people don't want to know the truth that may come out of me." However, his request was denied. Warren and Ford did not want to hear what he had to say, especially if it meant the possibility of a conspiracy.

Once again, a key witness was not allowed to give his testimony. The only difference is that Jack Ruby quite possibly was the most important witness in the entire assassination scenario. By assassinating Oswald, he deprived our country of the opportunity to have a trial in a court of law to determine if the real assassin had been found. In addition, by not being allowed to be heard before the Warren Commission and not being allowed to leave the city of Dallas as he had requested, we were again deprived of very valuable testimony indicating a potential conspiracy.

Ruby, during a television interview in 1965, said, "Everything pertaining to what's happening has never come to the surface. The world will never know the true facts of what occurred, my motives." When asked if the facts will ever come out, Ruby declared: "No, because unfortunately the people who had so much to gain and had such an ulterior motive to put me in the position I'm in will never let the true facts come aboveboard to the world."

I don't believe I could be accused of reading too much into these statements by saying that Jack Ruby was declaring that there was a conspiracy responsible for the assassination of John F. Kennedy. Unfortunately, he never lived long enough to tell more and perhaps reveal the facts about who really killed JFK.

He was granted a retrial by the Texas Court of Criminal Appeals on October 5, 1966, with a change of venue to Wichita Falls as the site of a new trial. Ruby was finally going to be moved from Dallas, something he had wanted (and been refused by the chairman of the Warren Commission). He had been incarcerated in Dallas for nearly two and one half years.

Jack Ruby died on January 3, 1967, thirty-three months after he was originally sentenced to death. Ruby entered Parkland Hospital on December

9, 1966, with the original diagnosis of pneumonia, which was then quickly changed to advanced cancer. He died less than one month later.

Was this an accurate diagnosis? Did he die of natural causes or is there a possibility that Jack Ruby was also murdered? This is something we do not know, although Ruby charged that he had been injected with cancer cells. We do know Ruby never again left Dallas while he was alive.

This was also the time that Jim Garrison, attorney in New Orleans, was reopening the Kennedy case. Ruby's knowledge of the conspiracy would never be revealed. Ruby carried the information about the conspiracy to his grave. It has been said that Oswald's assassination basically brought an end to the official governmental investigation into the assassination of John F. Kennedy.

Both Lee Harvey Oswald, who called himself a patsy and Jack Ruby who considered himself a scapegoat were vital components of the JFK assassination conspiracy. However, it is highly probable that neither of them were instrumental in planning the events of November 22, 1963. They were both being used by powerful people. So far, the cover-up was successful.

John F. Kennedy

The president in deep thought.

JFK as president, husband, father.

Collage of the assassination.

X

The Dallas Police Department and the Secret Service

The Dallas Police Department, the Federal Bureau of Investigation, and the Secret Service were all responsible for protecting the president. Yet all three groups seemed to be markedly inefficient in preparing for Kennedy's trip to Dallas, let alone protecting him once he was there.

Let's discuss the police department first. The Dallas police never investigated the anti-Castro groups known to be in Dallas at the time. Among these were Alpha 66, an extremely militant group, and the John Birch Society. Both were strongly anticommunist and disliked JFK.

Alpha 66 was composed of Cuban exiles and anti-Castro Cubans who were affiliated with the failed Bay of Pigs operation. Some members of Alpha 66 willingly accepted assignments to assassinate Fidel Castro. (Attempts had failed.) This group of exiles also felt betrayed by Kennedy during the Cuban missile crisis. It was Kennedy, they reasoned, who ultimately banned all raids against Castro and his dictatorship.

Hopes Are Dashed

Since Cuba was to be left alone and not invaded, these people felt abandoned with no hope of ever regaining their native country. It's also interesting to note that the leader of Alpha 66 announced that Lee Harvey Oswald attended some of their meetings.

How did Dallas police *drop the ball* and fail to investigate and watch this group? The police simply said they had no information about Alpha-66, the John Birch Society, or Lee Harvey Oswald.

Omissions Multiply

There were other glaring omissions that cast doubts on the police doing a proper job. Shortly after the assassination, Oswald left the TSBD and went to his boarding house. He would leave shortly thereafter to go toward the Texas Theatre. While he was at the boarding house, his landlady saw a police car stop in front of the house, the horn was honked twice, and the driver pulled away.

What type of signal was Oswald receiving and from whom? Why were there no notes, records, or tape recordings made of Oswald during his extremely long interrogation, which was conducted by the police and other law enforcement agencies?

A stenographer was never present and neither was a lawyer, although he reportedly asked for one. Throughout his interrogation, Oswald denied that he had anything to do with either assassination (the president's or Officer Tipitt's). It seems he was already considered guilty by all those who wanted this case to end.

These actions would be illegal and unheard of in our current judicial system A parallel to Oswald's supposed guilt which could be considered current, would be the prisoners in Guantanomo Bay who initially were also denied their legal rights.

Ruby's Timely Arrival

How was Ruby able to walk down the ramp leading to the basement of the city jail at precisely the time that Oswald was brought down to be transferred to the county jail?

It was well-known that Ruby was on friendly terms with virtually the entire police department and would often entertain them at his renowned Carousel Club. It was probably no coincidence that Ruby and Oswald were both in the basement at the same time. Ruby had to be assisted by someone on the inside, presumably a police officer, with whom he had close personal contact.

There were three assassinations in Dallas within a span of forty-eight hours. Obviously the police department did not or could not protect any of the victims.

The FBI Vacillates

The second group dealing with internal security and which certainly should have had a role in protecting the president was the FBI. We have already seen this intelligence agency had its own personal file on Oswald dating back to when he returned from the Soviet Union. Yet agents claimed they had no knowledge of Lee Harvey Oswald until after the assassination.

A few weeks prior to JFK's assassination, Lee Harvey Oswald walked into the Dallas FBI field office and asked to talk to Special Agent James Hosty. When he was told he could not, Oswald left a note threatening to blow up the office. No bureau agents followed up on this even though they knew that Oswald was working at the TSBD at the time. In addition, the FBI failed to notify the Secret Service about the incident. Following the assassination, Hosty was ordered to destroy the note written by Oswald.

What could this be but a move to disclaim any connection between Oswald and the FBI prior to the assassination?

Secret Service Knows Nothing!

The other agency that had the most significance in protecting the president was the Secret Service. In fact, guarding the president and assuring his safety was its number one responsibility. The Secret Service had not received information on Lee Harvey Oswald by either the FBI or local authorities regarding his presence in Dallas. However, the FBI as well as the CIA knew of all his activities, both in Dallas and New Orleans. Neither group communicated with the other. As a result, both kept information on Oswald quiet or, to use the CIA's term, *covert*. (This lack of communication between the FBI and the CIA is not unusual. In fact, we heard about the same scenario directly after the tragedy of 9/11, 2001.)   Neither agency took the time to investigate Oswald's reason for being in Dallas on November 22. Therefore, the Secret Service was never warned.

There was another incident abut two weeks prior to the arrival of the president in Dallas. Adlai Stevenson, the ambassador to the United Nations, was attacked in Dallas. *Yet no one deemed this serious enough to investigate or to identify the perpetrators.*

The Secret Service simply maintained they had no listing in the protective research file of anyone who might pose a threat to the president. By definition, this included anyone who had previously threatened the president or had been convicted of a violent crime or had joined a group that advocated assassination as a political weapon.

This was only the beginning of inexcusable mistakes, mishaps, or omissions made by the Secret Service. It has been documented that several Secret Service agents assigned to protect the president were out drinking the night before. Regulations prohibit the use of intoxicating liquor while involved in White House detail in travel. This would be an immediate cause for dismissal from the service. However, none of the agents suffered any disciplinary action. Supposedly, it was feared they would be blamed for the assassination if they were reprimanded. Four of the agents who participated in the partying the night before were assigned to ride in the follow-up car to the presidential limousine.

None of the agents involved in protecting Vice -President Johnson consumed alcohol on the evening prior to the assassination. *One can only speculate on the impact of this fact.*

Another point of conjecture is whether the response or reaction time of the agents assigned to guard the president was slowed because of alcohol consumption. It certainly would not be increased. In fact, the agents in the follow-up car did appear to freeze during the six seconds of gunfire. The only agent who did respond was Clint Hill, Jackie's personal agent. About two to three seconds after the last shot (the fatal head shot), Hill climbed on the back of the limousine and pulled Jackie down back into her seat to protect her. Jackie was attempting to retrieve part of her husband's skull and brain, which had been blown out by the fatal shot. Some had thought that Jackie was attempting to get out of the car, but Hill had said this was not true. Hill blamed himself for not reaching the limousine sooner and even stated that he wished that he had taken the fatal shot himself.

What about the speed of the limousine once the shots were fired? The Secret Service agent driving the car was William Greer and the agent seated next to him was Roy Kellerman. Their reaction time to the shots also appeared very slow as verified by testimony from several eyewitnesses. Upon making the sharp 120-degree turn onto Elm Street, the limousine was forced to slow down well beyond its desired speed. This was against Secret Service regulations, which state that the vehicle must be going at a reasonable speed to make it a more difficult target. At the sound of the shots, many eyewitnesses stated that the car slowed to a virtual halt. It has also been stated that William Greer, the driver, after hearing the first shot, turned around to view JFK. This would have been devastating, because if the limousine had stopped, this would mean that the president was in direct aim of the sniper(s). Unfortunately, the final shot (occurring about six to seven seconds after the first shot) exploded in the president's head. The president's wounds were survivable until he received the head shot. If only the driver of the limousine had taken some type of evasive action, the outcome may have been altered.

The Secret Service did not adhere to other regulations as well. One of these stated that all "critical" points along the motorcade route, including anything higher than the motorcade itself, be "closed." In addition, spectators were not to be allowed on balconies or near windows during the motorcade. None of the potential sniper nests along the route were checked out by the advance team of the Secret Service. These included the Texas School Book Depository, numerous other tall buildings along the route in Dealey Plaza, the bridge overlying the Triple Overpass, and the storm drain and picket fence area on the Grassy Knoll. These last two, located in close proximity to one another, were thought to be the source of shots fired from the front. Witnesses who made that claim were to become conspiracy theorists.

In addition the House Committee on Assassinations in 1979 based on its own acoustical evidence, concluded there was a fourth shot originating from this area on the Grassy Knoll. Many witnesses who were located in Dealey Plaza believed that shots were fired from in front of the presidential limousine. They even went so far as to point to the picket fence on the Grassy Knoll, which was located to the right front of the limo during the shooting. Unfortunately, much of this eyewitness testimony was either changed or ignored. Many of these witnesses were not even called to testify before the Warren Commission.

Another deficiency of the Secret Service was its neglect in checking the open windows in the buildings along the route that allowed spectators to view the proceedings. This entire area of the Grassy Knoll located in Dealey Plaza could certainly not be considered secure. Yet this is the area from which the assassination did occur.

There are other points, probably not as significant, which do add to the lack of protection for the president. The bubble-top was not used over the limousine (reportedly the president made this request). Although the top was not considered bulletproof, it might have deflected the bullets. In addition, there were no agents on the running boards on the back of the limousine. Thus, a shot from behind could not have been blocked. The motorcycles were situated at the rear of the limousine rather than on the flanks, leaving the president more open to possible crossfire.

In other presidential motorcades, the police motorcycle escort rode on both sides and in front of the limousine, thereby forming a shield around the car and making it harder for potential assassins to shoot the president. This was obviously not done during the Dallas motorcade, and the results were disastrous.

The President's Limousine

The limousine of the president was the responsibility of the Secret Service, even after the assassination took place. Unfortunately, the Secret Service continued to err even after the murder of JFK. Bullet and skull fragments were found in the vehicle, and it should have been considered a vital piece of evidence in the investigation. However, the Secret Service apparently did not feel this way. The limo was quickly washed of all blood before any detailed forensic examination could be conducted. In addition, there are initial photographs of a bullet hole in the front windshield, which would indicate a shot fired from the front. However, the limo was flown back to Washington D.C. for repair before it could be thoroughly investigated. Subsequent photographs show that this bullet hole had miraculously disappeared. The cover-up seemed to be in high gear as significant evidence in this case was already being changed.

Many people lined up on Elm Street to watch the procession and upon hearing the shots, rushed toward Dealey Plaza and the Grassy Knoll. They obviously believed this was the source of the shots. There they confronted people with Secret Service badges who quickly turned them away. Of those Secret Service agents who were in Dallas on that date, not one of them was assigned the Grassy Knoll area. Could these people have been the actual shooters posing as Secret Service agents? Unfortunately, at the time people were not suspicious enough to even doubt these men.

Many eyewitnesses were never interviewed by the police and several were intimidated and threatened if they even suggested they saw rifles or men shooting from the area of the Grassy Knoll or the picket fence. Information contrary to shots being fired from the Texas School Book Depository was ignored. At the time of the motorcade, there were many people who were filming the events. Photographs and film of the assassination were taken from their rightful owners and never returned.

What then was the role of the Secret Service in the assassination of John F. Kennedy? It certainly didn't protect the president. In fact, the House Select Committee on Assassinations in 1978 issued the following statement: "President Kennedy did not receive adequate protection. The Secret Service was deficient in the performance of its duties and possessed information that was not properly analyzed, investigated, or used in connection with the president's trip to Dallas." What more need be said?

XI

Lyndon Baines Johnson and the Warren Commission

Following the assassination of President Kennedy, two things happened in an expeditious manner. Within one or two hours of the shooting, Vice President Lyndon Baines Johnson was sworn in as the thirty-sixth president of the United States aboard Air Force One. Within the week, he established the Warren Commission.

Many people remember Lyndon Johnson taking the oath as president with Jackie Kennedy standing near to him. She was wearing her blood-stained suit and looking very solemn and distraught. She seemed out of touch and was probably in shock. It always seemed strange that Johnson requested, and even insisted, that Jackie be by his side when he took the oath as our new president.

What was the reason for this? It's highly doubtful that Jackie, through all of her grief, wanted to be a part of the ceremony where a new president was sworn in to take the place of her just-assassinated husband. Was this a ploy by Johnson to quickly affirm his newly acquired power? Was he taking some kind of revenge against the Kennedys?

It's interesting to note that a photograph taken during the swearing in ceremony shows Congressman Albert Thomas of Texas winking at Lyndon Johnson. Lady Bird Johnson was grinning broadly. Why would joviality be in evidence during such a solemn event? This was no time to celebrate if indeed the Johnsons were actually celebrating. It's as if Johnson finally achieved what he always wanted: the presidency. In one respect, the rapidity of the swearing in of the new president was reassuring to people. By being sworn in as president of the United States by Federal Judge Sarah Hughes so soon after the assassination of JFK, Lyndon Johnson let the world know that the Constitution was viable and that our country had the ability to persevere despite any emergency.

It was well-known, however, that Lyndon Johnson always wanted to be president of the United States. And, it was widely rumored that President Kennedy did not want Johnson as a running mate in the upcoming 1964 election. The vice president's integrity had come under scrutiny during the Bobby Baker and Billy Sol Estes scandals.

Friendship and Affiliations

Bobby Baker was Johnson's close friend and served as his right-hand man during Johnson's leadership period in the Senate and during the 1960 presidential campaign. Many of their business ventures were ethically questionable, and some probably were illegal. Johnson's business deals with Billy Sol Estes, a Texas-based entrepreneur, were similar to those he entered into with Baker.

The Kennedy perception of another JFK-Johnson ticket had changed. The reason Lyndon Johnson was originally chosen as the vice-presidential candidate in 1960 was purely political. John Kennedy needed the vote in Texas and the South, but by 1963 it appeared that Johnson would have trouble delivering his home state of Texas to Kennedy in the upcoming election. This coupled with the fact that there was discord in the Democratic Party in Texas were the main reasons for the president's November trip to Texas.

In addition to the intense pressure put on him by the Sol Estes and Baker scandals, it was feared that Johnson could be personally subject to criminal charges and prosecution. Johnson believed if he were dropped from the Democratic ticket in 1964, he wouldn't stand a chance of becoming the presidential candidate in 1968. Some people reasoned that the only way Lyndon Johnson would ever become president would be through the death of President Kennedy.

There was no love lost between Lyndon Johnson and the Kennedy brothers. In 1960 the office of vice president was considered a menial position, one which was subservient to the office of the presidency. In fact, JFK once told his aide Kenny O'Donnell, "I'm forty-three years old. I'm not going to die in office. So the vice presidency doesn't mean anything."

It's amazing how fate can change the course of history.

Some cabinet members had more clout than the vice president. In fact, Johnson didn't have any influence on foreign policy and wasn't considered part of the administration's decision-making process. Soon after the assassination, however, the Vietnam War became Johnson's war. He presided over a massive escalation of U.S. combat troops and reversed Kennedy's policy of gradual withdrawal from Vietnam.

Gulf of Tonkin Resolution

In August 1964 Johnson went to Congress and decried an alleged unprovoked attack on an American destroyer in the Gulf of Tonkin. The destroyer was said to be in international waters thirty miles away from North Vietnam.

The Gulf of Tonkin Resolution was passed unanimously by Congress, and it gave President Johnson the power to take any action he deemed necessary in Southeast Asia. Almost immediately, the United States attacked North Vietnam and the war escalated. Only later did it become clear that the Gulf of Tonkin incident resulted because U.S. ships provoked an incident by intruding into North Vietnamese waters, not the other way around. By then, it was too late. There was no turning back.

President Johnson was obsessive about Vietnam. He once said, "I am not going to lose Vietnam. I am not going to be the president who saw Southeast Asia go the way China went."

Lyndon Johnson didn't take criticism and embarrassment lightly. He was considered ruthless and had the means to get what he wanted—a trait he often exhibited as Senate majority leader. At that time, he was considered one of the most skilled, respected, and powerful men in Washington.

Johnson was very ambitious and had a pressing need for power. He considered the vice presidency the ultimate step to the presidency but "serving as Kennedy's second in command tortured the competitive Johnson." Johnson once said, "One out of every four presidents has died in office. I'm a gambling man, and this is the only chance I got." Johnson got his opportunity to be president at the age of fifty-five.

Lyndon Johnson had more to gain than anyone from the assassination of JFK. He assumed the presidency on Air Force One within a very short time of the fatal shooting. One year later, he scored a lopsided victory over Barry Goldwater, his Republican opponent. This was the biggest landslide in presidential history. At this point, one could say that Lyndon Johnson had finally arrived at his number one goal in life and he had public support. He was inaugurated on the steps of the Capital by the chief justice of the supreme court, Earl Warren. This was the same man who chaired the Warren Commission, the "fact-finding" committee which Johnson created to look into Kennedy's assassination.

The next four years of Johnson's presidency were not happy years. He found himself in Kennedy's shadow, something he couldn't avoid. Some of the measures he was able to pass through Congress, including the Civil Rights Bill, were actually a continuation of the work done by Kennedy. The Vietnam War escalated to tremendous proportions, and people blamed President Johnson. As someone who served in Vietnam, this author concurs with this opinion.

Not only did this war result in the tragic loss of thousands of lives, the Vietnam War became a 100-billion-dollar war. As occurs in all wars, there is always a group of people who derive a large financial profit. Was this a potential motive for Kennedy's assassination?

The Vietnam War was the undoing of Johnson, who in 1968 withdrew as his party's nominee for president in the upcoming election. A few months later, he was back on the viewing stand, witnessing the inauguration of Richard Nixon, his successor, but also the loser to his predecessor, John F. Kennedy.

The irony of it all doesn't go unnoticed.

Not a Crime in Texas

Was Johnson somehow involved in the assassination? He certainly had the means, opportunity, and motive to be a major player in its orchestration and subsequent cover-up.

The assassination of a president was not considered a federal crime in Texas at that time. Therefore, any investigation or autopsy would have been done in Texas, where he had an enormous amount of influence and power, and would basically be under his control. In essence, President Johnson did control the investigation (through the Warren Commission), but the autopsy was not done in the state of Texas.

The primary questions the public asked following the assassination of President Kennedy were simple but the answers were complicated.

1. Why did this happen?

2. Was it truly the work of a single-crazed gunman and, if so, what was his motive?

3. Why was the "assassin" (Oswald) assassinated? How could this happen in full view of millions of people who were watching on television?

4. If it wasn't Oswald, who killed the president?

5. Did Jack Ruby murder Oswald purely out of passion and grief because his president had been assassinated? Was he really the ultimate concerned citizen who performed the deed so that Jackie would come to believe the murder of her husband had been avenged?

6. Did Jack Ruby think he would be considered a hero and that the history books would record him as such?

Multiple committees had been formed for one purpose; (supposedly) to discover the truth behind the assassination. They include the Warren Commission and the House Select Committee on Assassinations.

* * * * * *

Records have been released from the National Archives and numerous books have been written on the assassination, as recently as within the past year or two. The books all favor the probability of a conspiracy as opposed to the idea of a lone gunman. Despite this the government doesn't budge from its original conclusion that Lee Harvey Oswald assassinated the president and acted alone. The media supports this finding.

Those who attack the "conspiracists" say it is within the realm of possibility that a lone crazed individual had the capability of assassinating the most powerful man in the world and that we should just accept it.

Every public opinion poll taken since 1963 verifies that most people do not accept this explanation.

Wouldn't it be more reasonable to first rule out a potential conspiracy before placing blame on a single individual? The Warren Commission concluded there wasn't any evidence to implicate a conspiracy. At the same time, members didn't say it wasn't possible.

I contend that from the onset, the purpose of the Warren Report was to frame

Lee Harvey Oswald as the lone assassin of President Kennedy. Members had no intention of looking for others who might be involved in this assassination.

Was There a Cuba Connection?

The immediate reaction of those people who felt Oswald had not acted alone was to consider the possibility that he was an agent for either Cuba or the USSR and that their governments (one or both) were directly responsible for the murder of our president. After all, communists, as exemplified by both the Soviet Union and Cuba led by Fidel Castro, were our archenemies in this time of the cold war.

Retaliation by the United States for the murder of President Kennedy against either Cuba or Russia could spell disaster for the entire world. The American people would not and could not "turn the other cheek" and allow a foreign government to kill their president without taking action. The only way to preserve our dignity and standing in the world would be to get to the truth of this assassination and respond accordingly.

Did President Johnson really believe the assassination was the result of a communist plot? He did make the following statement: "Kennedy tried to get Castro, but Castro got Kennedy first. It will all come out one day."

Or, was the new president just trying to target another patsy? Was he trying to protect himself?

This is where things get somewhat confusing. Lee Harvey Oswald was an ideal patsy because of his pro-Castro and pro-Russian leanings. Yet, the Warren Commission tried to disconnect any association he may have had to the Soviets and Castro in particular. Johnson did not want our archenemies of the cold war involved.

What's Wrong with This Picture?

If we did not want the Soviets or Cubans incriminated why did our intelligence agencies build the case against Oswald with emphasis on his connections to the USSR and Cuba? Like so much about this travesty, it simply does not make sense.

On the night before the assassination, there was a gathering in Dallas attended by many prominent individuals. Among these were Clint Murchison, a very wealthy Texan with interests in oil, banking, and publishing. Others in attendance were Richard Nixon, former vice president who was in Dallas that day attending a Coca-Cola convention; John McCloy, prominent banker who would eventually be appointed to the Warren Commission; H. L. Hunt, oil billionaire who had connections to the CIA; J. Edgar Hoover, director of the FBI; and Vice President Lyndon Baines Johnson. It was at this party that news of an assassination plot to kill John Kennedy in Dallas was revealed. Nothing was done by any of these people to thwart the plot. Does this make them co-conspirators? Were they participating in a cover-up by keeping this information to themselves and therefore committing treason? Or, did they simply dismiss the possibility and relegate it to rumor and nonsense?

Following the murder of Oswald, there were growing rumors of a conspiracy. It's ironic that these rumors occurred primarily because of Oswald's death. If he had lived, I believe the thoughts of an assassination conspiracy would have been less prevalent. In any event, Johnson wanted to put an end to these rumors and, as a result, quickly appointed a group of people who would be known as the President's Commission on the Assassination of President Kennedy. This cumbersome name was changed to the Warren Commission, named after its chairman, Earl Warren, chief justice of the supreme court. Its purpose, as stated by President Johnson, was to come up with the "truth" behind the assassination so that people would accept the conclusions of the Warren Commission as gospel. Of course, in the early 1960s few people questioned what government officials told them.

Initially, Chief Justice Warren did not want to be part of this committee. It was only after excessive persuasion by President Johnson that he finally consented. He was told that the country would be in grave straits with the threat of a major war (resulting in mass casualties) if the commission did not dispel some of the rumors that were circulating since Kennedy's assassination. Those rumors dealt with Oswald and his connections to Castro and the Soviet Union. Of course, Oswald's connections to our intelligence agencies, namely the FBI and the CIA, were not mentioned. The other members chosen by Johnson for this committee were Richard B. Russell, Democrat, senator from Georgia who had been in the Senate for over thirty years; John S. Cooper, Republican, senator from Kentucky and the ambassador to India; Hale Boggs, Democrat, congressman and majority whip in the House of Representatives; and Gerald Ford, Republican congressman from Michigan who was destined to become a future president of the United States. It was said that Gerald Ford looked out for the interests of the FBI on the Warren

Commission and kept Hoover fully informed of proceedings. Other members were John J. McCloy, former president of the World Bank and finally, Allen W. Dulles, former director of the Central Intelligence Agency and, in fact, the director who was fired by President Kennedy following the Bay of Pigs fiasco. As the intelligence expert for the Warren Commission, Dulles was able to minimize or erase evidence of CIA involvement. It was reported that Allen Dulles gave Warren Commission members books on the history of presidential assassinations that stated that "nearly every killer, would-be or successful, had been a lone psychopath." It appears that Dulles was trying to influence his colleagues.

These appointed members of the Warren Commission had other responsibilities and delegated research and investigation to their staff members. Unfortunately, none of them had much experience in criminal investigations. Staff lawyers conducted interrogations based upon their own contentions, ignoring accepted criminal interrogation standards. Committee meetings were conducted by this ancillary staff. The appointed commissioners missed meetings about half of the time. In fact, the seven members of the full commission were never present as a full body for one entire session. The truth behind the murder of President Kennedy did not appear to be high on their priority lists.

A Key Observation

The Warren Commission didn't conduct its own investigation. Staff members relied upon the reports of federal agencies to expedite their assignment. The FBI supplied information to the Warren Commission whereas the CIA disseminated propaganda. The commissioners were given only a few months to make a final report public. The deadline date was prior to the next presidential election. A definitive answer, accepted by the public, would relegate the JFK assassination to an event in history.

Theoretically this investigation was a monumental task and could not be completed quickly if other potential assassins were to be considered. The FBI reports were geared to the premise that Oswald was the lone assassin. Remember that J. Edgar Hoover declared within forty-eight hours of the assassination that Lee Harvey Oswald was the assassin and that he acted alone. Hoover called Robert Kennedy within four hours of the assassination to inform him that the assassin (Oswald) had been found. How could anyone make this statement so fast?

Was Hoover attempting to divert attention and suspicion away from the intelligence agencies? He demonstrated the FBI's indifference to any vital information offered by witnesses.

Helms Sticks to the FBI Dogma

Years later, Richard Helms, a future director of the FBI, said, "All of the speculation and conspiratology not withstanding, I have not seen anything, no matter how far-fetched or grossly imagined, that in any way changes my conviction that Lee Harvey Oswald assassinated Kennedy and that there were no co-conspirators. Furthermore, I know of no information whatsoever that might have any bearing on the assassination that has been concealed from the public."

Note: Sections One and Two of this book discuss most of what follows in great detail. Snippets appear below to serve as reminders and to provide a backdrop as the spotlight falls on the Warren Commission.

Over 500 witnesses were interviewed.

1. Many were intimidated or ignored if their statements pointed to a conspiracy.

2. Evidence was altered and manipulated and personal property (e.g., home films of the assassination) was taken and never returned.

3. Statements were changed and documents were forged or withheld.

4. All recorded information had to reflect the fact that the shots were fired from behind. Staff dismissed as speculation and rumor statements from witnesses that the Grassy Knoll in Dealey Plaza was the source of the shots. If this premise was accepted, it would indicate that Kennedy was shot from in front and would mean that there was more than one shooter, assuming that Oswald was one of the shooters.

5. Chapter I, Medical Evidence: Parkland vs. Bethesda details the enormous amount of discrepancy regarding the medical evidence. The commission stated the *doctors at Parkland were wrong*.

6. Two eyewitnesses who essentially were ignored by the commission

were Governor and Mrs. John Connelly. Each testified that after hearing the first shot, the governor turned to his right to view the president and see what had happened. Connelly consistently said that both he and the president were hit by different shots. *How could the commission justify such an omission?!*

7. The commission never called Lyndon Baines Johnson to testify. Being the new president should not have made him immune from testifying. In fact, the successor to a victim of such a crime should always be considered a prime suspect.

In short, everything was done to deliver a nice neat package: Oswald. The media had already accused Oswald and essentially convicted him of both murders (JFK and Officer Tippit) and other powerful forces lent support. The commission performed mop-up work.

I thought the law in our country stated that a man was innocent until proven guilty.

Here a Bullet, There a Bullet

Three bullet casings were found on the sixth floor of the Texas School Book Depository (TSBD). Supposedly they were from the Mannlicher-Carcano, the alleged murder weapon. To the lone-gunman enthusiasts, this meant that only three shots were fired. In addition, it was well documented that one bullet completely missed the president, since it careened off the foot of a bystander, a spectator named James Tague, who stood close to the Stemmons Freeway sign. This left only two bullets to be accounted for. However, the autopsy, as inaccurate and unprofessional as it was, placed two bullets entering the president, one hitting him in the upper back or lower neck (depending on where this wound was placed to fit the proper trajectory) and the other hitting him in the back of the head. Both of these shots, according to the autopsy report, were entrance wounds and, therefore, fired from the TSBD. This was in direct opposition to the observations made at Parkland. In any event, this would account for three shots fired from the sixth floor of the TSBD. The Warren Commission had to find a way to incorporate the autopsy conclusions (despite any information that proved to the contrary) into its own report.

There was one other detail that was vital to the case. Where did the shot(s) that hit Governor Connelly come from? If this were a separate shot, it would mean there were more than three shots fired and, therefore, there had to be a second shooter. This, of course, would knock out the government's case for a lone assassin. It would indicate Oswald had an accomplice and such important information needed to be kept from the public.

As a result, the single bullet theory was confabulated to account for some of the wounds in President Kennedy and all the wounds in Governor Connelly. In other words, one bullet would have to go through President Kennedy to cause all the wounds in Governor Connelly.

The author of this theory, which actually defies logic and common sense, is a man named Arlen Specter, then a commission assistant, and now a senator from Pennsylvania and head of the Senate Judiciary Committee. Specter's primary responsibility dealt with the medical evidence and autopsy findings.

The single bullet theory was key to the Warren Commission report in order to prove that one assassin fired three shots from behind the president's car. The final conclusions of the report mentioned that the first bullet missed the president, entirely. This is apparently the same bullet that hit James Tague. This saga is quite interesting and certainly vital to the conclusions circulated by the Warren Commission. James Tague was an automobile salesman from Dallas who came to watch the presidential motorcade and parked near the triple overpass. He reported being hit by a ricochet bullet or piece of curb hit by the bullet. He immediately reported this to the Dallas police and FBI (who ignored his statements) and later he gave his story to a Dallas newspaper, which promptly printed it. This so-called "stray" bullet then became public knowledge. The question was how did this bullet fit into what the Warren Commission was going to say? The commission was initially going to conclude that there were three bullets fired: one hit JFK in the back, one hit Governor Connelly causing his wounds, and the third hit the president in the back of the head fatally wounding him. However, there was now a fourth bullet that had to be accounted for, and that was the one resulting in the injury to Mr. Tague. Remember, if the number of bullets fired were indeed four, this would indicate multiple shooters and therefore, a conspiracy. It was then that Arlen Specter introduced the single bullet theory.

According to this theory, this second bullet which hit the president in the back of his neck, went through his body, exited through his throat (i.e., Adam's apple), continued forward to strike Governor Connelly in the right armpit, fractured his right fifth rib, collapsed his lung, and exited his chest via his right nipple, where it then entered and exited from his right wrist and eventually embedded in his left thigh. For the sake of the theory, this bullet then became the magic bullet, which finally exited from his thigh in a pristine or completely undamaged form and was found eventually on the governor's stretcher at Parkland. For one bullet to do so much damage (causing seven separate wounds and shattering two dense bones) and escape completely un-scathed is a little too much for our imaginations to embrace. In fact, some time later, the pathologist Pierre Finck (acting as the consultant pathologist at the autopsy) stated that "more lead was removed from Governor Con-nelly's wrist than was missing from the pristine bullet." The autopsists felt the single bullet theory was very unlikely because this pristine bullet could not explain the multiple metallic fragments found in the fracture wounds of the governor. In addition, the doctors who took care of Governor Connelly found it very unlikely that one bullet after hitting the president had enough velocity to inflict the governor's wounds and fracture his ribs and wrist. The Warren Commission ignored these professional medical witnesses. In reality, the single bullet theory defies the law of gravity, but that didn't seem to con-cern the commission.

What happened to the fatal shot? The Warren Commission said the third bullet hit the president in the back of his head (bottom right rear) near the ex-ternal occipital protuberance, traversed the cranial cavity, and exited through the right parietal bone, carrying with it part of the cerebrum. This is in direct contradiction to the Parkland observations where this posterior head wound was considered an exit—not an entrance—wound. The Warren Commission was thus able to account for the three bullets supposedly fired from behind the president. Commissioners proffered this theory to convince the public that one man had assassinated the president.

The Warren Commission tried to be in agreement with the results of the autopsy. Dr. Humes concluded that the president was hit by two shots fired from above and from behind. It is interesting to speculate how the pa-thologists arrived at this conclusion when they never were able to track the path of the bullet, in part, due to their inexperience in conducting autop-sies on gunshot-wound victims. They never had the opportunity to view the Zapruder film and its infamous head-snap shot. The Zapruder film showed the fatal head shot that sent the president slamming back against his seat and to his left. This was strong evidence of a shot coming from the front. In addition, a motorcycle policeman riding to the rear of the president's car was splattered with brain matter from the president. For this to occur, the brain had to be pushed back, again indicating that the shot came from the front. Finally, Humes learned from the Parkland physicians the morning after the autopsy that the throat wound was felt to be an entry wound and not an exit wound. Yet despite all of this, Humes said that President Kennedy was hit from behind.

Were the pathologists misled by some information they received prior to conducting the autopsy? After all, there were already press reports that incriminated Oswald as being the killer, and it was known that he was in the TSBD at the time of the shooting. In addition, there were people in the morgue shouting orders during the autopsy. These people were high-ranking officials with more authority than Humes or Boswell. Were Humes and Boswell told that the bullets had to come from above and behind and were they conducting the autopsy under the direction of others?

The Warren Commission verified Humes's findings. If it weren't for the single bullet theory, verification would have been totally impossible. There would have had to be at least four shots fired and more than one shooter involved. Two FBI agents were present during the autopsy, and their report was dependent on what they heard from the pathologists. They stated that there were separate shots that hit the president and the governor. This would be in addition to the shot that missed its target and instead hit James Tague. And it would mean there had to be more than three shots fired. One word sums it up: conspiracy.

JFK's personal physician, Admiral George Burkley, signed the death certificate, which stated there was a "nonfatal posterior wound located in the back, at about the third thoracic vertebrae." This location of the back wound (lower than the anterior neck wound) that was confirmed by several Secret Service agents would be too low to be the entry point for a bullet that exited from the throat, assuming that the bullet was fired from above and behind the president.

Specter ignored the original site of the back wound as described by Humes (along with the FBI report, Boswell's autopsy face sheet, the photographs of the shirt and jacket, and the death certificate). To account for the throat wound as the point of exit for the back wound, the back wound had to be raised by more than six inches. In fact, the site of the back wound was moved up (presumably by someone on the commission).

The single bullet theory requires the bullet to go through a zigzag direction, up and down, and right and left. *Excuse me?* Humes did not see the throat wound. However, the following morning he talked to Dr. Malcolm Perry, one of the Parkland physicians, and learned that there was a neck wound (described as an entry wound) that was used as the site for the tracheotomy. Humes then burned his original autopsy notes and rewrote the autopsy conclusions. He somehow had to make changes and connect the back wound (which he initially described as penetrating about one inch but not having an exit tract) with the neck wound he now said was an exit wound. Specter also chose to ignore the Parkland testimony that the anterior neck wound was a wound of entry that was obliterated by the tracheotomy.

The work of the Warren Commission resembled that of a crossword puzzle. The final product (conclusion that Oswald was the lone killer) was known, and all that was needed was to fit the matching pieces together (by ignoring anything that pointed to a conspiracy). The commission (including Arlen Specter) never examined the multiple photographs and X-rays taken during the autopsy, and they were eventually turned over to the Secret Service.

Not Until Years Later

The photographs and X-rays weren't seen again for several years. The failure of the Warren Commission to examine these materials (which should be considered vital pieces of information) suggests that this appointed group of influential figures had no intention of scrutinizing the findings (whether to agree or disagree). They felt that no one would question their reputations, let alone their conclusions. In fact, the first time that Specter saw the autopsy photographs was in 1999 at the National Archives. He said, "I saw the small bullet hole in the back of his head, which was fatal, blow out the top of his head. I saw the top of his head, that thick head of hair."

This physician-author contends that there was no possible way for that thick head of hair to remain in view after the devastating head wounds suffered by the president, as mentioned by both the Parkland and Bethesda contingents. When the Parkland personnel were finally shown the photographs years after the assassination, they uniformly denounced them as inaccurate and not representing what they had personally seen. Even the autopsists felt they were seeing photos that were different from what they had originally seen. These photographs showed that the huge opening in the rear of the president's head had become a small hole higher up on the head, in the cowlick area. One of the conclusions of the commission was that the fatal head wound had struck JFK from behind and had caused massive damage to the head, blowing out the right side. Hence, the photographs had to be fabricated to show this.

Specter's Remorse?

Years after the assassination, the creator of the single bullet theory began to question himself. Arlen Specter observed, "There has grown a tremendous distrust of the Warren Commission. I'm trying to tell people in America that there are ways of dealing with the government. I'd like to stem the free fall we've seen in voting and the tremendous skepticism. There are issues that we need to deal with to restore public confidence."

Is It Any Wonder?

The X-rays and photographs, which are routinely taken during an autopsy, weren't authenticated when they resurfaced. All were at variance with the autopsy report and eyewitness testimony. The photographs were of poor quality and didn't display case number, name, place, and date data. They would not be admissible in a court of law.

Throughout the entire inquiry, there was a collection of false evidence created for the specific purpose of incriminating Lee Harvey Oswald. Even the Zapruder film, the one piece of evidence that should have presented the clearest piece of documentation on the assassination, was altered in spots to deceive the public. Anticonspiracy advocates used the Zapruder film to try to make their case. By substituting and splicing certain frames (omitting and then putting them back together), they were able to make the backward head-snap into a forward motion, thus trying to prove a shot from behind.

In 1963, Dan Rather was the New Orleans bureau chief for CBS television. He had been sent by CBS to Texas to cover the president's visit. This well-respected newscaster and anchor man was there at the time of the assassination, and his employer asked him to review the Zapruder film. On Monday, November 25 (the same day that Oswald was assassinated), Dan Rather discussed his observations during two televised interviews. He gave detailed descriptions. This was somewhat surprising because he only viewed the film on one occasion. It was a short clip showing multiple events befalling the limousine occupants at the time of the shooting. Most people would probably need to see the film more than once to specify so many details. In any event, Rather described three separate shots: two hitting the president and one hitting the governor. What got most people's attention, however, was Rather's description of the final and ultimately fatal shot. He said, "His head went forward with considerable violence. He then slumped over Mrs. Kennedy." This statement—that Kennedy fell forward—was contrary to what anyone else who later viewed the film reported. The overall consensus was that the impact of the shot had caused Kennedy's head to move forcefully backward, consistent with a gunshot entry from the front, and not from the back as Rather had implied.

What caused Dan Rather to report that Kennedy's head flew forward rather than backward? Was he seeing a film that was altered? Was he indirectly part of the government cover-up, knowing that the American public would not see the film until years later? Or, did he simply make a mistake? Only Mr. Rather can answer these questions.

To this author, the most striking photograph was that taken of the rear of the president's head. The photograph showed that the back of the scalp was intact with the hair free of blood; something that is at complete odds with what the Parkland physicians and nurses as well as the Bethesda witnesses saw—a large defect (i.e., exit wound) in the posterior aspect of the head. Was this really a picture of President Kennedy's head or was it someone else's?

Did Dr. Humes (as he claimed) really burn the notes because they were stained with the blood of the president or was he ordered to destroy the notes? Was he told what to do during the autopsy, or more significantly, was he told what not to do?

The commission's final conclusions were based upon the navy's autopsy report as well as ballistic evidence. The shell casings found in the sniper's nest on the sixth floor of the TSBD were said to have come from the Mannlicher-Carcano rifle that was the rifle Oswald had obtained through an alias, from a sporting goods store. This is circumstantial evidence and was never verified. How do we know the casings and possibly even the rifle itself weren't planted there in order to build up the case against Oswald? Oswald's fingerprints were never found on the Mannlicher-Carcano rifle. The FBI lab in Washington

D.C., after a thorough search, found no prints. However, the following day, the Dallas police said they had found a palm print on the rifle. Could this have been planted? In addition, the nitrate test was negative. Normally, after firing a rifle, deposits of nitrate are present on the shooter's cheek. The fact that this test was negative indicated that Oswald did not recently fire this rifle.

Contradiction Reigns

The Warren Commission reached its conclusions despite an enormous amount of contradictory evidence. In addition to everything just mentioned, there were many witnesses standing along the motorcade route on Elm Street. These people claimed they heard shots or saw smoke coming from the area of the Grassy Knoll. They thought this was where the shots originated. Chief of Police Curry, at the sound of the shots, ran up the Grassy Knoll. Almost all the Sheriff's deputies did the same. Yet, the testimony of the witnesses was never mentioned in the Warren Report. In addition, people standing near the TSBD did not believe the gunshots came from there. Commission members simply said, "These witnesses are mistaken"—a rather outrageous comment considering the circumstances. The commissioners were even emboldened to say, "the doctors are wrong" after learning of the Parkland Hospital Report where all personnel administering emergency treatment to the president agreed there was an exit wound in the back of the head. This implied the shots came from the front. Apparently anyone who contributed information that threatened the commission's findings was wrong!

Even Admiral Burkley, JFK's personal physician, was not called to testify before the commission, yet he was the one medical man who was riding in the motorcade during the assassination, was in Trauma Room One at Parkland Hospital, was present during the autopsy, and was on the plane when it returned to Washington D.C. Nor did the commission take into account the personal testimony of Governor Connelly, who emphatically and repeatedly stated he was not hit by the same bullet that hit the president. There are photographs showing Governor Connelly looking straight ahead at the time President Kennedy is raising his hands toward his throat, indicating that he had been hit. The vastly different body language indicates both men were not hit by the same bullet.

Photographs Speak

Abraham Zapruder was a Dallas dress manufacturer who, using a small 8-millimeter motion-picture camera, photographed the motorcade as it passed down Elm Street and out of Dealey Plaza. He was standing on a short cement pedestal near the Grassy Knoll, in very close proximity to the picket fence. His entire film lasted only thirty seconds and was filmed in vivid color but didn't have sound. Through this film, the timing of the shots, positions of those in the limousine, and reaction of the onlookers could be determined. This has become the most famous film in history. Without this film, there would have been no way to time the shots. As a result, there would have been no controversy about Oswald's ability to fire the rifle that often and that accurately. The anticonspiracy enthusiasts said it was possible for Oswald to have fired the three shots in succession during the allotted period of time. The camera was set at 18.3 frames per second. The exact number of shots has never actually been determined although it has been thought that three shots were fired over a span of seven seconds.

According to scientific calculations based upon the Zapruder film, this meant that 2.3 seconds were required between shots. There are several points that refute the possibility of Oswald firing his rifle in this allotted time. First, Oswald was not considered to be a good marksman. In fact, as a marine, he was thought to be a very poor marksman. Several expert riflemen were asked to try to reproduce this task: firing a Mannlicher-Carcano rifle three times, allowing only 2.3 seconds between shots. Not one of them was able to do it and each was firing at a stationary target. To believe the Warren Commission statement that Oswald was able to hit a moving target on two occasions with the utmost accuracy is incomprehensible.

Some time ago, a man telephoned me at my office stating that he was one of the expert riflemen who had been asked to duplicate this feat and he emphatically stated that it was not possible! This from someone who had been firing guns most of his life. In addition, the alleged murder weapon, the Mannlicher-Carcano, was considered a very cheap inferior weapon even back in the 1960s. There was no way this generally ineffective weapon could be fired in that short period of time by an equally ineffective marksman through a clump of trees that obstructed his view and hit a moving target. Finally, the paraffin test taken on Oswald was negative and did not reveal the marks that would have to be present in order to prove that Oswald had recently fired this rifle.

In reviewing the Zapruder film, several things seem obvious. We can see the president's car, and both JFK and his wife are waving. The limousine traveling down Elm Street passes the Stemmons Freeway sign, and we then see the president clutching his throat and throwing his hands up. This has to be his first reaction to being hit by a bullet. We then see the explosion of President Kennedy's head into a red ball of dust. This was the fatal head shot. The president's head and body are thrown to the rear and to the left, where he comes to rest on Jackie's lap. The direction of the president's head upon the impact of the bullet was backward, as if he had just been hit from in front. This has been referred to as the "backward jerk of the head." This could not have occurred if the president had been hit from behind. The Warren Commission enthusiasts equate this "backward snap" to a "massive neuromuscular reaction" that can occur with severe trauma to the nerve centers of the brain, which would include the pons, medulla, and cerebellum, which are all located in the posterior aspect of the brain. This is also known as the brainstem. However, the Warren Report said that the right cerebral hemisphere was damaged, not the nerve coordination center. As a result, how could this neuromuscular reaction have occurred? Did the Warren Commission invalidate its own theory?

Telltale Comments

To the dismay of many, the Warren Commission report is considered the final "factual" report regarding the events of November 22, 1963.

After the report was issued, Chief Justice Warren said that all of the reports would eventually be made public. He was quoted as saying, "Never in our lifetime will we know the entire truth of what happened in Dallas. I am not referring to anything especially, but there may be some things that would involve security."

Could any statement more strongly suggest a cover-up?

Not all the commissioners agreed with the final conclusions of the report even though they all signed it. Hale Boggs, Richard Russell, and John Sherman Cooper all had doubts about the single bullet theory. In fact, Judge Bert W. Griffin, an assistant counsel to the Warren Commission said, "We accepted the answers we got, even though they were inadequate and didn't carry the battle any further. To do so, we'd have had to challenge the integrity of the FBI. Back in 1964, that was something we didn't do."

Was this truly a sign of the times, or does it fully reflect the limitations and ineptitude of the Warren Commission in finding out the truth about the assassination of the president of the United States?

Even though the Warren Commission information was based on the findings and observations of the FBI, there did seem to be certain discrepancies between the final reports of each. The two FBI agents who observed the autopsy submitted a report that was completely dependent on the report of the pathologists conducting the autopsy. One major difference concerned the site of the bullet in the back of the president (either entrance or exit notwithstanding). The agents' report stated that the bullet penetrated just below the level of the shoulder to the right of his spine at a downward angle of forty-five to sixty degrees. There was no point of exit, and the depth of the wound was only about one fingerbreadth. The bullet was never found, and the path for the bullet could never be demonstrated. In other words, it could not have passed through the president's neck to then enter Governor Connelly. It was thought that this bullet might have fallen out during the course of the CPR administered to the president at Parkland. In addition, on the basis of the location of the wounds in the president's jacket and shirt, the bullet hole was about five inches below the collar line. For this shot to have been fired from high on the sixth floor of the TSBD, it would have had to strike the president and then drastically turn upward if it were to exit from the neck area—definitely not a possibility. Therefore, if this bullet did not pass from Kennedy's neck to strike Governor Connelly, then Connelly had to be hit by a separate shot; proving at least four shots were fired, and that there had to be a conspiracy.

In contrast to the FBI report on the autopsy, the Warren Commission Report stated that the bullet hole was located just below the neck line and not inches below. Somehow it had just miraculously moved up about four or five inches. Without the single bullet theory, there would be absolutely no case to disprove a conspiracy. Therefore, the government's conclusions depended totally on Arlen Specter's theory.

The Warren Report concluded that Lee Harvey Oswald had acted alone in the assassination of President John F. Kennedy.

The commission has found no evidence that either Lee Harvey Oswald or Jack Ruby was part of any conspiracy, domestic or foreign, to assassinate President Kennedy. The possibility of others being involved with either Oswald or Ruby cannot be established categorically, but if there is such evidence, it has been beyond the reach of all the investigative agencies and resources of the United States and has not come to the attention of this commission.

Was the commission somehow trying to get out of a very uncomfortable position and placate all involved parties? It was known that not all commissioners believed in the feasibility or reality of the single bullet theory, and yet none of the members voted against the final conclusions of the Warren Report. This conduct could be considered dishonorable.

What They Didn't Know

Evidence was withheld from the Warren Commission by the main investigative agencies, the CIA, FBI, and the Secret Service. Foremost among this evidence was the Mafia-CIA coalition set up to assassinate Fidel Castro. If this fact had been known to the commission, its conclusions would probably have been different. Certainly, the perception of Oswald as the sole assassin would have been reconsidered.

The Warren Commission had a duty (as laid out by President Johnson), in a time of extreme stress, to comfort the people about the strength and stability of our society and to dispel any fears the entire country experienced since November 22. It's obvious that the passage of time has created extreme doubts and multiple questions that still beg to be answered.

Publication Oddities

When all was said and done, the Warren Commission convened its work after ten months in September 1964. The summary report consists of 888 pages including photographs and drawings. Overall, there were over 17,000 pages placed in twenty six volumes. It isn't well organized, doesn't have an index, and hasn't been widely circulated or, one may assume, read. It gives the impression of being detailed, thorough, massive, and accurate. The truth is the report contains extraneous material, much of which is insignificant and inaccurate. This material helps to fill up space.

No Trial by Jury

In a murder trial, there is a prosecutor to establish the guilt of the defendant, and a defense lawyer to try to exonerate the defendant and argue against certain witnesses and their testimonies. That person tries to protect the rights of the defendant and attempts to expose lies and inconsistencies. Here, the Warren Commission acted as judge, jury, prosecutor, and defense counsel.

Lee Harvey Oswald never had the benefit of a defense lawyer. As a result, there was no way to cross-examine a witness. There was no possibility for the defense to introduce or refute evidence. Lee Harvey Oswald was determined guilty from the start; he was not innocent until proven guilty. The truth could not and would not be revealed.

If Oswald had lived, the American standard of justice should have allowed him to exercise his full rights. He would have had a defense lawyer or more likely, a team of defense lawyers. He would have been presumed innocent until proven guilty beyond a reasonable doubt. He would have been allowed to give his testimony and participate in his own defense. Much of the testimony against Oswald if given today would be considered inadmissible in court and not used against him.

Oswald had been interrogated by the Dallas chief of homicide, Will Fritz, for over twelve hours. Yet, there weren't any handwritten notes or tape recordings kept of the proceedings. An attorney for Oswald was not present to inform him of his rights. Certainly, the Dallas police would have realized that legally his testimony would be invalid. Was Oswald's fate decided at the time he was arrested? Did the people who interrogated him know he would never live to stand trial?

Some would say that this "trial" was different because the defendant was dead and, therefore, the same rules could not apply. The fact that the accused was assassinated should make this trial even more important. After all, the president of the United States was dead and so was the alleged assassin. We needed to be 100 percent certain about all the events of the assassination and not base conclusions on presumptions or circumstantial evidence.

Mark Lane, a very prominent but controversial lawyer, had been asked by the mother of Lee Harvey Oswald to defend her son posthumously and uphold his interests. Her request was denied by the Warren Commission. Today's citizens would not tolerate this false justice and should not be expected to accept the same type of bias and propaganda that was spoon-fed to citizens forty years ago.

XII

J. Edgar Hoover and the FBI

J. Edgar Hoover was a man of average size, physically speaking, but his public image was that of a giant. He was the head of the Federal Bureau of Investigation (FBI) for nearly fifty years and held this appointed position through nine different presidential administrations.

He was a powerful and arrogant man who relished being in control. He felt 100 percent secure in his job and believed he would always command respect. He feared no one. People feared him.

The Stuff That Blackmail Is Made Of

Hoover was able to obtain personal information about anyone. He kept it on file and let it be known he had *the goods* on many high-level individuals including congressmen, senators, other politicians, celebrities, and especially presidents. No public figure was immune from Hoover's snooping. He gathered the kind of information that, if revealed, could ruin a public figure (e.g., alcohol or drug addictions, sexual indiscretions, and skeleton-in-the-closet family secrets). These private files gave Hoover leverage and control over very powerful people—even the president of the United States.

His was a subtle kind of *blackmail* that went unchallenged for what seemed like an eternity. It wasn't until John F. Kennedy became the president that Hoover's dynasty began to show signs of eroding.

Fighting Communists

Hoover was a staunch anticommunist and would have liked a communist-free America. He was very much involved in the House Un-American Activities Committee, which equated much of the film industry with communism.

Cold war fears of the 1950s made conditions ripe for the incriminating hearings conducted by Senator Joseph McCarthy. Senator McCarthy was notorious for labeling people communists with little (if any) valid evidence.

Russia had become our archenemy. Fighting communism, by identifying sympathizers, became an obsession for Hoover and McCarthy, and many innocent people suffered. Hoover even aided McCarthy by supplying him with various FBI files that dealt with the communist predilections certain people might harbor. In this way, Hoover helped McCarthy make his case.

Hoover had no fondness or respect for Martin Luther King Jr., who he considered to be an agitator. He was not in favor of the civil rights movement and felt it was fueled by communist propaganda. Still, Hoover didn't believe his agency had the jurisdiction or man power to get involved in civil rights issues. Because the FBI was an agency of investigation, Hoover didn't believe his job was to protect Black people. In the 1960s a segregated Southern city or state was not considered illegal. On the contrary, at that time, the civil rights activists were considered the ones who were breaking the law.

Organized Crime: Fiction or Fact

J. Edgar Hoover initially refused to acknowledge the existence of organized crime—at least publicly. As a result, little was done from a law-enforcement perspective about the Mafia's growing criminal activities. It was allowed to function independently with few restrictions. In actuality, Hoover was a friend to organized crime while claiming he didn't know of its existence. He never thought of the so-called Mafia as being against the law. He carried on many of his activities in the company of Mafia figures and became addicted to racing and gambling, the two primary sources of revenue for the mob.

It was rumored that many horse races were *fixed* so that Hoover was often successful in his betting. The Mafia actually did its own blackmailing when it came to the director of the FBI. It has recently been brought out (but long suspected) that J. Edgar Hoover was a homosexual, a fact known to certain leaders of the mob. In fact, certain mob leaders possessed photographs of Hoover in *compromising positions,* which they could expose if they felt threatened. This information was used for decades to keep Hoover and the FBI from bringing members of the mob to justice. In that era, Hoover couldn't afford to have this personal fact of his life known to the public. He would have been humiliated and rendered weak and ineffective. In a word, he would have been destroyed.

As soon as John Kennedy became president, he was a thorn in Hoover's side. He placed the FBI under the control of the Justice Department and then appointed Robert Kennedy the new attorney general. The Justice Department expanded the fight against organized crime by dramatically increasing the number of agents working in New York and Chicago. Hoover tried to resist this because he wanted the fight to be exclusively against communism and not organized crime. But the president's brother was now Hoover's boss and threatened his power and influence. Earlier attorneys' general, for well over thirty years (since the administration of President Franklin D. Roosevelt), were considered Hoover's superiors in theory only. Hoover answered only to presidents up until the time that Robert Kennedy became attorney general. There was now a layer of authority that separated Hoover from the president. Hoover's autonomy and influence with the president was diminished, and he reasoned the way to regain it would be to find information he could use to blackmail the president. In no time at all, he had what he needed.

The Wolf Guards the Henhouse

Deception, blackmail, and a lust for power became Hoover's hallmarks. It's ironic that the FBI played a fundamental role in investigating the president's assassination. The agency resorted to tactics such as falsifying and nullifying testimony and intimidating witnesses.

I contend that Hoover played a large part in the cover-up of JFK's assassination as well as in protecting his own agency from any involvement with Lee Harvey Oswald prior to the shooting.

Hoover had an extensive file on President Kennedy and his sexual activities. "Reckless womanizing was a flaw in Kennedy's character that imperiled everything he strove for, and Edgar was one of the first to spot that flaw."

It is no secret that the president had several sexual encounters with several different women both before and during his presidency. This has been extensively discussed in other books, and to my knowledge, no one has ever come forth to refute this.

In the 1960s the office of the presidency was considered sacred. Kennedy's private life was never discussed in the media. The predominantly male press corps believed a politician's private life was his own business, and they didn't write about it. Even though the media, various governmental aides, and others especially close to the president knew of his liaisons with those of the opposite sex, these were never disclosed to the public. If the public was made aware of his sexual prowess, this could have become a very important issue during the 1964 election. Even the Secret Service chose not to disclose what it knew about the president's private life. Their function was to protect the president. Almost everyone viewed the office of the presidency with a great deal of respect—a far cry from the attitude of the media today.

In recent years the press and television media pounced on rumors surrounding former President William Clinton. He was essentially convicted by the media, whose primary goal was one of sensationalism. It didn't matter who got hurt in the process. This is not to condone the sexual exploits of a man as powerful as the president. However, in the 1960s, the public was much more concerned with the events of the country, which included the threats of the cold war, as well as the segregation issue and the Vietnam War.

In the late 1990s, the focus was on the personal life of the president, and the true issues our country faced took a backseat. The times had certainly changed over this span of about forty years.

Secrets

What did Hoover have in his large personal file on President Kennedy? Among the first of several *indiscretions*, which Hoover found especially suspicious and revealing, was Kennedy's sexual relationship with a Stockholm citizen, Inga Arvad. This was in the early 1940s while Kennedy was in the navy and working for Naval Intelligence. Inga was pro-Hitler and considered a possible German spy. Hoover used his information to appeal to Joseph Kennedy Sr. The senior Kennedy felt that Arvad could pose a threat to his son's political future, and as a result, JFK wound up being shipped off to the South Pacific where he eventually gained notoriety for the *PT-109* incident. As mentioned earlier, this was the scenario whereby Kennedy's ship was attacked by the Japanese and he became an instant war hero by risking his own life to save the lives of his crew.

Another sexual liaison affecting JFK that Hoover found out about through bugs and wiretaps was with a woman named Judith Campbell Exner. Not only was she bedding the president, but at the same time, she also was the mistress of Sam Giancana, the head of the Chicago Crime Syndicate.

This could be very embarrassing to the president if the public were to find out. Hoover's admission to the Kennedys that he knew of this affair, no doubt, prompted an end to this affair.

Finally, there was the famous liaison between President Kennedy and the most known and "desired" actress of that time, Marilyn Monroe. This affair continued throughout his presidency and was actually known to many, not just the FBI director. In fact, in 1986 a British Broadcasting Company documentary was made entitled *Say Goodbye to the President: Marilyn Monroe and the Kennedys*. This affair apparently was not kept a close secret. Marilyn Monroe's death (August 4, 1962) has been the object of many rumors and controversy, and some believe that her death was not suicidal and, in fact, was intimately related to the Kennedy assassination.

Hoover had a personal dislike for the Kennedys (some might even call it a hatred) that was intensified by his fear of being removed from his leadership position in the FBI upon reaching retirement age. The mandatory retirement age for federal officials was seventy years old. Hoover would be seventy years old on January 1, 1965, only weeks after the 1964 election. It would take an executive order to prolong Hoover's tenure at the FBI. Above all, Hoover wanted to remain the director of the FBI for life. In his inaugural address, John Kennedy declared "the torch has been passed to a new generation of Americans, born in this century." Hoover believed he would be left out of serving in this new administration if it were not for all the incriminating information he had accumulated.

As soon as he acquired the necessary information, Hoover informed one of the Kennedy brothers about a potentially embarrassing revelation about the president's personal life. He wanted his "victim" to know what information he had in his possession. Surely, if he had a file on the president, he could put together a file on virtually anyone.

On the other hand, Hoover was extremely close to Lyndon Johnson. They were close personal friends as well as neighbors in Washington D.C. He knew that if Johnson were president, his job would be secure. In fact, it could be said that Kennedy's assassination resulted in Hoover's political survival. However, to be on the safe side, Hoover also had a personal file on Johnson. It contained information about dealings with Bobby Baker and Billy Sol Estes, which obviously Johnson would never want revealed. As mentioned in an earlier chapter, this dealt with illegal business encounters the vice president had with both of these men and which if exposed to the public, could end Johnson's political career.

Did Hoover have any direct connection to the plotting of the assassination? This author believes the answer is no, but I also believe Hoover played a major role in the subsequent cover-up after the murder, which continued for several years.

The basic source of information for the Warren Commission was through the FBI and, therefore, through Hoover. The commission did not conduct its own investigation and instead relied on the records of the bureau, at least those records the FBI chose to release. The FBI donated voluminous reports to the Warren Commission, much of which was irrelevant. The commission did not have enough time to go over all this data and, as a result, seemed to concentrate primarily on reports concerning Oswald. After all, its main function as stated in a previous chapter was to prove that Oswald was the sole assassin.

The FBI had learned of multiple allegations and threats about the potential assassination of John F. Kennedy. There were reports of two assassination plots on the president in early November 1963: one in Chicago and one in Tampa, Florida. Both plans were uncovered in time by federal authorities and thus averted. The trip to Chicago was cancelled, but the trip to Tampa was not and proved uneventful. However, five days before the assassination, a teletype came into the New Orleans FBI office warning of a potential assassination attempt on Kennedy in Dallas on November 22.

The FBI didn't follow through, and the Secret Service was never notified. This turned into more than just a threat and unfortunately, proved fatal. Hoover had also received previous information about the possibility of a mob conspiracy to assassinate the president. He ignored this as well.

Asleep at the Wheel

As director of the FBI, he was obliged by federal law to notify the Secret Service of all threats against public officials. By neglecting to do this, Hoover could have been considered an accessory to the crime.

Hoover also knew of Guy Bannister's and David Ferrie's connections with Oswald and Carlos Marcello. He knew of the probability of the Oswald imposters. He had knowledge of many of the characters who, in one way or another, were involved in the assassination. He kept the information to himself. Would it have made a difference on November 22, 1963, if he had disclosed what he knew? We can only speculate.

Case Closed

Hoover virtually closed the case after Oswald's assassination. He concluded very quickly that Oswald was the killer, had no accomplices, and acted as a crazed lone gunman. He had no interest in discovering the truth or bringing the guilty party to justice. He ignored or suppressed all evidence suggesting that a conspiracy was involved. Why was Hoover eager to blame Oswald so quickly and terminate the investigation?

I conclude he felt his job as chief of the FBI would be in serious jeopardy if Kennedy remained in office. Now that Kennedy was eliminated, he wanted to close this chapter as soon as possible.

He also knew that an assassination conspiracy theory was likely to implicate Lyndon Johnson as well as the FBI. His position as permanent director of the FBI would be in grave jeopardy.

It turned out that fate was on Hoover's side. The government agreed with Hoover's notion of Oswald being solely responsible for the assassination.

In May 1964, President Johnson waived the mandatory retirement age provision for the director of the FBI. Hoover now had a lifetime position.

The FBI had a fully stacked case against Oswald even before he was charged with the murder of the president. *Could this have been prepared prior to the assassination?* I say *yes, especially if Oswald was used as a patsy as Oswald himself claimed.*

The FBI had contact with Oswald prior to the assassination. Special Agent James Hosty of the FBI Dallas field office was given a file on Lee Harvey Oswald in March 1963 and asked to investigate him as a security risk. Yet the FBI later tried to cover up its dealings with Oswald and dispel any knowledge about its connections to this lone marine who by now was known to the entire world.

The FBI knew before the assassination that Oswald was in Dallas and working at the Texas School Book Depository. Despite the fact that they knew Oswald was a Marxist with communist leanings, they didn't notify the Secret Service of his presence. This was the cold war era and any known communist (i.e., Oswald) would certainly pose a threat to the president. Yet they did nothing to deter the president from visiting Dallas.

Following the assassination, letters and documents linking Oswald with the FBI were destroyed, including a personal letter Oswald had written to Hosty. Hoover needed to convince the Warren Commission that Lee Harvey Oswald, acting alone, killed both JFK and Officer Tippit and that Jack Ruby, also acting alone, killed Oswald out of patriotic duty.

Hoover made certain that mob threats against JFK (by Carlos Marcelo, Santos Trafficante, and James Hoffa) never came to light. After all, a mob connection to the assassination would be an embarrassment to both the FBI and to Hoover.

Hoover's primary motivation following the assassination seemed to be to protect the institution and prestige of the FBI rather than to investigate the murder. Within two or three hours following the actual shooting, Hoover telephoned Robert Kennedy to inform him they had captured the man who killed his brother and his name was Lee Harvey Oswald. This was before Oswald was charged, let alone booked, and before there was any investigation. Only two days after the assassination, Hoover drew up a memo stating that he wanted something issued to convince the public that Oswald was the real assassin. Hoover seemed obsessed in getting these statements out as soon as possible even to the point of not allowing his FBI agents to conduct a normal investigation. Hoover sent a letter of general instruction to his field divisions stating, "We're only going to prove that Oswald was the guy who did it. There were no co-conspirators, and there was no international conspiracy."

Hoover kept the nation focused on Oswald's quick capture and guilt and diverted attention from the FBI and its failure to protect the president.

Too Good to be True

Oswald is murdered, and within forty eight hours, Hoover informs President Johnson that there was no conspiracy and that Oswald was the lone assassin. How could anyone arrive at this conclusion so soon? Could this conclusion have been planned before the assassinations? Was Hoover aware of JFK's fate on November 22, 1963, long before that date arrived? *It's certainly possible.*

The FBI (as well as the CIA) had connections to Lee Harvey Oswald. The intelligence community had helped create Oswald's background. Following the assassination, they needed to manipulate and destroy evidence that would connect Oswald to their respective agencies.

This strategy carried over to the James Garrison investigation in New Orleans and the subsequent trial of Clay Shaw (1967). Both the bureau and the agency helped Shaw by conducting clandestine operations against Garrison. His headquarters was infiltrated and his witnesses were harassed. Prospective jurors were intimidated. Clearly certain "higher-ups" in our government were becoming very concerned about Garrison's progress. They needed to stick to the conclusions of the Warren Commission that there was no conspiracy. As it turned out, Garrison lost his case, but he was the first investigator to actually accuse someone other than Oswald for the assassination. As a result, the public started to think about the possibility of a conspiracy.

Finally on November 25, 1963 (three days after JFK's assassination and only one day after Oswald's murder), Deputy Attorney General Nicholas Katzenbach, a member of Robert Kennedy's staff, stated in a written pronouncement that the "public must be satisfied that Lee Harvey Oswald was the lone assassin and there were no confederates still at large. The evidence must be made that if he were still alive, he would have been convicted. We must convince the people that the killer has been caught and is now dead himself. There was no conspiracy. We need to make the entire case go against Lee Harvey Oswald."

The President had been assassinated and no one really wanted to uncover the truth. The "patsy" was accused, tried, convicted and assassinated.

XIII

The Role of the Media and the
Importance of the Movie *JFK*

In the 1950s and1960s, the media in the United States was predominately anticommunism. Widely read publications including *Time Magazine, Newsweek, US News and World Report, Readers Digest, the New York Times, Washington Post,* and *New York Daily News* appeared to be obsessed with communism, and the topic received nonstop attention. The administration's cold war policy was considered soft on communism and called un-American.

Many journalists and management at their respective publications didn't like what they perceived to be JFK's appeasement policy with the Soviets. This included his lack of aggression against Cuba during the Bay of Pigs crisis and the Cuban missile crisis and his agreement to the Test Ban Treaty with the Soviets.

Engaging ... Likeable

Nevertheless, the media had a great deal of regard for the man. He was the first president to make the weekly televised press conference a common occurrence. He always made himself available to reporters for interviews and actually seemed to enjoy these meetings. There had been no other president who was so accessible and well-liked by the media. They enjoyed being around such a young, vibrant, and charismatic individual. "He was accessible, he was quotable, and he had a special reverence for language—he was in a phrase, good copy."

With Reverence

Coverage of the assassination and funeral were handled in a very professional manner. This, no doubt, helped the American people get through this horrible ordeal. Print and broadcast personnel went the extra mile to dispel the spread of frightening rumors. These communicators knew that in times of tragedy and shock the public depended on them for information. The timing for the advent of news reported over television could not have been better. In addition, the news media took responsibility to calm national anxiety and minimize confusion regarding the country's future and its new president.

Nobody's Business But His Own

The media respected the office of the presidency. Certainly a percentage of the people assigned to follow President Kennedy, as well as certain members of the media who were closest to him, knew of his personal indiscretions and yet would never make these public. They did not engage in sensationalism. The media of the 1960s essentially ignored the extramarital affairs of the president. His womanizing did not become public knowledge until many years after the assassination. Times have certainly changed as exemplified by the 1998 near impeachment of President William Jefferson Clinton following his involvement in sexual scandal. The media generated massive amounts of publicity about this president's indiscretions and unacceptable behavior.

I believe the press, radio, and television crews did a good job of reporting the news as they learned it on that fateful day of November 22, 1963. This carried over for the next two days when the alleged assassin, Lee Harvey Oswald, was murdered. Television actually came of age when this horrific crime took place. Ninety-six percent of the country's households tuned into a television network for the coverage of the assassination. The average viewer watched nine hours a day. We all saw a national funeral attended by well-known figures and felt as if there had been a death in our own family. Our grief was overwhelming.

I believe the media began to fail readers and viewers when the official Warren Commission Report was released. This became clear when the possibility of an assassination conspiracy was raised. The national media was unrelenting in putting forth the opinion that the Warren Report delivered the ultimate truth despite all the controversy. For years, no major news outlet would print any word of doubt. When individuals began to question the findings of the Warren Report, members of the media were not among them.

A Different Drummer

The pioneer in questioning the government's conclusions about the assassination (even before the Warren Report) was Mark Lane, noted Kennedy researcher, who first raised his suspicions as early as December 1963. He believed the case against Oswald was made too rapidly and was filled with contradictions.

Soon after the release of the Warren Report, other writers began to express their doubts about the way the government was portraying the assassination. Among them were Josiah Thompson in his famous book *Six Seconds in Dallas* and Sylvia Meagher in her noted book *Accessories After the Fact*. Both books were written in 1967 and paved the way for hundreds of other writers who would voice their views criticizing the government's conclusions. Despite the fact that authors, historians, and book publishers cast grave doubts about Oswald being a lone assassin, the media stuck to its original premise. They supported the findings of the commission that was appointed by President Kennedy's successor.

Chicago Tribune

In 1991, my wife, Kris, and I went to Chicago to attend a conference. It focused on the assassination of President Kennedy and was well attended. A reporter from the *Chicago Tribune*, a popular big-city newspaper, was seated at our table. She seemed very friendly and stated she was just there to observe. Her exact words were, "I want to learn." The symposium dealt with various conspiracy theories all of which were in sharp contrast to everything the media asserted. She asked everyone, "Why are you here?" We answered her questions, not giving them a second thought. We appreciated what we perceived to be her genuine interest.

About two weeks later, a lengthy article ridiculing the conference and all of us who attended was published in the *Tribune*. We were called, "fanatics" as well as other derogatory names such as "JFK junkies."

I was thoroughly offended. This was the first conference of this type I had attended, and I was there to observe and learn. I did not consider myself eccentric and believed I had the right to question the government's conclusions. Unfortunately, this reporter (and colleagues at her paper) were unwilling to question, or even doubt, the findings of the Warren Commission.

I wrote a rebuttal letter to this reporter and her editor, but neither replied. I assumed they were afraid to confront me. They didn't know or refused to learn enough facts about the assassination to confront anyone who had an opposing view. Of course, there's another way to assess their response, but I didn't consider it at the time. It could be the media (especially top management and owners) were participating in a cover-up. Thirty years had passed since JFK was assassinated, but nothing in this regard had changed.

The media decreed that Oswald was the lone assassin and the single bullet theory was accepted even though it was refuted by the public. In fact, all the polls since 1963 have shown that people believed there was a conspiracy and Oswald was a likely patsy.

Why, Why, Why?

- Why didn't the media go along with public opinion or at least acknowledge that perhaps the public was correct?

- Why would the media be afraid of the idea of a conspiracy? Why would it be so defensive and not want to hear (or report) anything that was contrary to the Warren Commission Report? The idea of a conspiracy to assassinate President Kennedy could be the biggest news item in history. After all, wasn't the media supposed to report the facts to the public?

- Why couldn't the media accept the possibility of a conspiracy or at least recognize its potential?

The reasons, no doubt, are linked to threats and vested interests.

The media is operated and controlled by big business conglomerates and the intelligence community (CIA, the government, and the military) as well as private interest groups. These groups are referred to as: "higher ups," "power elite," "the establishment," or "military-industrial complex." These are different labels for the same people.

The media was (and actually still is) compelled to uphold the Warren Commission findings. After all, the Warren Commission was appointed and directed by the government. The media was probably told by "higher ups" that a bias suggesting a conspiracy would constitute a breach of national security. Such statements could be considered irresponsible and lead to negative legal consequences.

It's not surprising that a smear campaign was directed against conspiracy advocates Mark Lane, Josiah Thompson, Jim Garrison, and Oliver Stone.

Hindsight

Noam Chomsky, a major linguist as well as writer on political and contemporary issues, has described the evolution of the media. He wrote that in the 1920s in the United States, radio was under the auspices of private powers and not public interest groups. Wealthy people held power and dictated policy. The same scenario existed in the 1960s when television became the "darling" of the media. Television was corporate funded and represented the interests and power of a class-conscious business system. This core group made all the decisions. They desired a "passive and obedient population of consumers and political spectators." They limited the content of what was reported and the people on the air did their biding.

Under these circumstances, objectivity isn't possible, and much of what is reported is propaganda. Unfortunately, the average citizen accepts what he hears or sees as a truth because he generally does not know the background of the writer or newscaster and probably doesn't have reason to doubt that person.

To say that the media deals in intellectual dishonesty would not be far-fetched. Journalists cannot give their honest opinions if they're contradictory to the group that pulls the strings for fear they won't be printed. The "power elite" sees to it that the public is told what it should know or believe.

These were the circumstances at the time of JFK's assassination when the media declared Lee Harvey Oswald the lone assassin. The easiest thing to do to avoid embarrassment was to continue to blame Oswald rather than to aggravate an already tense situation by looking for a second shooter. We had just missed being at war with Russia during both the Cuban missile crisis and the Berlin crisis. To attempt to report on the potential of a possible conspiracy in the blatant murder of our president would have been a sticky situation, to say the least.

In the spring of 1964, a census revealed that one third of Americans favored the theory that Oswald acted in concert with others to carry out the assassination. Twenty years later, the percentage of Americans favoring a conspiracy theory had risen to 80 percent. To my knowledge, there have not been any recent polls. I suspect if the public were asked the question again today the overwhelming answer would be no, that Oswald did not act alone. It's interesting to note that even Lyndon Baines Johnson once said he never believed Oswald acted alone.

The CIA's Tentacles

The Central Intelligence Agency maintains hundreds of reporters on its payroll. In 1967 the CIA issued a memo that virtually ordered broadcasters to counter and refute any attacks made by Warren Commission critics and conspiracy writers. Book reviews and feature articles to discredit the arguments were written and circulated. Most anticonspiracy advocates had ties to the CIA. So, the media's reports ignored anything suggesting a potential link to the agency. This behavior was so pervasive that even if the CIA had been behind the assassination, the media wouldn't expose it.

For or Against

Never before in the history of movies had a movie received so much negative press coverage prior to its release than Oliver Stone's movie, *JFK*. Even David Brinkley, a foremost news anchor at that time, ridiculed the conspiracists and said they were wrong, saying, "Oliver Stone's movie JFK offered a ridiculous account of a murder plotted and executed by the Mafia, CIA, and an assortment of right-wing characters from around the world."

Why was this movie purported to be ridiculous? What proof did the media have that this tragedy couldn't occur as portrayed?

Several large newspapers printed articles asserting that Stone was misstating history and exaggerating the truth. Yet none challenged the FBI or CIA regarding the "lost brain" or for ignoring multiple eyewitnesses.

Warren Commission conclusions were based on bias and preconceived notions because pertinent information was ignored. There were no separate investigations. There was no trial or defense mounted. There was a botched autopsy, and some eyewitness testimonies were altered. Then, too, the lack of evidence pointing to a conspiracy is not synonymous with proving that Oswald was the perpetrator.

A Question of Patriotism

In 1991 Gerald Ford (member of the Warren Commission and later to be president of the United States) and David Belin (Warren Commission counsel) reported in *The Washington Post* that the investigation of the murder of JFK with the talk of a conspiracy after so many years and after the government had already given its conclusions was a form of "desecration to the memory of President Kennedy, a desecration to the memory of Earl Warren, and a fraudulent misrepresentation of the truth to the American public." It's amazing to see how the government and the media can twist ideas and words to suit their purposes.

It's one thing to critique a movie and give an appraisal that's either pro or con. It's assumed this provides the public with information upon which to base a decision about whether or not to see a movie. The heavy-handed negative reviews of Stone's movie may have had the opposite affect. The movie *JFK* introduced the mysteries of the assassination to vast numbers of people, including new generations not yet born in November 1963.

The media was not the only group that tried to discredit Stone's movie. David Belin, a former Warren Commission counsel, said the following: "By ignoring pieces of evidence and misrepresenting others, it's a shame that a man as talented as Stone had to go to such lengths to deceive the American public."

I find this statement ironic and contrary to fact. Belin's words describe the Warren Commission's performance. Oliver Stone was not interested in deception. We can't say the same about the Warren Commission.

With the advent of the movie, it became possible for people of all ages to be exposed to the details of this unsolved murder.

Linking Generations

Oliver Stone's movie *JFK* appealed to two generations of people. The first were those who vividly remembered the events of November 22, 1963. This is my generation. Their interest, fascination, and concerns were rekindled. They had become skeptical of information received from the government so many years ago. The second group to whom this movie had special appeal was the "nonrememberers," the group not yet born or too young to have memories of the events of that historic day. They were so impressed by the movie that they led the way to open up government files and clamored for a new investigation. These are the so-called baby boomers and the first generation to seriously question government authority. This generation wanted the real truth and would accept nothing less.

Due to Stone's movie, a true distrust of our government came into play and people were eager for the opportunity to view a large-scale replay of the events of November 1963.

I saw the movie *JFK* on four separate occasions and strongly support many of the ideas that were put forth in this movie. Stone's film was obviously dramatized, but it was based on extensive research. Many of Stone's statements are factual even though they disagreed with the official government version.

I've read most of the books written about the assassination, and much of what Oliver Stone put into his movie also appeared in these thoroughly researched books.

The media never slammed these individual books as it did *JFK*. However, it did try to make a mockery of the investigative work done by Jim Garrison, district attorney for the City of New Orleans.

Why Slam Jim Garrison?

Garrison's investigation into the New Orleans connection to the assassination began in late 1966 and ended with the Clay Shaw trial in March 1969. Garrison felt that Lee Harvey Oswald, David Ferrie (a man with Mafia, CIA, and FBI connections) and Clay Shaw (a prominent New Orleans businessman who also had CIA connections) were all involved in a plot to assassinate President Kennedy that originated in New Orleans. Oswald was already dead at the onset of the investigation, and Ferrie died prior to the trial. This left Clay Shaw as the only one left for Garrison to attempt to convict.

Oliver Stone's movie was largely based on work done by Garrison. Even though Shaw was acquitted of participation in the assassination, Garrison became the first person to actually convince a jury there was a conspiracy in the assassination. The movie put the media on the defensive.

I Like Ike

Stone incriminated many organizations (or people affiliated with them), holding them potentially responsible for JFK's assassination. They included the CIA, FBI, Mafia, anti-Castro Cubans, Cuba, Fidel Castro, and the so-called military-industrial complex that former President Eisenhower named in his farewell address as president.

Eisenhower spoke of a clandestine group of people composed of military and scientific-technological individuals who could become sufficiently powerful and take control of and endanger the nation. During the cold war and technological revolution, a permanent armaments industry of vast proportions had been created. Eisenhower warned:

> This conjunction of an immense military establishment and a large arms industry is new in the American experience. The total influence of this is felt everywhere. We must guard against the acquisition of unwarranted influence, whether sought or unsought, by the military-industrial complex. The potential for the disastrous rise of misplaced power exists and will persist. The military-industrial complex should never be allowed to endanger our liberties or democratic processes. We should take nothing for granted.

This was spoken by a military man who had spent his life defending freedom and achieving peace.

Each of these groups mentioned by Oliver Stone had their own potential motive for the assassination. Nobody has ever said that they were all involved (or that a certain group as a whole was involved.) I believe that certain select members from some of these organizations did conspire to kill the president.

Keeping Secrets

Many conspiracy antagonists argue that with so many potential groups involved a leak of information is inevitable. How could this have been kept secret for so many years?

What if only a handful of people were involved in the actual planning and implementation of the assassination? What if each group had a specific job and was unaware of what other groups were doing? Then, too, several people potentially associated with the assassination plot died—either naturally or unnaturally (i.e., murder). Isn't this what happened to both Oswald and Ruby?

The critics of the movie (those advocating Oswald as the lone assassin) say that Stone blames everyone for the murder of the president. In fact, he merely illustrates there were many in our society who disliked Kennedy enough to consider assassination.

He shows how certain people from select groups had the means, motive, and opportunity to kill the president. John F. Kennedy made many enemies during his short term in office. His primary obligation was to the American public, and he made decisions that alienated some people in high places. John F. Kennedy disturbed their status quo. To use an old cliché, Kennedy tried to "buck the system." He showed exceptional courage by knowing when to say no. He prevented potential nuclear war on several occasions. Contrary to the beliefs and desires of many of his advisors (especially those affiliated with the military), Kennedy opposed reliance on nuclear weapons. He was reluctant to expand the fighting in Vietnam (in contrast to his successor) as he always vowed not to send combat troops. His goal was to preserve peace and not wage war. On the other hand, Kennedy was prepared to go to war if necessary. The safety of our country and its people was always foremost in his mind. To his misfortune, there were others in our country who did not feel this way.

I had the opportunity to express my feelings to Oliver Stone in Dallas in 1993 while attending a seminar on the assassination of JFK. He seemed appreciative of my praise for his movie.

I credit Mr. Stone with having the guts to direct and make a movie of this magnitude. Countless viewers were prompted to open their eyes and question the government's position for the first time.

Oliver Stone was interviewed by *Playboy Magazine* in November 2004. He discussed *JFK* and what he was attempting to do when he produced the movie. In answer to his critics he said, "It's a hypothesis, a philosophical inquiry into what is truth and what is reality. There is an entire book with footnotes to explain our sources. We made every effort to be honest, and we were raked over the coals."

Oliver Stone is an inspiration to those who search for the truth. He asked the public to question dogma and made the role of the government, both in the assassination as well as the eventual cover-up, suspect. Of course, the present-day reader or viewer is more sophisticated. Today people are quick to question information disseminated by government officials.

At My House

In addition to my young daughter, Kennedy, whose name is instilled in the title of this book, I have two older sons. Each of my children was born years after the assassination. My sons were intrigued by the movie, which caused them to question the events surrounding President Kennedy's death.

Naïve No More

The public's mistrust of government was compounded as the following events unfolded:

1. Watergate. The most notorious of the events was the Watergate incident, which led to the downfall and subsequent resignation of President Richard Nixon.

2. Sanctioned assassinations. There was the revelation in the mid-1970s by the House Select Committee on Assassinations that the FBI, CIA, and the Secret Service all withheld strategic information from the Warren Commission. If this had been known, earlier findings related to the JFK assassination might be different. There were other committees assembled around this time to further investigate the assassination as well as delve into the possibility of a CIA conspiracy and potential CIA illegal activities. Among these were the Church Senate Select Committee on Intelligence Activities and the Rockefeller Commission appointed by President Gerald Ford who prior to his presidency served on the Warren Commission. It was learned that the CIA was in the business of assassination, but supposedly this concerned only foreign leaders. Among the victims were Rafael Trujillo (Dominican Republic on May 30, 1961), Patrice Lumumba (Congo in January 1961), and Rene Schneider of Chile. It is also believed that the CIA was instrumental in the assassination of Ngo Dinh Diem, president of South Vietnam, only two weeks prior to Kennedy's assassination. Finally, the CIA plan in alliance with the Mafia to kill Fidel Castro has been well documented. In fact, the assassination of four of these five leaders of foreign countries was successful. The only one that failed was that of the Cuban dictator. The revelation that our strongest international intelligence agency was in the business of assassinating foreign leaders would certainly add to our mistrust of government.

3. The Pentagon Papers, released in 1971, let us know we were being lied

to about Vietnam. We were not winning this war, contrary to what we had been led to believe by the government.

4. The Iran-Contra affair in 1985 led to more mistrust. In this case, missiles were sent to Iran in exchange for the release of hostages being held in Lebanon.

5. Finally, during the most recent War on Terror (September 11, 2001), there was the revelation that our intelligence agencies, the CIA and the FBI, had little communication among themselves and withheld important information from each other. This seems quite similar to the scenario of the 1960s where the intelligence agencies did not co-operate with each other, let alone share information.

6. The most recent event has been the war in Iraq, which has again caused the American public to question the government and the way it reports to the people. These examples show that citizens have repeatedly been led down the "garden path" and they know it!

I believe the events surrounding the assassination of John F. Kennedy are not any different than these other examples.

The Opposite View

Over the past several years, there have been two primary authors who have continued to back up and agree with the Warren Commission and its conclusions that Lee Harvey Oswald acted alone and that there was no conspiracy to assassinate President Kennedy. As you are already aware, I strongly disagree with this contention and thoroughly question the so-called evidence both authors claim. The first of these authors is Gerald Posner and his book *Case Closed* (1993). This book received a very positive review by the media. However, it was severely criticized by Posner's contemporary authors who believe that much of his evidence was fabricated and made to appear as the truth, just to fit his own hypothesis of the lone assassin. In other words, eyewitnesses were not interviewed if it appeared that their testimony would favor the idea of a conspiracy.

Various researchers assert that many of the people that Posner purportedly quoted were never interviewed by him. An example would be when Posner claimed that he had interviewed the Parkland physicians and they told him that they all agreed with the autopsy findings and that their own original observations were made under great stress and were distorted by conspiracy writers. Posner tries to make us believe that these physicians, all highly expertise in treating victims with gunshot wounds (in contrast to the autopsy physicians), recanted their original statements. Despite my own extended research, I have yet to find another author (either proconspiracy or anticonspiracy) who questions the testimony and subsequent integrity of these Parkland physicians (other than, of course, the Warren Commission). Of course, the Warren Commission conveniently circumvented these doctors' testimonies simply by ignoring them.

Posner's book *Case Closed* has been touted by the media to be the final word on the assassination. Every time there's a serious disclosure of new information suggesting the possibility of a conspiracy, Gerald Posner appears on our television screens to refute such claims, even though he has no proof to support his allegations. The anticonspiracy assertion that "the lack of the findings of a conspiracy must mean that Oswald had to have been the assassin" simply defies logic and intelligence. Yet, this is the philosophy which those speaking against a conspiracy believe. They never attempt to prove or disprove the guilt or innocence of Oswald. In other words, the lack of a conspiracy does NOT mean Oswald was the assassin. In August 2001 Posner was interviewed on a television show that was showing the Zapruder film. When again questioned about the potential of a conspiracy in the assassination, he answered he is surprised that the entire population does not believe that there may have been a conspiracy. That's right—surprised! Maybe he is finally beginning to see the light, or at least, maybe he is beginning to realize the truth.

In an attempt to ridicule those who believed in a conspiracy, he once said, "The debate is no longer whether JFK was killed by Lee Oswald acting alone or as part of a conspiracy. It is instead, which conspiracy is correct?"

One major magazine, *US News and World Report*, carried a book review on *Case Closed* that filled more than twelve pages. Naturally, the review favored the book. I don't believe there has ever been such a large review for any book in the history of man. I guess we were supposed to believe this book gave the only factual account of the events of that day. If we didn't believe the Warren Report, then we most certainly had to believe this book. In fact, I contend that Mr. Posner's book was nothing more than a reiteration of the

Warren Report with the same faulty conclusions. Gerald Posner was relatively unheard of prior to the appearance of his book, but all of a sudden he had become an expert on JFK's assassination. He became a popular television personality and the "darling" of the media. In fact, he has also written a book abut the assassination of Martin Luther King Jr., in which he referred to James Earl Ray as the lone assassin, again a very controversial and unproven hypothesis.

The second author who has gained recent prominence in also believing that Oswald was the lone assassin is Vincent Bugliosi, initially of *Helter Skelter* fame. His first book entitled *Reclaiming History: The Assassination of John F Kennedy* (2007) is an extensive, nearly 1,500 page treatise of the events surrounding the assassination—long and detailed and in my opinion lacking accuracy. His second book entitled *Four Days in November: The Assassination of John F. Kennedy* (also 2007) is basically drawn from the larger book, apparently to appeal more to the general population. I must always question a book of the magnitude of *Reclaiming History*. First of all, very few people will read a book of this size unless they are true Kennedy scholars. An analogy would be to read the total Warren Report, which consisted of twenty-six volumes and 17,000 pages. Very few people have read this, and I guarantee that this includes the members of the Warren Commission itself even though they signed off on it. Be careful of extraneous material and insignificant information just to increase the size of a book. It may look impressive but can very deceiving. I am not accusing Mr. Bugliosi of doing this, but I am accusing the Warren Commission of padding their report.

Both books were advertised as presenting new revelations and information in proving the single assassin and no conspiracy theory. In other words, the Warren Commission with its report is again vindicated, and its conclusions are again substantiated. These books, as the media would like us to believe, will end the controversy about the Kennedy assassination once and for all. End of discussion! End of controversy! End of speculation! In other words, case closed. This is a real play on words. If we do accept this, than the truth will never be found out, and the deception will go on, except now in our children's minds.

Just as I have with Mr. Posner's conclusions, I must also disagree with Mr. Bugliosi and his conclusions. Mr. Bugliosi is a prosecutor by trade and who better qualified to gather incriminating information against a defendant (i.e., Oswald) than a prosecutor. I thought that *Fours Days in November* was well-written and actually read like a John Grisham novel—a page turner, so to speak. However, after reading both books, I found absolutely no evidence (old or new) put forth to show that Lee Harvey Oswald was an assassin, let alone a lone assassin. The questions remain the same, and the answers still remain unanswered.

I do not have the writing credentials of these two established authors but nonetheless, I also believe that my opinion and conclusions are just as significant and should not be ignored. I have devoted several years of my life to finding the truth. I want my children to know the truth as they grow during their lifetimes. Only then can they be proud of their country. History is the premise upon which our future depends. We must know what has happened in the past, and it must be the truth. If not, then we continue to deceive ourselves as well as everyone we care about.

Section Four

A BREATH OF FRESH AIR

XIV

And So My Daughter, Kennedy

It's 2008, and students who look up information about the assassination from sources such as textbooks, history books, encyclopedias, and the Internet come away with the impression that Lee Harvey Oswald acted alone and assassinated President John F. Kennedy. As you've already seen, this has never been proven and evidence strongly points to the contrary.

What Really Happened?

After all, JFK was one of our most popular presidents. Yet, the: *who, what, why, and where* questions about his assassination still don't have official answers that reasonable people can accept.

Why didn't this young and vital man live to serve out his term of office? And, there's more to ponder. He was the youngest president ever elected to office, and one supposes that after his presidency, he would have had a long and productive life. How we might have benefited, we shall never know. How the world might have benefited, we shall never know. It's highly conceivable that mankind would have benefited greatly from all that *might have been,* and we know that. With the exception of some "closed" countries, where news never filtered through to the citizens, people the world over mourned his loss.

It's shocking when anyone is assassinated, but, all of us who were adults at the time were devastated by what happened and what followed. It may help you to better understand our genuine affection for the man if you know a little more about him—not only about his death or the likely means and motives for his assassination, but more about him. Books about him continue to be published, and you can find them with ease. (I hope you'll read some of them. I read all of them!) What follows "about him" here is limited, but it is information you should have.

JFK was the first Roman Catholic to be elected to this high office. He once said he was not running as a Catholic but instead was a man who was running for high office who just happened to be Catholic. JFK had to overcome three outstanding adversities when striving for the highest elected office in the land: his youth, religion, and inexperience.

Clearly he appealed to the masses, whether Catholic, Protestant, or Jewish, black or white, well educated or not, young or elderly. Not only did he have the courage to give people the hope they hungered for, but his charisma and personality enabled him to *tell it like it was*. Election time was exciting because he made it exciting, and people all over this great nation let him know they favored him when they voted. His popularity continued to grow after his untimely death. The Kennedy Era following his death became known as the time of Camelot.

Camelot was the title of Kennedy's favorite musical show. There is a notable verse in one song: "For one brief shining moment, there had been a chivalrous kingdom known as Camelot." Kennedy had his brief shining moment. He had a glittering style, which he and his wife brought to the White House.

The British prime minister at that time, Harold McMillan, said during his eulogy for the late president: "Was it not because he seemed, in his own person, to embody all the hopes and aspirations of this new world that is struggling to emerge—to rise from the ashes of the old?"

People still talk about John F. Kennedy as if he were here today, even though our direct contact with this respected and beloved president ended over forty years ago. If he were still alive today, he would be your grandfather's age.

Today and Tomorrow

JFK's place in our history is marred when available reading material about this famous man is skewed. And, *skewed* (i.e., twisted, distorted, partial, off-center) is a polite description of what's out there.

For example, *Colliers Encyclopedia* in 1995 stated, "The shots which killed President Kennedy and wounded Governor Connelly were fired by Lee Harvey Oswald." In essence, this supports the single assassin and single bullet theory. Additionally, you'll read, "Warren Commission found no evidence that either Lee Harvey Oswald or Jack Ruby were part of a conspiracy, whether domestic or foreign, to assassinate President Kennedy." This was the same premise the average person entertained for several years following the assassination. People were told what to believe by the powers that be, and it was regurgitated by the media.

The *Encyclopedia Britannica* also quoted the findings of the Warren Commission, but, in the *Britannica* you'll read, "Oswald probably was not the only gunman involved in the assassination, and he was probably part of a conspiracy." This observation is based upon a special committee report from the U.S. House of Representatives in 1979. It concludes, "Kennedy assassination, the most notorious political murder of the twentieth century, remains a source of bafflement, controversy, and speculation."

World Book Encyclopedia also admits, because of the House Select Committee report, that Kennedy was probably assassinated as a result of a conspiracy. *The American National Biography* printed by the Oxford University Press said the following: "John F. Kennedy was struck in the head and throat by a bullet fired from a window on the sixth floor of the Texas School Book Depository. The bizarre circumstances of the assassination caused conspiracy theories to proliferate. The Warren Commission concluded that Oswald was solely responsible for the assassination. Although many suspect that the murder was a conspiracy planned by others, the weight of the evidence supports the original finding of the Warren Commission."

In 1999, the *World Book of American Presidents* tried to appease all factions. It quoted the Warren Report and its conclusion that Oswald acted alone though it added that many observers disputed this and thought that he was part of a group that planned the assassination. It then added that in 1978, the Committee of the House of Representatives, on the basis of acoustical evidence, concluded that Kennedy was "probably assassinated as a result of a conspiracy." However, it reversed itself by offering that in 1982 a National Research Council disputed the second gunman theory, thus essentially indicating that the assassination was accomplished by a single gunman.

Confused? Why wouldn't you be?

Finally, *The Complete Idiot's Guide to the American Presidents 2000* contains a short chapter entitled "Staying off the Grassy Knoll." It concludes the following: "The assassin was Lee Harvey Oswald. The Warren Commission was convened to investigate Kennedy's assassination, and members concluded that Oswald was the lone gunman and was not part of a conspiracy." In 1979 the House Select Committee on Assassinations believed in a conspiracy but stated that "all the conspiracy theories would be a book unto themselves, so let's leave it at that."

Even television got into the act. ABC news in a program on the assassination in November 2003 on the work done by the Assassination Record Review Board (1992) reported, "In all these years, there has never been any evidence to prove a conspiracy." This totally ignores the fact that there never was any concrete evidence to prove that Oswald was the lone assassin. The government bases its case on discrediting the conspiracy theorists rather than on proving that Lee Harvey Oswald was the killer. Its rationale is that if a conspiracy cannot be proved, it would stand to reason that Oswald must be the assassin. I'm not a lawyer, but even I know this way of thinking would never hold up in a court of law.

Finally, the Internet has spread the same false information. To quote from a website regarding the assassination: "This website is dedicated to debunking the mass of misinformation and disinformation surrounding the murder of JFK. If you believe in Oswald as the lone gunman, you are likely to enjoy the website, since most of the misinformation and disinformation has come from conspiracists. But if you are a sophisticated conspiracist, you likely understand that the mass of silly nonsense in conspiracy books and documentations does no service to the cause of truth in the assassination, and simply buries the 'case for conspiracy' under layers of bunk." Though this is a single opinion appearing on the Internet, it could bias people who know little about the assassination and want to know more.

Deprivation

Students, young or old, after reading these summaries, are likely to believe that Kennedy was assassinated by Lee Harvey Oswald. They may entertain the thought that he had an accomplice. However, a nagging thought isn't enough to make them believe there was a conspiracy. If some hunger for more, they'll find only crumbs that allude to other responsible parties or potential conspirators. They'll be deprived of historical "facts" and theories. These seekers of knowledge will come away with the idea that Lee Harvey Oswald, at the least, was one of the killers.

I don't believe Lee Harvey Oswald ever fired a shot at JFK.

As described in the *Graphic Story of the American Presidents* by David Whitney in 1975, Lee Harvey Oswald was an "emotionally unbalanced former U.S. Marine who believed in communism, had previously renounced his United States citizenship to live in Russia, and had been arrested as the assassin after he killed a Dallas policeman while trying to evade arrest."

What else is a young person to think after reading blanket statements such as these? It will not dawn on anyone that Oswald might not have had anything to do with this historical crime other than being in the wrong place at the wrong time. He may have been the patsy he claimed to be.

School textbooks as well as history books publish biased information about the assassination. That's because textbooks are designed to avoid controversy and perpetuate ideas that are safe, comfortable, and uncomplicated. School officials routinely avoid buying books that have ideas considered to be dangerous to the norm and status quo. Major textbook publishers will often omit content that might offend certain political constituencies. Our school system deals with events, dates, and names rather than details and controversy concerning these events.

New Information: Keep Out

Historians are suspicious of the reinterpretation of facts, but things change and modern tools (e.g., DNA testing) can provide us with new information. Therefore, historical *truth* cannot logically be viewed as fixed and permanent. There's nothing wrong with disagreements among history professionals. Each generation should reexamine history when there's reason to do so. Data should be updated in response to new findings. This should be a constantly evolving process and not one that's static.

Within a very short time after the assassination, a great amount of information about Oswald was revealed to the public. This included his pro-Castro tendencies as well as other details of his life such as his defection to Russia and his attempt to renounce his American citizenship.

Who Knew?

The most logical explanation is that Lee Harvey Oswald was watched by our intelligence agencies, especially the CIA and the FBI, from the day he joined the marines to the day he was assassinated. Surely, his dossier was compiled with care. If a report had been prepared before the assassination, it could be released when news of the shooting was released or when Oswald was captured. He was essentially tried and convicted for this assassination before he was accused.

The students of today will probably never learn what actually happened in November 1963 unless they search for it. They can't rely solely on ordinary textbooks, history books, encyclopedias, or even the Internet. *It is primarily for this group of students that I write this book.* They have a right to know what really happened on that fateful day and to know more about the period of time leading up to and following the assassination. I also write this book for members of my own generation, to reawaken memories so *you* do not labor under false pretenses.

At the Time

You already know that JFK was elected president at the age of forty-three. During his one thousand days in office, he made wide-reaching decisions, some that increased his enviable popularity and others that helped create the hostile atmosphere that undoubtedly led to his death.

Kennedy was prophetic when he said, "To be a great president, maybe you have to die in office." He also believed that greatness depends on the courage to face the challenges of life.

In a Nutshell

- Bay of Pigs, 1961: This was an attempt to overtake Cuba and get rid of its communist dictator, Fidel Castro. The entire operation was planned prior to the inauguration of Kennedy as president. It was essentially set up by Eisenhower and Nixon and primarily involved the CIA to direct and train the anti-Castro Cubans. The invasion was a failure because Kennedy refused to give it the air support it needed. Kennedy felt he was totally misled and should have discussed all aspects of the invasion with trusted advisors before it was attempted. Even though Kennedy assumed responsibility for its failure, he drew the wrath and hatred of both the CIA and the anti-Castro Cubans. In addition, organized crime was a loser in the failed attempt in Cuba.

These three groups go to the head of the list of Kennedy's potential enemies. Following the Bay of Pigs, Kennedy threatened to disband the CIA and in fact, did dismiss Director Allen Dulles. Authority to deal with the cold war was taken away from the CIA and given to the joint chiefs at the Pentagon. All of this occurred within four months of Kennedy assuming office. It was not an auspicious debut! A Cuban exile leader once said: "CIA agents were more dangerous than the Kennedy administration. The Kennedy administration would end, but CIA agents always stayed and their memory was longer than the memory of elephants and they never forgot or forgave."

- The Berlin Issue: At a summit meeting in Vienna in late 1961 between President Kennedy and Nikita Krushchev, the head of the USSR, Krushchev threatened to sign a peace treaty with East Germany which would give it control over the city of Berlin. This would threaten our access rights to West Berlin and our relationship with the people of West Germany. Krushchev acted this way because of the large exodus of people from East Berlin to West Berlin. Included in this group were many highly educated individuals; especially scientists.

- The Soviet Union could not afford to lose its hold on these people by having so many move to the United States sector. The Communist threat to have East Germany control the city of Berlin nearly led to a confrontation between the two world powers. The fear was that this would mean a nuclear conflict between the US and the USSR. In fact, President Kennedy prepared our country for war. Our defense budget and our military capability were dramatically increased. People were encouraged to build shelters. The situation in Berlin was one of the reasons JFK did not support the Bay of Pigs project. He feared if the United States directly intervened in Cuba, there would be a good chance that Russia would make a retaliatory effort in Berlin. In any event, a nuclear war was prevented when the Soviet Union decided to build a large wall separating the two factions of Berlin. In actuality, all this wall did was prevent the East Germans from moving over to West Berlin. This wall remained a sore point to the "free world" for nearly forty years, but it probably prevented a nuclear disaster and World War III. President Kennedy had shown his strength in his dealings with Krushchev. Did Krushchev actually back down in his original threat to Kennedy or, was this actually the beginning of a cooperative venture between the two most powerful countries in the world? If so, did this mean that JFK was "soft" on communism? Some powerful American groups clearly interpreted it that way.

- Cuban missile crisis: October, 1962: This has been known as Kennedy's greatest triumph. Soviet missiles were found on the island of Cuba ninety miles off the coast of Florida. The Russians stated the missiles were there as a defensive strategy to defend Cuba. Why did they feel that the United States was a threat to Cuba? Here's why: The Bay of Pigs was considered a direct invasion of Cuba. The fact that it failed did not mean the United States was a friend to Cuba. Secondly, since 1959 the CIA and Mafia had collaborated in attempts to kill Fidel Castro. Cuba was removed as a member of the Organization of American States as the United States began to show loyalty to the rest of Latin America. Finally, the United States was increasing defense spending and accelerating military maneuvers. As a result, the USSR claimed the missiles were in Cuba to protect this small country (i.e., purely defensive) although it was the perception of leaders in the United States that the missiles were offensive and poised to attack.

Most of our military and intelligence agencies as well as most of his advisors urged Kennedy to attack Cuba and destroy the Soviet missiles aimed toward the Florida coast. Kennedy, however, realized the hazards of mounting such an attack and feared that the world could be devastated and possibly destroyed.

Despite advice to the contrary, Kennedy announced a strict quarantine on all offensive military equipment (i.e., weapons, missiles, and ships) that were bound for Cuba. He called for a prompt dismantling and withdrawal of all offensive weapons in Cuba under the supervision of the United Nations. This would have to be done before the quarantine (naval blockade) could be lifted. Kennedy warned that his government would regard any nuclear missiles launched from Cuba as a direct attack upon the United States, and, in turn, would launch a full retaliatory response against the Soviet Union. He called upon Krushchev to halt this provocative threat to world peace.

Kennedy warned people of this immense danger and acted accordingly.

Ships were to be intercepted five hundred miles off the coast of Cuba, which was designated the Quarantine Zone. For several days, there was a battle of the minds between the two most powerful leaders in the world. It was Kennedy versus Krushchev in a diplomatic and potentially disastrous mental confrontation. Finally, on October 28, 1962, the USSR dismantled the missiles and withdrew them. The United States agreed not to invade Cuba. Kennedy won the respect of his countrymen and women as well as the respect of our allies. His youth and experience in world affairs no longer appeared to be issue. Krushchev was also a "winner" since he knew that Cuba would be safe from a direct attack by the United States.

While Kennedy's popularity hit an all-time high, both nationally and internationally, it had a very negative effect on several high ranked statesmen, intelligence agencies, and the military. Many feared Kennedy was soft on communism and did not have the courage to defend our country. Was Kennedy going against our doctrine of dealing with the cold war, our policy of being totally against communism?

This was the second time Kennedy decided not to attack Cuba and rid it of its communist dictator. And, it was learned that Kennedy agreed to remove our missiles that were deployed in Turkey and faced the Soviet Union. Many people who felt betrayed by the Bay of Pigs incident felt betrayed for a second time.

- Nuclear Test Ban Treaty, August 1963: This was an agreement between the United States, Great Britain, and the Soviet Union forbidding the atmospheric testing of nuclear weapons. This treaty was considered the first international agreement to control nuclear arms and again showed Kennedy's willingness to negotiate with the Soviets. Once again, this was in direct opposition to the philosophy of many government leaders, intelligence agencies, military personnel, and certain business tycoons.

- Alliance for Progress: This coalition gave aid to Latin American countries in order to improve economic development and education. Cuba was excluded. This reinforced Kennedy's stand against the growth of communism. It also showed his continued animosity toward Castro.

- Southeast Asia: The situation in Vietnam was becoming desperate and extremely discouraging. When Kennedy became president, there were

700 U.S. "advisors" in Vietnam, whose purpose was to teach and train the South Vietnamese in their battle against the North Vietnamese and Viet Cong invaders. This number quickly increased to 17,000 troops. Their reason for being in Vietnam remained advisory and supportive. After the assassination and under the leadership of Lyndon Johnson, we became totally involved in this battle (never officially declared a war).

We sustained a high number of casualties and by the end of the war we lost over 59,000 American soldiers. They had either been killed or were missing. To this day, many remain MIA (missing in action).

Up Close and Personal

I spent 1969–70 in Vietnam. I was a physician at the time and was fortunate to come back to the states intact, both physically and mentally. Many were not so fortunate.

Why were we in Vietnam in the first place? The idealistic answer was to keep communism from taking over Southeast Asia. This was the premise under which I served. I was there to preserve democracy and prevent the flow of communism to other parts of the world. However, as time went on, we began to realize we could never win this war, and other reasons for our continued involvement surfaced. First, we wanted to save face and not admit we were losing this war. I was an officer during my year in Vietnam and attended daily meetings to assess our success or lack of success. The *measure* that determined success was the "body count." If more enemy Vietnamese were found killed compared to the number of daily U.S. casualties, we were said to be successful. Because there were more North Vietnamese and Viet Cong in this country compared to U.S. soldiers, the number of casualties didn't tell the story and this emphasis gave a false sense of assurance. This deception depended on a deliberate inflation of enemy casualties, captured weapons, and number of enemy defectors as well as a deliberate deflation of enemy strength. If there was an impression that we were winning this war, there would be less discussion of withdrawing from Vietnam and at the same time, there might be more discussion about getting more Americans and materials directly involved. This fantasy of apparent success benefited the military-industrial community as well as our intelligence agencies.

A second reason, and possibly a more realistic one for our continued presence in Vietnam, was an economic one. The war provided financial profits
to many individuals and companies. Somebody has to build the helicopters,
provide the weaponry, build the barracks, supply the food, cigarettes, alcohol,
and so on. The war cost our government over one million dollars per day and
"somebody" benefited *big time*.

The availability of illegal drugs (heroin) was a major problem for our
troops in Vietnam, but it was also a lucrative and profitable business for
some people, including the CIA, organized crime, and the military-industrial
complex. The heroin network included Vietnam, the warehouse of the raw
opium, under the direction of Ngo Dinh Nhu (the brother of the Vietnamese president); the Marseille mob from France, which distributed the refined
heroin; and our own Mafia, which sold this heroin to addicts in our country.
Our withdrawal from Vietnam would kill this business.

Eventually President Kennedy realized we could not be victorious. We
were losing financially, but above all, we were losing more Americans every
day we remained there. The public didn't support the war. The South Vietnamese government was corrupt (e.g., accused of misappropriation of U.S.
funds as well as involvement in the opium market) and was weak despite our
assistance. South Vietnamese President Nyugen Diem was widely disliked
and distrusted. The final straw was Diem's brutal treatment and repression of
the Buddhist population in Vietnam, especially because the Buddhists were
in the majority. Eventually, there was a coup and Nyugen Diem was assassinated. His successor's behavior was odious, too. President Kennedy, seeing
the futility of our continued involvement, called for the gradual withdrawal
of our troops. He promised that if he were reelected in 1964, we would be
out of Vietnam within one to two years. The proposal was tagged NSAM 263
and the date was October 1963. Unfortunately, he never lived long enough
to see it happen. Shortly after his assassination, the new president, Lyndon
Johnson, reversed Kennedy's proposal and escalated the U.S. involvement in
this war. This new proposal was NSAM 273, and by 1969, there were over
550,000 U.S. troops in Vietnam.

- Civil rights movement: In the early 1960s, we were also involved in a
  domestic battle. It was the civil rights movement under the leadership
  of Martin Luther King Jr. In 1954 the Supreme Court made a deci-

sion (Brown vs. Board of Education) that stated segregated education was inherently unequal and American schools needed to be desegregated. By 1960, however, only 10 percent of the blacks in the South attended integrated schools. Segregation in this part of the country was everywhere: restaurants, washrooms, drinking fountains, buses, and so on. At first, JFK did not want to take a direct stand on the issue of civil rights, probably for fear of antagonizing voters in the Deep South. JFK was more comfortable dealing with foreign affairs and economic issues. It must be remembered that the civil rights movement was heating up at the time the Vienna Summit with Krushchev and the Cuban missile crisis were underway. Kennedy didn't believe the integration issue warranted priority attention.

He soon realized, however, this was not an issue from which he could hide. What started as a peaceful march in Birmingham, Alabama, turned into a violent confrontation because of the interference of southern whites and independent organizations such as the Ku Klux Klan. There are films showing police using fire hoses and snarling riot police dogs to repel Black women and children. The consciousness of the entire nation was awakening as public sentiment was aroused. This violent scenario was captured by television cameras as the world looked on.

How can the world situation be solved if we cannot solve the problems in our own country? This question is the same question we ask today.

In short order, JFK became a strong advocate of the civil rights movement. He was brilliant when it came to expressing himself, and this was exemplified in his speeches concerning integration and segregation issues. He declared that "all people should be treated equally and have the same opportunities, regardless of the color of their skin." He realized that blacks were risking their lives in Vietnam, just like whites. He stated in one of his speeches that the "rights of every man are diminished when the rights of some are threatened." In another speech he said, "We have a right to expect that the Negro community will be responsible and uphold the law. Yet they have a right to expect that the law will be fair and that the Constitution will be color-blind." He stated that "any student of any color should be allowed public education of his choice and that any American consumer should be given equal service in places of public accommodation, which included restrooms, hotels, restaurants, and retail stores." The President delivered a great deal of rhetoric on the subject and backed up what he said with actions. (At present, I am unable to recall the exact source of these quotes. I am asking for your trust that they were actually said. After all, my main focus is to expose the truth, not hide it.)

He formed the committee on Equal Employment Opportunity and appointed Black people to government positions. He sent in federal troops to enforce integration at both the University of Mississippi and the University of Alabama. James Meredith, a Black man, served as a prototype when he enrolled at the University of Mississippi. Other Black students enrolled at what had previously been segregated schools. This was a bold and revolutionary concept during the 1960s! It widely increased Kennedy's popularity but, at the same time, had a negative effect on segregationists everywhere. Could this negative effect have been enough to create further hostility towards this young president? Could it have been enough to make some people conspire to assassinate the president?

With all the people and groups who felt threatened by Kennedy, Lyndon Johnson probably benefited the most from the assassination. It was rumored that Johnson would not be asked to be Kennedy's running mate in 1964. If true, this spelled the end of Johnson's political career. Johnson had power as majority leader of the Senate but quickly lost power when he became vice president. He considered the vice presidency merely a step to the presidency, and Kennedy's death propelled him into the office.

President Kennedy had many enemies, and yet we were told he was murdered by a lone assassin named Lee Harvey Oswald who had no motive for the assassination. *What's wrong with this picture?*

Enter Howard Brennan

A man named Howard Brennan, one of the government's prize witnesses, said he saw someone at the window of the sixth floor of the depository. He described this man as five foot, ten inches tall, weighing 170 pounds, and appearing to be thirty years of age. This matched the description given by the police within fifteen minutes of the shooting. Mr. Brennan must have had *tremendous eyesight* to be able to describe someone from six floors below and who was in a crouching position, because the windows were partially shut and the shooter was not able to stand upright. It's interesting to note that

Brennan was unable to identify Oswald in a police lineup when he was much closer to him.

There was no confession from Oswald. In fact, he said he was being used as a patsy and was framed for the president's death. Oswald's fingerprints were not found on the Mannlicher-Carcano rifle, if indeed this was the weapon used in the assassination. Oswald was considered a poor marksman by marine standards, and it's doubtful that he fired three shots in rapid succession through a group of trees at a moving target with any degree of accuracy. This feat was attempted by several expert riflemen, and they were unable to accomplish it even while shooting at a stationary target. Oswald was assassinated two days after the president was killed. If he was a lone gunman who murdered the president, why would someone want to kill him? I doubt many people believed Ruby's claims that he killed Oswald to spare the president's wife from the hoopla a trial would invite.

Isn't it likely that Oswald was a man who just happened to be in the wrong place at the wrong time? He was picked to take the blame and divert attention from the real killers. He was murdered to avoid a trial and the "snooping" that would attend it.

Coincidences?

There were two more assassinations in the 1960s. Martin Luther King Jr., the spokesman for the civil rights movement, and Robert Kennedy, the president's brother and the attorney general during JFK's term of office, were shot and killed. Robert Kennedy was a leading candidate for the Democratic nomination for the presidency in 1968. Both men died in 1968, and each were said to have been the victims of lone assassins. James Earl Ray murdered King and a man named Sirhan Sirhan murdered Robert Kennedy. We're led to believe that within a five year span of time three lone gunmen assassinated three prominent people, but the assassins were not linked to one another in any way whatsoever. Never before in our history have we endured such tragic "coincidences."

Ten years after the assassinations, committees were finally formed to re-investigate the events of November 22, 1963. The first two committees were the Rockefeller Commission and the Church Committee (1975). To the surprise of many, investigators unveiled illegal activities being carried out by our intelligence agencies. These included wiretapping and bugging, infiltrating groups to spy on participants, and mail interception programs. Of special concern was the discovery of a program conducted by the CIA to assassinate foreign leaders, specifically Fidel Castro. A CIA-Mafia connection was revealed. Unfortunately, the committees found nothing further regarding John F. Kennedy's assassination.

In 1976 the House Select Committee on Assassinations (HSCA) was formed to look into the assassinations of the Kennedy brothers and Martin Luther King Jr. Members seemed to concentrate on the president's death. The purpose was to look into a potential conspiracy. Their investigation was hampered by the CIA's refusal to cooperate. The CIA hampered all the official committees investigating the assassination of President Kennedy. Could it be there was something to hide? The HSCA, like the Warren Commission, had a time constraint for reaching its conclusion. It produced a report that didn't offer anything new and certainly didn't cast doubt on the Warren Commission findings.

As Good As the Parts

The committee based its conclusions on false medical evidence. The X-rays and photographs of the autopsy were "probably" falsified, because they showed the back of the president's skull completely intact even though the medical personnel at Parkland Hospital in Dallas agreed the back of his head had been obliterated. The HSCA stated that the Parkland physicians and associated personnel were incorrect. The HSCA was probably the only group of individuals who felt the photographs were authentic.

There were two other pieces of information that the HSCA could not suppress. The first dealt with the Zapruder film, which was probably the most critical piece of documentary evidence produced in the Kennedy case. Abraham Zapruder, an amateur photographer, was standing on a pedestal on the Grassy Knoll at Dealey Plaza as the presidential motorcade passed by. His 8-millimeter film lasted twenty-eight seconds. It *is* the one witness that cannot lie and that is not subject to human defects. It shows the president waving and smiling and then suddenly reaching for his throat and slumping over toward Jacqueline Kennedy. He had been shot. One to two seconds later (determined by the known film speed in frames per second and the number of the frame seen), Governor Connelly is hit, and three seconds later, we see the fatal head shot where the president is mortally wounded and there is a backward deflection (head snap) of the president's head. The HSCA concluded this was a neuromuscular reaction indicative of a shot from behind. The primary fallacy here is that a neuromuscular reaction would cause a snap or sudden movement of the entire body and not just the head. For all those who have seen the Zapruder film, it is obvious that at the time of impact, it is only the head that is seen to suddenly move backwards. Several neurologists agreed that the bullet had to have come from Kennedy's right side, the grassy knoll, in order to explain the violent thrust of his body to the left side. The kinetic energy imparted by the bullet as it moves through the body would cause a movement away from the path of the bullet. A backward head snap would indicate the shot originated from the front.

On the basis of the Zapruder film, these shots were fired in rapid succession with only a 2.3 second interval between shots. This result could not be reproduced by expert riflemen, let alone by Lee Harvey Oswald, who was not considered a good marksman. This eventually led to the single bullet theory, which attempted to prove that both the president and Governor Connelly were hit by the same bullet. This would account for three bullets fired, and in turn would match the number of fired casings found on the sixth floor of the Texas School Book Depository (TSBD). This theory would be worthless if a fourth shot could be verified. It would indicate a conspiracy by placing more than one shooter at the scene.

The most important piece of evidence which the HSCA could not suppress was that of the acoustical evidence. There was a Dictabelt recording of the number of gunshots heard during the actual assassination. This tape was recorded from a motorcycle microphone (which had been left on during the assassination) located a few cars to the rear of the president's car as it proceeded west on Elm Street, past the TSBD, and toward Stemmons Freeway. As the world knows, the car never got that far before shots rang out. In any event, the sounds of all the shots were recorded by the Dallas Police Department's Dictabelt tape. After synchronizing the sounds of the gunshots to the video of the Zapruder film, it was concluded there were at least four shots fired: three shots from the area of the TSBD and at least one shot fired from the area of the Grassy Knoll. This would indicate there were at least two shooters and, therefore, a conspiracy in the murder of John F. Kennedy. The HSCA did not totally disagree with the Warren Commission. It did agree that Lee Harvey Oswald was the assassin and that he had fired three shots from the sixth floor of the TSBD; the first missed entirely and the second hit the president in the back and exited through the governor's body. In order to do this, however, the HSCA decided the autopsy diagram of the back wound was wrong. This wound needed to be placed higher in the neck so that both men could be hit by the same bullet. Finally, the third shot hit the president in the back of the head, and this was the fatal shot, fired from above and behind. These conclusions are the same stated by the Warren Report.

One difference was concluded based upon Dallas police radio traffic recordings at the time of the shooting. A fourth shot was fired from the Grassy Knoll, but this shot missed its target. It concluded there was a high probability that a second gunman fired at the motorcade from behind the picket fence on top of the Grassy Knoll to the front and right of the limousine. It believed the conspirators were "probably" connected to the Mafia.

This final HSCA "proclamation" did not receive much attention. Even today, when the words "Kennedy assassination" are brought up in conversation, most people recall that Lee Harvey Oswald was the assassin.

The primary purpose of the Warren Commission Report in 1964 and the House Select Committee on Assassinations Report in 1979 was to pacify the public and allow the nation to come to terms with grief as well as to divert attention from a possible foreign government participation in the assassination. *The truth* was never sought, demanded, or obtained. Neither group conducted its own investigation. Most of the "eyewitnesses" were never called to testify especially if their testimony might favor a conspiracy.

In February 1964, Earl Warren, the head of the Warren Commission, was asked by a reporter whether all the testimony would ever be made public. He responded by saying, "Yes, this will come in time, but it might not be in your lifetime." Was he "diplomatically" hiding something?

Now You See It, Now You Don't

The cover-up of the assassination of President John F. Kennedy was successful. Throughout my research I have come across several quotes that exemplify the government position all these years:

- "What the public wants is not necessarily what it gets."

- "Congress wants to get away from the assassination and not delve into it."

- "Political survival is the priority in Congress, and there is no political profit in investigating the JFK assassination."

- "This is a no-win situation, so why bring it up again."

The government and its respective agencies were wrong in deceiving the people. On the other hand, the people were wrong in so easily accepting the information they were spoon-fed.

Groups that may have conspired to kill the president would likely be implicated in the postassassination cover-up. The Mafia is one of these groups although it would have no way to alter the medical evidence to make it appear that the bullets came from behind. The same could be said for the Cuban exiles and the pro-Castro Cubans. Most likely, however, rogue elements from both these groups did play a role in the assassination.

In his book *Bound by Honor* author Bill Bonano states that the families outside of Marcello-Trafficante-Giancana knew that the mob was associated with the JFK assassination after seeing Jack Ruby kill Lee Harvey Oswald. In addition, certain members of the Dallas Police Department were on the payroll of Carlos Marcello. The scenario apparently was for Officer Tippit to kill Oswald, but when this backfired, Ruby was ordered to kill Oswald.

After the assassination, Johnson realized he had to reunite the country and be accepted as the new president. He had to proceed with care. He could not speak against President Kennedy because of his marked popularity. Johnson needed to make everyone believe he respected and admired the late president as much as they did.

Johnson also needed a closure to the investigation of the assassination. Johnson feared a nuclear war if either Russia or Cuba were found to be involved. Revenge and retaliation could be rampant. He needed to convince people there was not an international conspiracy to kill Kennedy. The dye had been cast. Lee Harvey Oswald had been chosen to be the patsy by JFK's assassins. President Johnson suspected a conspiracy but was supposedly reassured by Hoover that Oswald was the lone gunman. Johnson did not pursue the matter further.

The security agencies (CIA, FBI) most certainly participated in the cover-up by wrongly stating they had no knowledge of Oswald prior to the assassination. Oswald most likely was a contact or agent for one or both groups, because after his discharge from the marines he was able to leave the United

States, renounce his citizenship, go to Russia, marry a Russian girl, and then come back to the United States. In this cold war era, travel between the United States and Russia was severely restricted. The relative ease with which Lee Harvey Oswald traveled hinted at his connections.

Those people who President Kennedy should have trusted the most in the CIA and FBI never tried to dissuade him from making the trip to Dallas. People in both agencies had known of potential death threats against President Kennedy. They knew Oswald was in Dallas at the time and any professed communist would always present a security risk to the president. There was also the potential retaliation by Cuba because of the CIA-Mafia collaboration to get rid of Castro. The CIA had to keep this secret and therefore withheld all information from the Secret Service. If news of the CIA mingling with the Mafia was revealed, President Kennedy would be livid. The FBI also ignored the potential danger to the president by not acting on the Castro intelligence activity in both New Orleans and Dallas, the two major cities where Oswald resided.

JFK was told by some of his advisors and personal friends that the trip to Dallas could be dangerous. Dallas was a very hostile city as exemplified by the rude reaction United Nations Ambassador Adlai Stevenson received only a few weeks earlier. Shortly before Kennedy's arrival in Dallas, handbills and signs, strongly critical of him, were widely circulated. He was accused of being a traitor. This city was a haven for several radical groups including the John Birch Society and the Minutemen. These organizations were strongly anti-Kennedy. It should be remembered that in the election of 1960, Kennedy barely won the support of Texas and he lost Dallas. Dallas was a city of extremists, and one issue many of its citizens were adamant about was segregation. It is easy to see why many considered this trip a risk for the president.

If the Secret Service had learned of the dangers to President Kennedy in Dallas, would the trip have been cancelled and the assassination avoided? If the Warren Commission had been made privy to the information held by the intelligence agencies, would it have concluded that JFK was assassinated as the result of a conspiracy rather than by a lone gunman?

There is another element of our society that deserves mention in a discussion about the assassination conspiracy and cover-up. President Eisenhower on January 17, 1961, in his farewell address spoke about our response to Soviet communism. In order to maintain peace and retain freedom, the United States had to build a huge military establishment and encourage a large arms industry. He warned against the potential excesses and growing power of this military-industrial complex. He believed that economic strength was as important a deterrent as military strength.

Eisenhower feared President Kennedy would agree to the buildup of a military system of unlimited complexity and expense. He warned that the president must be on guard against impulsive action even though it may be popular. He went on to say "every citizen should be kept well informed because it is only an alert and informed citizenry which can keep the abuses from coming about."

Genuine

By 1960 military expenditures had reached $350 billion, more than twice the defense budget under former President Truman. The Defense Department (Pentagon) had become the primary buyer of arms in the world and the world's largest corporation, with assets of over $60 billion. Peace and an end to the cold war (as advocated by JFK) would result in a complete change of our economy. The resultant progressive drop in military expenditures would cause many people to be out of work and many towns would stop flourishing. Animosity towards the president was a likely by-product.

Imaginary

The Soviet economy was barely functioning, and the Russian populace was in desperate straits. Technology was primitive. Despite this, our intelligence (CIA and the Pentagon) perceived the USSR as a true world power. Did our intelligence system fail or did this become an imaginary power, one that was reported to be more of a threat than it was? The military-industrial complex would certainly benefit financially from Russia becoming an overinflated threat. This would mean larger budgets for the military services, bigger contracts for the military suppliers, and more money for the so-called "experts" needed to combat the enemy.

Who Has the Power?

Presidents do not chart new courses or ignore older ones. This is all part of a continuous process, limited by precedents, public opinion, the Constitution, and the international scene (i.e., our world allies and enemies). A president is in office for only four to eight years. However, the milieu, both domestic and international, is shaped prior to the new president and will continue after he leaves office. During his short period as leader of our country, he will make decisions, which are essential to our well-being and to our daily lives. However, does he really shape the course of history or is this something that is in the hands of a group of individuals with global connections? Was this the reason that John F. Kennedy was assassinated? Did he single-handedly try to change the course of the world or, the course of the United States? Was he truly soft on communism as has been suggested?

John F. Kennedy attempted to improve relations between the USSR and the United States. This could only be done by a disarmament program and an eventual end to the cold war. However, this, in turn, would completely change our economy. The Defense Department and many industries (through their military contracts) would be hurt. In addition, JFK ordered a reappraisal of the entire defense system and strategy with an emphasis on capacity, commitment, and need, given the potential danger of the cold war. Kennedy replaced the military philosophy of massive retaliation with a strategy of flexibility and diplomacy. He believed our economy must not be dependent on a large military establishment, similar to what former President Eisenhower had espoused. JFK felt that diplomacy and defense must complement one another.

Assume Nothing

Why didn't the Kennedy family demand a full investigation, and why did they accept the Warren Commission's version as to what did happen? In fact, the Kennedys did not accept the conclusions of the Warren Report although they were probably afraid to admit it. Jackie Kennedy was still in a state of shock, and her sole priority became her two children. Bobbie Kennedy was devastated by his brother's death. His initial reaction at hearing the horrible news (told to him by Hoover) was, "'*They*' got him. I thought '*they*' would get me."

He was referring to more than one assassin. He thought the assassins were leaders of organized crime. He then went on to say, "I thought they'd get one of us. But Jack, after all he'd been through, never worried about it. I thought it would be me."

It has been reported that Bobby asked the CIA director, John McCone, if the CIA had killed his brother. He had his doubts even when McCone told him the CIA did not have anything to do with the assassination. Bobby felt that embittered Cuban exiles, deployed by elements of the CIA, may have had a role in the assassination. The attorney general had many suspicions regarding the death of his brother. You might say he knew too much. He was well versed in the dealings of the CIA and the Mafia, but too much was at risk for him to act. It was known that patriarch Joseph Kennedy Sr. had business dealings with the mob during Prohibition and had made an arrangement with organized crime for assisting JFK in the 1960 election. Mob influence in West Virginia and Chicago, Illinois, helped JFK win the election albeit the Kennedy brothers probably didn't know about their father's involvement at the time.

There were the CIA-Mafia plots to kill Castro, with no intervention from JFK, and the president's many extramarital affairs. One of the *other women* was Judith Campbell Exner, who was mistress to Chicago mob boss, Sam Giancana. JFK also had a relationship with Marilyn Monroe, the most famous actress of that time. Robert felt he had to protect his brother. An open and independent investigation into the death of the president could reveal too many embarrassing improprieties. Accordingly, Robert Kennedy chose not to pursue any differences he might have with the Warren Report. He once claimed he had never read the Warren Report. Yet, in his own mind, he did not believe that Oswald was the assassin.

Doctor, Doctor

To the physicians both at Parkland and Bethesda, President Kennedy was a patient. Despite his stature and the horrific event that had occurred, it was imperative for the physicians to deal with him in the most objective manner. Emotions could not play a role.

The president was virtually "dead on arrival" at Parkland. Nevertheless, both groups of physicians were required to perform the basics of medicine in caring for this patient. This is where the immense differences of opinion arise. I, as a physician, contend that this is where the proof (or disproof) of a conspiracy lies.

The victim's condition *informs us* there was more than one shooter in the Dealey Plaza vicinity on that fateful day. Whether one of the shooters was in the TSBD remains conjectural; personally, I don't think there was. *I base this on my medical interpretation of the findings of the two distinct groups of physicians involved.*

Thirty Years Later

In 1992 the *Journal of the American Medical Association (JAMA)* came out with a series of articles edited by George D. Lundberg, MD, in which the two former U.S. Naval pathologists who performed the infamous autopsy made public statements. They were Drs. James Humes and J. Thornton Boswell. A short time later, the third pathologist, Dr. Pierre Fink, was interviewed. Why did it take these men nearly thirty years to defend their findings?

The chief pathologist was James Humes with Boswell acting as his assistant and Fink as the consultant. Humes initially thought the autopsy should be done at Walter Reed Memorial Hospital, the apex of military pathology. This suggests his reluctance, which is understandable, owing to his lack of experience in this arena. Humes stated he was told through the ranking naval officers that he was to find the cause of death. The cause of death was a "fatal gunshot wound to the head," and this was obvious to all. What was not obvious, however, was the number of bullets fired and the direction from which they originated.

As a physician, I find several facets about the autopsy to be troublesome.

First, Humes states that the room where the autopsy was being conducted was filled with people. Various high-ranking officials were talking on phones and radios. They were loud, verbose, and probably abusive. Some were giving orders. Many of those present in the autopsy room outranked the pathologists. How could Humes perform a thorough exam when he was distracted by so much commotion? Didn't he say he was instructed to find the cause of death? Was this his sole function? If so, could this have caused him to hurry and not conduct a complete exam? The people who were intimately involved with the autopsy (the pathologists and their supporting staff) should have been the only ones allowed in the room. They should have had all the time they needed to perform the task with efficiency. *One wonders who really was in charge of the autopsy.*

Second, the autopsy report indicated the fatal head shot had blown out 70 percent of the right hemisphere of his brain. However, the brain weighed 1,500 grams, basically the size of a normal brain for a man of this stature. *How could his brain weigh so much after sustaining so much damage?* Were two different brains autopsied? The autopsy findings indicated the major portion of the right cerebrum had been lacerated and was exuding from the large skull defect. In the *JAMA* interview Humes stated, "The head was so devastated by the exploding bullet and the gaping jagged stellate wound it created—it blew out thirteen centimeters of skull bone and skin—that we did not even have to use a saw to remove the skullcap."

Yet, the facial features as seen on the autopsy photographs were intact despite the massive head wound. It is difficult to believe that a head wound of such a large magnitude (whether inflicted from behind or from in front) would not cause any distortion of the facial features. A bullet entering the rear of the head on a right to left trajectory (which would have to be the case if the bullet was fired from the east window of the sixth floor of the TSBD) would exit around the front of the left cheek. Yet the photographs of the back of the head as well as the face show these areas to be intact. Contrary to the belief of the HSCA, *I contend the autopsy photographs are not authentic and are therefore evidence of a cover-up.*

The Parkland group (total of twenty-six men and women) stated there was a large defect in the back of the right side of the head (occiput) through which brain tissue could be seen. They concluded this had to be an exit wound because of its extremely large size. In contrast, Humes at Bethesda stated that the fatal shot entered the back of the president's skull and exploded away a six-inch section of the right front side of his head. Of interest is the fact that the defect in the skull as reported during the autopsy was at least three times as large as that described in Dallas. The Parkland Hospital doctors recorded the diameter of the head wound to be two and three-quarter inches, whereas the autopsy doctors at Bethesda recorded the same wound to be seven inches in diameter. *Were they were looking at the same head?*

Speechless

In spite of glaring discrepancies, the Warren Commission and HSCA announced the observations, testimony, and "diagnoses" by the physicians at Parkland were wrong (i.e., the opposite of right, incorrect, off-the-mark).

They discarded eyewitness reports and ignored testimony if it favored a conspiracy. *Wrong! Wrong! Wrong!*

What would the Parkland contingent have to gain by falsifying what they saw? The back of the head was blown away. This was their observation. It was not wrong.

The Bethesda contingent had to falsify some of their observations to fit the hypothesis that the shooter was located behind the presidential limousine. It's as if the physicians conducting the autopsy had preconceived ideas of what they were supposed to find and so that's what they found. (That was wrong!)

The Warren Commission still had to contend with the Zapruder film showing the backward head snap. It indicated the fatal shot was fired from a direction located in the front of the limousine. The Zapruder film was the one eyewitness the government could not ignore although it certainly tried when it came to stating its conclusions.

Third, Humes initially mentioned a bullet that had supposedly entered at the base of the neck. However, its exit track was not apparent and the president's neck was not dissected because it was thought "not important." What type of autopsy would fail to track the course of the bullets that had resulted in the assassination of the president of the United States? This was either a poorly prepared autopsy done by inexperienced people who lacked know-how or who *did know* ahead of time what they were supposed to find. In other words, they knew what to look for and what *not* to look for.

Fourth, two other major items which Dr. Humes bungled during the autopsy were his notes and communication protocol. He burned the original notes (and later had to rely on his memory to recreate observations for a medical artist). He didn't consult with the physicians at Parkland before beginning the autopsy. Why would he not want to inquire as to what the Parkland physicians saw and did during the resuscitative efforts? Were these oversights or errors in judgment? Were they an admission that he was not there to conduct a complete autopsy but only determine the cause of death? (An autopsy conducted in good faith would not support the lone gunman argument.)

Times Change

In the 1960s, people trusted their government. The idea of officials lying to them was not something they could envision. It wasn't until the presidency of Richard Nixon and his subsequent downfall with the Watergate incident that people began questioning their leaders. The media became more critical of government decisions and policies. This attitude is alive and well today.

The Watergate affair may actually have been a continuum from the Kennedy assassination. Two of the Watergate burglars were Frank Sturgis and E. Howard Hunt, both CIA trained and key figures in the CIA-sponsored anti-Castro operations. In addition, each had a definite resemblance to one of the *three tramps* who were temporarily taken into custody shortly after the assassination and who were hiding in a railroad car just beyond Dealey Plaza. Could these Watergate burglars have had a connection to the events of November 22, 1963?

Richard Nixon was in Dallas on the day of the assassination. That's not an accusation, but it's interesting to note that after the Watergate fiasco was revealed, one of Nixon's closest associates, H. R. Haldeman, threatened the CIA director with revealing how the Bay of Pigs disaster had an impact on JFK's assassination.

It's Criminal!

The official government position as stated by the House Select Committee on Assassinations in 1978 was that there was more than one shooter responsible for the assassination of John F. Kennedy. There was evidence that James Hoffa, Carlos Marcello, and Santos Trafficante, the three primary targets for criminal prosecution by the Kennedy administration (Bobbie Kennedy, in particular), had discussed the murder of the president with their subordinates. There are witnesses, affiliated with the mob, who have verified these statements. Frank Regano, a mafia lawyer, states he was told by Hoffa to let Marcello and Trafficante know that they had to get Kennedy. In addition, Regano states he was present at the death-bed confession of Trafficante, when he said, "They got the wrong Kennedy."

These statements are forceful, believable, and incriminating, although alone they don't constitute proof. These men certainly did not like the Kennedy's and did have a motive for the assassination. Still, it would have been virtually impossible for the Mafia to alter medical evidence. And, it's likely the powers that be would gladly toss Mafia figures to the wolves if they were solely responsible for JFK's murder.

The doctrine of the media, in agreement with the Warren Commission, has always been that Oswald acted alone. The anticonspiracy literature is given much more credibility by the media and gets more press coverage.

Oliver Stone's Movie

How can a movie be completely bombarded and ridiculed prior to release unless someone is afraid of the truth? This is what happened to Oliver Stone's movie *JFK*. Despite this negative publicity, the movie was welcomed by the public. It rekindled interest in the events of November 22, 1963. It raised questions by people who were either too young to remember or who were not even born at the time (currently, the largest part of our population).

* * * * * *

With the publication of this book, another source of accurate information is available to future generations as well as present and past generations. New generations of Americans need not live with false information about what is arguably the greatest crime of the twentieth century.

When I was a young man learning about the history of our country, I was taught there was a president who was shot by a single assassin. Abraham Lincoln had been shot by John Wilkes Booth. There was no mention of a conspiracy, and this is what I accepted and tucked into my memory. In recent times, it has been reported that Booth was involved in a conspiracy and that even though he was the one to pull the trigger, he did have multiple accomplices. I believe the same conclusions will eventually be accepted as "official" in the JFK assassination. The difference will be that I do not believe that Lee Harvey Oswald was the one to pull the trigger.

Most of the recent JFK books published over the past ten years dwell on the president's life and politics or on Jackie Kennedy or on the family in general. Fortunately, within the past year, there has been more written about the assassination, including the possibility of a conspiracy. Have we settled into a mode where we truly believe and have finally accepted as fact that Oswald did assassinate Kennedy by himself? Is it that we don't care anymore and don't want to be bothered? After all, the crime did occur over forty years ago. In addition, most of our current population was not even born by 1963. Admittedly, the truth about the assassination is not the number one priority in the lives of people today. *But truth should always be a priority for without it we risk facing dire consequences*—now as much as ever. We cannot afford to be lulled into complacency by the passage of time or anything else. A wake-up call was sounded by the tragedy of September 11, 2001. The events of November 22 were as much a shock to the generation of the 1960s as the terrorist attack was to the current generation.

* * * * * *

The assassination of John F. Kennedy was the single most traumatic public event in my lifetime.

XV

Straight Talk and the Historical Record

The actual killers of John F. Kennedy are probably no longer alive. Those people who planned the assassination, however, may indeed be alive. It is this second group that holds the key to the assassination and a true account of what actually occurred on that tragic day in November 1963.

If you've been reading this book from the beginning, you're already aware of most of what follows in this chapter. If you skipped to Section Four: A Breath of Fresh Air, to see how it ends, you'll probably want to read early chapters carefully to obtain details.

Most of what we've been asked to believe about who was responsible for this beloved president's death is so preposterous you may have shrugged it off as a fairy tale. Nevertheless, it remains the government's official explanation, and so we're going to wrap up this book with many important highlights in one place. The intention is to give you the full impact of how much doesn't add up!

Reliable information about the assassination of JFK is scarce.

Witnesses died.

Evidence was altered. Evidence was destroyed. As a physician, I'm especially appalled by how much medical evidence comes under this banner. Medical practitioners are expected to maintain high standards at all times. They frequently work under less than optimum conditions (i.e., chaos). Therefore, the disregard for safeguarding medical evidence is without a legitimate excuse.

In the thirty years following JFK's murder, more than 115 witnesses died. This may not seem unusual until you know that most were murdered or committed suicide. The deceased (i.e., witnesses) either saw events unfold in Dealey Plaza or had a strong connection to people who were implicated in the crime. The likelihood of so many mysterious deaths in this group is peculiar, to say the least.

For more than forty years there has been a deluge of misinformation offered to the public. It's difficult to change perceptions and question information that sits in the "accepted" category for so many years. The one bright spot on this horizon is that nearly all public polls favor/favored a conspiracy as opposed to the lone assassin theory.

Objective and Unbiased

When I started to dig and poke at the JFK assassination circumstances, I didn't personally have anything to gain or to lose. I was simply an interested party. When my admiration for this man came to call, I set it aside and recognized that if I didn't, it could cloud my interpretations and my findings.

At the same time, nothing would come of the probing if I didn't use logic, heed and follow-up on my suspicions, and let my ethics support me as I assessed information that came to my attention. After all is said and done, however, I recognize the Kennedy assassination will probably never be fully explained to everyone's satisfaction.

Subjective and Biased.

I stepped into the investigation without an agenda but frequently felt this was not true of the historians whose books I was reading.

Historians generally do not speak favorably of JFK. They find it hard to accept his immense popularity among the American people. In their opinions, he was too soft on communism and exacerbated the cold war by his stand during the Bay of Pigs. They minimize the value of his domestic policy and question his civil rights policy, which was actually passed after the assassination. They talk of his possible connection to Sam Giancana, an organized crime boss, as well as his various sexual exploits. Some blame him for the escalation of the war in Vietnam, though Kennedy was planning to end our commitment in Vietnam, not enlarge it. During his last two years in office, there were less than sixty U.S. advisors killed in Vietnam. After his assassination, over 59,000 Americans died in this remote country. Surely, this demonstrates our true involvement in Vietnam began after President Kennedy was assassinated.

In spite of his detractors, John F. Kennedy was the most popular president we ever had. The public saw a different man, someone who radiated youth, self-confidence, and commitment. They saw someone who symbolized optimism, idealism, and promise. They saw a man who was an individualist and who brought hope and appealing aspirations for the future not only in the United States but also for third world countries. John F. Kennedy's death was a tragedy but his life was a triumph.

Remembering

No matter how history tells the story, those of us who lived through it with JFK remember his immense popularity and universal appeal. We judge him now on what he promised to do rather than by his actual accomplishments. We realize the attainment of his goals was thwarted by assassins' bullets. We admired his youthfulness, which stood out in contrast to the aging rulers of the Soviet Union and Western Europe. We forgave his shortcomings because he gave us so much hope for the future. He helped us to envision the future as one of peace and prosperity and some of his attempts to attain a peaceful coexistence with the Soviets worked. We witnessed it all.

Name Calling

Those who believe in conspiracy are "nuts," fanatics, and unwilling to accept the truth. This is what many historians put into print. Earlier in this book, I wrote about the time my wife and I were called fanatics in a newspaper article simply because we attended a conference on the JFK assassination. Our only *crime* was in listening to speakers discuss possible alternatives to the government's conclusions. All arguments against conspiracy rely upon the Warren Report as the *gold standard*. Opposing reports have been repeatedly and loudly discredited. (*Say it long enough and loud enough and people will believe it. Won't they?*) Anticonspiracists say that in all these years there has not been any concrete evidence to prove a conspiracy. They play fast and loose with good judgment when they attempt to discredit the idea of a conspiracy rather than prove that Lee Harvey Oswald was the sole assassin. They dismiss eyewitnesses and Parkland physicians by stating they "were wrong." They ridiculed the movie *JFK* and its producer Oliver Stone even before the movie was released. They completely blast Attorney Jim Garrison and his New Orleans investigation because his conclusions are contrary to the government's version that cites Lee Harvey Oswald as the lone killer.

In reality, there is probably nothing more unbelievable and contrived than the Warren Commission Report. It is full of lies and contradictions. I find it extraordinary that anyone could accept that a single bullet could cause seven separate wounds in two different men and remain in a pristine or unscathed condition. It doesn't take a rocket scientist to follow the dots! Yet this has been the government's official version for over forty years.

What's New?

Just prior to the fortieth anniversary of the assassination, ABC television presented a documentary entitled, *Kennedy Assassination, Beyond Conspiracy* moderated by Peter Jennings. It was claimed that this documentary would reveal the "truth" behind the assassination. New information had apparently been discovered and was about to be revealed. I viewed this television special and was thoroughly disappointed and disgusted. Watching the program was the same as reviewing the Warren Commission Report. The magic bullet theory remained the primary piece of information to support the government "case" and without it, the explanation that favored a conspiracy would prevail.

Fortunately, 75 percent of the population has never believed or accepted this theory. "We" are not that gullible. Still the official government explanation, riddled with holes though it may be (pun intended), still stands.

Who Was Lee Harvey Oswald?

Lee Harvey Oswald was a poor person from a broken home who was raised by his single mother. He moved from place to place and school to school. His psychiatric history (taken when he was quite young) records he had a tendency toward violence. He joined the marines, became disenchanted with the United States, and subsequently moved to Russia (our prime enemy at the time). He married a Russian citizen named Marina but then became disenchanted with life in the USSR. He and Marina moved to the United States. This is the "evidence" that argues that Lee Harvey Oswald was a bad man and, therefore, was able to kill our president. These days, this might be called *profiling.* I recognize it as a way to choose a patsy. This ploy certainly benefited some people, albeit not Lee Harvey Oswald!

There is no proof that Oswald ever fired a gun at the president.

I repeat: *there is no proof that Oswald ever fired a gun at the president.*

Yet historians "say so" in their books about the assassination.

As youngsters, we memorize history lessons and act out roles as prominent characters in school plays. As adults, we commemorate special days in history by celebrating them, declaring a day off from work.

We rarely question the *whys and wherefores* of past events and when we do, we should pay attention to what else was happening during that period of time. If a historian claimed that news spread quickly in the days of the Pony Express we would question his statement. After all, we are people of the computer age and know what "quickly" means. We can better judge assertions based upon our grasp of the big picture. The same is true regarding the murder of John F. Kennedy.

What was the world *climate* at that time?

The United States had ascended to the position of the most powerful military nation in history and the Central Intelligence Agency was established as our primary defense against communism, our *archenemy* in the cold war. By the 1960s, the CIA had become extremely powerful. There's reason to believe this group felt it could overrule the president and be responsible for all decisions regarding our country's defense. Through its clandestine operations, it became the most effective assassination machine in the world.

Conflict of Interests

In 1960, a president (JFK) was elected who seemed to regard the entire human race with compassion. He wanted détente with Russia and acted accordingly when dealing with the Bay of Pigs, Cuban missile crisis, and the Nuclear Test Ban Treaty. His actions ran counter to the philosophy of the power structure whose purpose was to win the cold war, not to end it. Accordingly, Kennedy alienated himself from two of our country's most powerful groups: the CIA and the military.

When asked about his view of the future, JFK replied: "We need men who can dream of things that never were, and ask why not." He also said, "Let us step back from the shadows of war and seek out the way of peace. Let history record that we, at this time, took the first step." While Kennedy concentrated on bringing an end to the cold war (i.e., peaceful coexistence with Russia and maintenance of the status quo with Cuba), the CIA continued its fight against communism and Castro.

Could all this have been the "last straw" that led to his assassination?

Military-Industrial Complex

In January 1961, President Eisenhower warned against the military-industrial complex. He felt its power and influence was becoming the dominant force in our country. (If you *follow the money to better understand who benefits,* you'll discover there was a time when defense spending exceeded the profits of all American corporations combined. Business was good for purveyors of defense goods and services! Change would devastate them.)

Kennedy's philosophy of favoring a peaceful diplomatic solution as opposed to direct military action was already contrary to what many of Kennedy's advisors, the CIA, and Pentagon officials preferred. When he proposed withdrawal from Vietnam, he definitely added fuel to the fire. During a commencement address given at American University in Washington D.C. in June 1963, he said, "The United States and Soviet Union must live together peacefully on one small planet." He felt that world peace was the "most important topic on earth" and that his primary task as leader of this country would be to pursue this. He proposed a strategy of peace leading toward nuclear disarmament, involving both the United States and the Soviet Union.

Kennedy offered to stop nuclear testing in the atmosphere with the hope that the threat of nuclear weapons would draw people closer, not push them farther apart. In July 1963, both Kennedy and Krushchev agreed on a Nuclear Test Ban Treaty. Was this difference of opinion between President Kennedy and the cold war proponents enough motivation to have led to his assassination?

At the moment that Lee Harvey Oswald died, thousands of potential answers to questions about the assassination of John F. Kennedy were obliterated. The assassination was the event that elevated JFK to a primary place in our history. His death pricked the political consciousness of the world, and he became a legend after his death. His tragic death at such a young age influenced people's perceptions of his deeds. Those most affected by him were adults during his presidency. Others need to rely upon written history to appreciate our thirty-fifth president.

Accounts should reflect that the assassins and co-conspirators are not really known, even after forty years. Lee Harvey Oswald probably doesn't fall into either category. Surely, the assassination was the result of a conspiracy and not a single individual. The public's private assessment (i.e., favoring the conspiracy theory) should not be in direct opposition to the official government pronouncements; not after forty years!

Throughout this book, I have attempted to reconstruct events surrounding the assassination showing that a conspiracy was responsible for the act itself as well as the cover-up that followed. Further, that JFK was assassinated by a small eccentric group of individuals because of his stand on communism and because of his attempts to bring together the United States and the Soviet Union for the purpose of a peaceful and safe coexistence.

For well over twenty years, beginning in 1940, the hallmark of American public and political life was to battle against communism. All aspects of our society (e.g., professionals, labor unions, the media, religious groups, various interest groups) were anticommunists. Fighting communism had the highest priority apropos our foreign policy and became the primary focus of our defense and intelligence agencies. To their dismay, the youngest president ever elected was trying to change things.

John F. Kennedy strongly disagreed with communism and its basic philosophy. Yet, for him the threat of nuclear war and subsequent devastation of the world was a reality. With this possibility ever present, he attempted to avoid a direct confrontation with the Soviet Union whenever possible, and even though powerful advisors and adversaries urged him to do the opposite, Kennedy didn't bend. His strong convictions and confident leadership likely caused the president his life.

Throughout this book, I have discussed various groups who had the opportunity, means, and possible motives to assassinate the president. Ironically, the one thing that is certain is that John F. Kennedy was not assassinated by Lee Harvey Oswald. Oswald was the fall guy in a plot that was extremely well planned and orchestrated. In addition, the cover-up has proved to be a success. If the public could be made to blame Oswald, they would not consider the possibility of other assassins. This sounds simple but in reality was difficult to achieve. Nevertheless, achieve it they did—at least so far! The Warren Commission was supposed to alleviate the fears of the American people, but instead it aggravated our psyche and made us mistrust our government; a trait that unfortunately persists today.

If It Wasn't Oswald, Who Was It?

All of the groups mentioned in this book had motives with the exception of Oswald. An international conspiracy (i.e., Russia with Krushchev or Cuba with Castro) would make no sense in view of the fact that Kennedy was trying to reach some type of peaceful settlement with both men. Krushchev also feared a nuclear war, and Castro knew there would be immediate retaliation by the United States if he had a direct hand in the assassination. The same could be said for the anti-Castro Cubans who would not have the means to orchestrate this assassination by themselves though certainly could be persuaded to assist in its implementation. If the perpetrators were not from outside our country, we are then faced with the possibility of a domestic conspiracy.

Though doing a very poor job of guarding the president, the Secret Service didn't have a motive to want the man dead. However, assisting the assassins by not protecting the president is not beyond the realm of possibility. It raises the question of *who* had the power to limit the security provided for the president during his fateful drive through Dallas.

Another group mentioned is the Federal Bureau of Investigation led by J. Edgar Hoover. Hoover feared losing his job as director if JFK remained president, but would this be enough to have him arrange an assassination? He certainly had enough power, but I doubt he could get enough support from the higher echelon. It's highly likely, however, that Hoover knew of the assassination beforehand and did nothing to prevent it.

What about Lyndon Baines Johnson, the thirty-sixth president of the United States? It was well-known that Johnson wanted to become president, and it was rumored that he would not be Kennedy's running mate for another term. Moreover, he was implicated in two very serious business scandals that could have ruined his political career and possibly land him in jail. Johnson was *standing at the edge of a cliff* but would this have caused him to orchestrate a complex assassination plot and cover-up? It is true that he was the one person who gained the most from Kennedy's assassination. Personally, I don't believe he was a completely innocent bystander, but nothing solid leads me to brand him a conspirator.

Finally this leaves a group of individuals, probably with global tentacles, who carry enormous weight and influence. Since World War II and the bombing of Hiroshima, the military had emerged as the dominant force in our government. Coinciding with this was the growth of the industrial complex necessary to supply the equipment for the preservation and defense of the cold war. Joining this enormous group was the CIA, considered to be the clandestine arm of the military-industrial complex. Collectively these groups formed an organization wielding extreme power and influence.

John F. Kennedy was not a sympathizer or supporter of communism, yet he did have respect for its leaders. This respect and fear of a nuclear confrontation guided the president and influenced his policy choices. Those who strongly disagreed with his actions are the likely perpetrators.

I don't believe President Kennedy made poor decisions. After all, we have not been involved in a nuclear war and generally have lived a good and peaceful life (until the events of 9/11). We have prospered, and our children have been safe. Who is to say what the world would have been like if JFK had not acted as he did? We can only speculate by examining what happened in Vietnam after the assassination.

His assassination prolonged our involvement in Vietnam. This cost us many thousands of lives, all innocent young people who really didn't know what they were fighting for or why they were there to begin with. It is tragic that government leaders following JFK did not share his vision, realize the futility of the war, and decide that our withdrawal from this war was the best thing to do. The Vietnam War officially ended on January 27, 1973, meaning that the United States continued its involvement for nearly ten years after the assassination of John F. Kennedy. With the administration of Lyndon Johnson, the number of our troops being sent to Vietnam increased at an enormous rate and, there was a marked increase in our casualty rate. The longest war, which our country has ever been involved in, cost the lives of over 59,000 American soldiers. How many of these lives could have been saved if President Kennedy had not been assassinated and, as a result, been allowed to withdraw our troops by 1965? We'll never know.

Which Part of This Don't We Understand?

The case for a conspiracy in the assassination of John F. Kennedy is overwhelming. At the same time, the argument that Oswald was a lone gunman is as strong as a house of cards. There isn't evidence against Oswald that would be accepted in a court of law. Of course, those who conspired to assassinate the president also made sure that Oswald never stood trial.

If we can officially say the president was killed as a result of a conspiracy; our history books, textbooks, encyclopedias, and historical information disseminated on the Internet and anywhere else would be of value to those who seek knowledge and truth. The facts regarding a conspiracy are admittedly speculative, but at least they're based upon solid information and clear thinking.

The hardest part to believe in this entire scenario is that the accused party was an impoverished and inept lone gunman who had no motive but had the ability to create the greatest cover-up in history.

People and groups mentioned throughout this book were frightened by what JFK's policies and actions were doing to our country and to them. I believe a subset of individuals from some of these groups believed they could and must impose their collective will on the American people. They arranged for the assassination and cover-up.

British statesman and philosopher Edmund Burke long ago stated that, "Those who don't know history are destined to repeat it."

The events of November 22, 1963, cannot be changed, but certainly the stating of these events must be accurate. If some people know more than has been revealed to date, can they be encouraged to step forward? Can records sequestered in the archives be revealed now rather than later? It's widely accepted that a political assassination (if this is what we have) is a very secret endeavor with the participants knowing only their own roles. (It mirrors the principle that *the whole is equal to the sum of its parts*.) It's also interesting to note that a CIA assassination training manual contains these words: "All planning must be mental; no papers should ever contain evidence of the operation. No assassination records should ever be written or recorded."

And So My Daughter, Kennedy …

You've had a look at this special man who became president. (He is no longer only someone who long ago died a violent death.) You've been exposed to potential motives for his murder. Likely conspirators have been fingered. You probably agree, at this point, that Lee Harvey Oswald was not part of the conspiracy. You know there was never a trial by jury. As a matter of fact, information, whether true or false, was never presented in any court of law. You've seen that the Warren Commission served as a tool to divert public attention away from the true assassins.

I have raised and answered questions about the most horrific event that took place in your daddy's lifetime. Members of my generation owe you and members of your generation the truth. We're still waiting for those who know who *really killed* JFK to step out of the shadows and put the matter to rest.

If we grow weary of our search, if we ask who cares anymore, and then if we answer that we don't care, the cover-up will be complete. I cannot look into your beautiful blue eyes and agree to that.

I would not be setting a good path for you to follow if I tossed up my hands and looked away. I would be cheating you. I cannot teach you about morals and ethics and believe you will heed what I say if I cheat you.

For more reasons than you (dear reader) may wish to know, I cannot do this to my daughter, Kennedy, or to my other children, or to anyone's children.

Can you?

> We owe respect to the living;
> to the dead we owe only the truth.
> —*Voltaire*

Notes

Introduction

2   "We …assassin" Summers, *Official and Confidential,* p. 317

I: "Medical Evidence : Parkland vs. Bethesda"

9   "In 1963...crime in Texas" Manchester, *Death of a President.*

10   "blood splattered pink suit" O'Donnell and Powers, *Johnny, We Hardly Know Ye.*

10   "I want...done to Jack" Lubin, *Shooting Kennedy,* p. 118

11   "I know the back...but blood" *American History : Assassination of JFK, 2003,* p40.

11   "Jackie … blown out" Groden, *The Case For Conspiracy*

11   "Right rear portion … was exposed" *American History: Assassination of JFK, 2003,* p.40.

11   Ibid

13   "threat of losing … even their lives" Crenshaw, *Trauma Room One,* p.12-13.

13   "Crenshaw's book" Crenshaw, *Conspiracy of Silence.*

14   "Humes and Boswell … really inept" Wrone, *Zapruder Film,* p.233.

14   "three doctors … exit wound" Wrone, *Zapruder Film,* p.234.

14   "This defect … and forward" Fetzer, *Murder in Dealey Plaza*

15   "dissecting the neck … been criminal" Fetzer. *Assassination Science,* p.99.

16   "an example … what to say" Tague, *Truth Withheld.*

16   'The initial notes … from his memory" Meagher, *Accessories After the Fact.*

17   "He placed … base of the neck" Groden, *JFK : Case for Conspiracy.*

19   "The pathologists … as they remembered" Groden and Livingstone, *High Treason 2*

20   "It was later … a forgery" Galanor, *Cover-up*

21   "Humes … X-rays apparently showed" Fetzer, *Murder in Dealey Plaza.*

21   "This was photographed … back of the skull" Bennett, *Conspiracy, Plots, Lies, and Cover-ups*

22   "In addition, … splattered with blood" Groden, *JFK-Case For Conspiracy*

24   "Best Evidence", Lifton, *Best Evidence*

25   "There are … around the head area" Hurt, *Reasonable Doubt*

25   "Where did this surgery … come from" Lifton, *Best Evidence,* p.449.

28   "In 1992 … findings of the assassination" Breo, *JAMA — JFKs Death,* pp.2794-2807.

29   "Conspiracy of Silence" Crenshaw, *JFK, Conspiracy of Silence.*

29   "This … not true" *Neurosurgery,* Nov. 2003, p.1023

31   "Humes … two-thirds … missing" *JAMA*

31   "Brain weighed … age 40-49" DiEugenio, *The Assassinations*

31   "President Kennedy … through his head" Lifton, *Best Evidence,* p.45

31   "not to dissect the back wound" Kurtz, *Crime of the Century,* p.73

32   "About two weeks … and Finck" Lifton, *Best Evidence*

32   "This could … surgically cut" Lifton, *Best Evidence*

33   "In October, … were missing" Posner, *Case Closed*

33   "substantiated … Warren Commission" *JAMA,* Vol.267, No.20, p.2800.

34   "He was located … Elm Street" Trask, *Pictures of the Pain,* p.60

34   "Yet the agent … evidentiary value" Trask, *Pictures of the Pain,* p.80

35   "It was determined … Oswald" *The Warren Commission Report,* p.106

35   "Zapruder frame show … less than 2.3 seconds" Meagher, *Accessories After the Fact,* p29

37   "By the way … Marine's standards" O'Leary and Seymour, *Triangle of Death.*

37 "At the time ... kill us all" Connelly and Herskowitz, *From Love Field*, p.08

38 "The impact ... source of the shot" Tague, *Truth Withheld*, p14

II: "A Step Back In Time : JFK, Pre-Presidency Years"

40 "money ... to everything" Quirk, *Kennedys in Hollywood* p.16

40 "They will always ... want to be" Quirk, *Kennedys in Hollywood*, p.17

40 "This tirade ... political career" Mailer, *Kennedys, America's Emerald Kings*

41 "He was convinced ... American political life" Leamer, *Sons of Camelot*

41 "We must carry on ... work to be done" Smith, *Hostage to Fortune* p.599

41 "We don't want ... accept second place" Smith, *Grace and Power*, p.37

41 "someone ... never absent" Ibid, p167

41 "His most serious ... back pain" Ibid

42 "During WWII ... Solomon Islands" Donavan, PT-109

42 "While convalescing ... Courage" Kennedy, *Profiles in Courage*

42 "vindication ... principles" Hellman, *Kennedy Obsession* , p.78

43 "They felt the public ... severely hampered" Mills, *John F Kennedy*

43 "senior thesis ... Why England Slept" Kennedy, *Why England Slept*

45 "at the request ... infamous journey" Klein, *All Too Human*

46 "Nobody asked me ... last mission" Leamer, *The Kennedy Men*, p.429

46 "Through his nomination ... vice-president" Spies, *John F. Kennedy*

47 "Twenty percent ... $3,100 a year" Blum, *Years of Discord*, p.149

47 "Nixon ... shadow" Mathews, *Kennedy and Nixon*

48 "Of the many times ... JFK" Harrison and Gilbert, *Word For Word*, p.17-21

III: "Moving Right Along : The Bay of Pigs and the CIA"

51 "This struggle ... diplomatic conflict" Levering, *The Cold War*

52 "The Central Intelligence ... project" Farren, *CIA- Secrets of the Company*

52	"to gather ... national security" Quirk, *The Central Intelligence Agency*, p 94-95

53	"It had become ... of the United States" Jeffrey-Jones, *CIA and American Presidency*

53	"known as plausible denial" Lane, *Plausible Denial*

53	"executive ... by President Ford" Jeffrey-Jones, *CIA and American Democracy*, p214

54	"This was ... Pigs." Wyden, *Bay of Pigs*

54	"The attack ... 200,000 men" Freedman, *Kennedys Wars*, p137

55	"larger invasion ... be necessary" Trento, Secret *History of the CIA*

56	"Kennedy feared ... regarding Berlin" Freedman, *Kennedy's Wars*, p132

57	"JFK felt ... 140 killed" Ibid, p145

58	"Those names ... crime" Blakey, *The Plot to Kill the President*

IV: "The Cuban Missile Crisis"

60	"they clearly demonstrated ... an attack" Sorenson, *Kennedy*

61	"openly displayed ... Hoffa in particular" White, *The Kennedys and Cuba*

62	"He assumed ... whole world" Freedman, *Kennedy's Wars* p195

63	"At the same time ... move on Berlin" Ibid

63	"What, if any ... close to destruction?" Ibid, p181

64	"A later ... agreement" Dobbs, *One Minute to Midnight*

65	"Kennedy feared ... Missile Crisis" Alterman, *When Presidents Lie*

65	"I thought ... had been killed" Kennedy, *Thirteen Days*

66	"matter of Berlin") Beschloss, *The Crisis Years*

66	"So he ... out of me" Mahoney, *Sons and Brothers*, p131

66	"Following this latest ... up to 75 percent" Smith, *Grace and Power*

V: "Vietnam"

68	"In the final analysis ... struggle" O'Brien, *John F. Kennedy - A Biography*, p862

70	"I am frankly ... support of the people" Winkler, *The Cold War* p11

71	"Our total involvement ... Tomkin incident" Alterman, *When Presidents Lie*

72 "It preys ... ethnic conflicts" Kennedy, Robert, *The Pursuit of Justice* p112

74 "The final ... Americans" Alterman, *When Presidents Lie*

76 "We can prevent ... nothing equivalent" Bradlee, *Conversations with Kennedy* p42

78 "He felt ... South Vietnamese governments" Freedman, *Kennedy's Wars*

79 "It was until 1971 ... involvement in Vietnam" Sheehan, *The Pentagon Papers*

79 "This money was ... communist rule" Farren, *CIA-Secrets of the Company*

80 "The first (NSAM 263) ... withdrawal by 1965" Newman, *JFK and Vietnam*

81 "It's just the biggest ... ever saw" Alterman, *When Presidents Lie*, p.149

VI: "Organized Crime and It's Partner, the CIA

83 "In fact, J. Edgar Hoover ... the Mafia" Gentry , *J.Edgar Hoover: The Man and the Secrets*

84 "Sam ... Democratic machine" Giancana and Giancana, *Double Cross*

85 "Ferrie was ... Oswald" Oglesby, *The JFK Assassination*

85 "The mobsters ... per year" *True Crime : Mafia,* Time-Life Books

86 "In 1954 ... Guatemala" , Winkler, *The Cold War*

87 "Rafael Trujillo ... Republic" Farren, *CIA: Secrets*

87 "Patrice Lumumba ... Africa" Mahoney, *JFK: Ordeal in Africa*

88 "The plan was ... Mongoose" Bamford, *Body of Secrets*

89 "This contrasts ... suspected mobsters" *True Crime : Mafia,* Time-Life Books

90 "Also occurring ... the Mafia" Ibid

90 "Other reports ... anticrime crusade" Davis, *Mafia Kingfish*

91 "Frank Ragano ... Kennedy assassination" Ragano and Raab, *Mob Lawyer*

91 "Johnny Roselli ... Dealey Plaza" Bonano, *Bound by Honor : A Mafioso's Story*

91 "reports ... JFK" Dankbaar, *Files on JFK*

92   "FBI informed ... death threats" Donavan, *The Warren Commission Report on the Assassination of John F. Kennedy*, p57

92   "Security risks ... not included" Fox, *Unanswered Questions About President Kennedy's Assassination*

92   "In 1966, an investigation ... Warren Commission" Garrison, *On the Trail of the Assassins*

94   "..Permindex ... political assassinations" Benson, *Who's Who in the JFK Assassination*

95   "The mob also ... anti-racketeering legislation" Scheim, *Contract on America*

95   "President Johnson ... most Americans" Beschloss, *Taking Charge*

VII: November 22, 1963

101   "Can't you ... we could have" Walsh, *Air Force One*, p73

102   "Kennedy ... traitor" Maier, *The Kennedys*

102   "There are many ... assassination" Lane, *Plausible Denial*

102   "From 1961-1962 ... Texas " Spies, *United States Presidents*

103   "All one had to ... such an attempt" Waright, *What They Didn't Teach You About the 60s*, P.136

104   "I find it ... presidential car" Trost and Bennett, *President Kennedy Has Been Shot*

104   "Now, it would be ... Grassy Knoll" Melanson and Stevens, *The Secret Service*

105   "Mr. President ... love you" Connally, *From Love Field*, p07

107   "..single witness, Helen Markham ..." Bishop, *The Day Kennedy Was Shot*

109   ".. Hoover telephoned ... his brother, the President" Summers, *Official and Confidential*

110   "There are ... assassination"

110   "It has been ... term of office" Mathews, *Kennedy and Nixon*

113   "..witness for the government ... sixth floor of the TSBD" Benson, *Who's Who in the JFK Assassination*

113   "His face ... preoccupied" Posner, *Case Closed*, p248

114   "It was well researched ... many years " Stone, *JFK-The Book of the Film*

115 "Ruby corrected ... Cuba Committee" Miller, *The Assassination Please Almanac*

115 "It was well-known ... Crime" Scheim, *Contract on America*

VIII: Lee Harvey Oswald

117 "He had ... assassin" LaFontaine, *Oswald Talked* , p52

117 "He was not ... society" Meaghner, *Accessories After the Fact*

118 "Yet he was ... job" Benson, *Who's Who in the JFK Assassination*

119 "He was sent ... job" Ibid

119 "The Central ... Watch list" Newman, *Oswald and the CIA*

120 "One ... Nosenko" Summers, *Not In Your Lifetime*

121 "Oswald was not ... CIA" The Warren Commission Report, 2003, p659

121 "CIA lied ... Assassinations" Newman, *Oswald and the CIA*

122 "FBI Agent ... him and Marina" Lance, *1000 Years for Revenge: International Terrorism and The FBI*

123 "The embassy ... imposter" Eddowes, *The Oswald File*

124 "A patsy ... and the conspirators" Belfield, *The Assassination Business*

125 "Kennedy ... free world" Fritz, The Kennedy Mutiny

125 "She feared ... they wanted" Maars, *Crossfire*

125 "Lee Harvey Oswald ... asssassassination" Mallon, *Mrs Paine's Garage*

126 "From the conspirators ... necessity" Fetzer, *Murder in Dealey Plaza*

126 "His presence in the lunchroom ... witnesses" Groden and Livingstone, *High Treason* p150-

127 "His face ... distorted" Posner, *Case Closed*, p267

128 "Oswald then arrived ... 1:04 PM" Ibid p268

130 "I am ... arrest" Groden and Livingstone, *High Treason*

131 "Today, this could ... commission" Southwell and Twist, *Conspiracy Files*

132 "He told ... occasions" Groden and Livingstone, *High Treason 2* , p458

132 "I have ... violence" Groden and Livingstone, *High Treason*, p138

133 "When the rifle ... Mannlicher-Carcano" Meagher, *Accessories After the Fact*

134 "..this was contradicted...missed its target" Tague, *Truth Withheld*

149 "By definition … political weapon" Melanson and Stevens, *The Secret Service*

150 "It has been … night before" Groden and Livingstone, *High Treason*

150 "Hill blamed … shot himself" Wallace and Gates, *Between You And Me*

150 "At the … virtual halt" Melanson and Phillips, *The Secret Service*

151 "One of these stated … closed" Nechiporenko, *Passport to Assassination*, p152

152 "In addition, there are … from the front" Melanson and Stevens, *The Secret Service*

152 "Of those Secret … Knoll area" Wrone, *The Zapruder Film*

153 "The Secret Service … trip to Dallas" Melanson and Stevens, *The Secret Service*

XI: Lyndon Baines Johnson and the Warren Commission

154 "It's interesting … Johnson" Lubin, *Shooting Kennedy*

155 "The vice-president's … Estes scandals" Unger, *LBJ: A Life*

155 "I'm forty-three … mean anything" Smith, *Grace and Power*, p15

156 "I am not … China went" Alterman, *When President's Lie*, p175

156 "..serving as … competitive Johnson" Wallace, *Character*, p104

156 "One out … chance I got" Smith, *Grace and Power*, p15

159 "Kennedy tried … out one day" Fontava, *Fidel*, p95

160 "It was at … revealed" Smith, *Conspiracy*

160 "It was said … of proceedings" North, *Act of Treason*

161 "It was reported … psychopath" Holland, *American Heritage*, Nov 95, p58

161 "The appointed … time" Lubin, *Shooting Kennedy*

161 "Remember … acted alone" Tague, *Truth Withheld*

162 "Furthermore … from the public" Helms, *A Life in the Central Intelligence Agency*, p229

164 "As a result, … theory" Specter, *Passion For Truth*

164 "James … overpass" Tague, *Truth Withheld*

165 "more lead … bullet" Thompson, *Six Seconds in Dallas*, p148

165 "In addition, … ribs and wrists" Meagher, *Accessories After the Fact*

166 "The FBI … pathologists" Ibid

166 "JFK's personal ... vertebrae" Groden and Livingstone, *High Treason*, p111

167 "I saw ... hair" Lamb, *Booknotes*, p366

168 "There are issues ... confidence" Ibid p367

169 "He then ... Kennedy" Wrone, *The Zapruder Film*, p101

170 "These witnesses ... mistaken" Kurtz, *The JFK Assassination Debates*

170 "the ... wrong" Ibid

170 "Nor did ... president" Connelly and Herskowitz *From Love Field*

172 "Never ... security" Fetzer, *Murder In Dealy Plaza*, p415

172 "To do so, ... we didn't do" Gentry, *J Edgar Hoover*, p539

173 "The possibility ... this commission" "The Warren Commission Report" 2003

175 "Her request ... commission" Lane, *Plausible Denial*

XII: J. Edgar Hoover and the FBI

177 "He was not ... propaganda" Strober, *The Kennedy Presidency*

177 "In actuality, ... existence" Summers, *Official and Confidential*

177 "It has recently ... mob" Ibid

178 "But the ... influence" Furiati, *Zr Rifle*

178 "Reckless ... that flaw" Summers, *Official and Confidential p270*

179 "Among the first ... Arvad" Kessler, *Bureau, FBI*

179 "Another ... Exner" Demaris, *Judith Exner*

180 "In fact, ... Kennedys" Brown and Barham, *Marilyn*

180 "In his ... century" Harrison and Gilbert, *John F. Kennedy*, p17

181 "There were reports ... Florida" Waldron, *Ultimate Sacrifice*

181 *"However, five ... November 22"* Smith : *JFK: Say Goodbye to America*

182 "He ignored ... involved" Fritz, *The Kennedy Mutiny*

182 "Special Agent ... security risk" Hosty, *Assignment : Oswald*

182 "The FBI ... Depository" Hack, *Puppetmaster*

183 "Within two ... Oswald" Wrone, *The Zapruder Film*

183 "We're only ... conspiracy" Summers, *The Secret Life of J. Edgar Hoover*, p317

184 "We need ... Oswald" North, *Acts of Treason*, p437

XIII: The Role of the Media and the Importance of the Movie "JFK"

185 "He was ... copy" Dallek and Golway, *Let Every Nation Know*, p105

186 "The average ... a day" Brinkley, *Brinkley's Best*

187 "Among them ... Dallas" Thompson, *Six Seconds in Dallas*

187 "Among them ... Fact" Meagher, Accessories After the Fact

187 "About two ... Tribune" *Chicago Tribune* , Friday, June 3, 1992

187 "We were ... junkies" *Hammond Times*, June 29, 1992

188 "The media ... groups" Bishop, *You Are Being Lied To*

189 "Noam ... media" Chomsky, *Secrets, Lies, and Democracy* and *What Uncle Sam Really Wants*

190 "It's interesting ... alone" Stone, *JFK: The Book of the Film*

190 "The Central ... payroll" DiEugenio, *The Assassinations*

190 "In 1967 ... writers" Miller, *The Assassination Please Almanac*

190 "Even David ... the world" Brinkley, *Brinkley's Best*, p199

191 "In 1991 Gerald ... public" Stone and Sklar, *JFK: The Book of the Film*, p254

191 "David Belin ... public" Ibid p206

193 "We should ... granted" Ambrose, *Eisenhower: Soldier and President*

194 "It's a hypothesis ... over the coals" *Playboy*, November 2004

195 "In fact ... was successful" Giancana, Hughes, and Jobe, *JFK and Sam*

197 "Posner ... original statements" Posner, *Case Closed*

197 "In an attempt ... correct" Ibid pX

XIV: And So My Daughter Kennedy

204 "For one brief ... Camelot" Mathews, *Kennedy and Nixon*, p244

204 "Was it not ...ashes of the old" Schlesinger, *A Thousand Days*, p1028

205 "This observation ... Representatives in 1979" Smith, *Conspiracy*

206 "In all these ... conspiracy" Nightline ABC News, *The Kennedy Assassination : Beyond Conspiracy*

206 "This website ... layers of bunk" Website : McAdams, *The Kennedy Assassination*

207 "That's because ... uncomplicated" Kick, *You Are Being Lied To*

207 "Historians ... facts" Fosner, *Who Owns History*

XV: Straight Talk and the Historical Record

Bibliography

Alterman, Eric. *When Presidents Lie: A History of Official Deception and Its Consequences.* New York: Penguin Group, Inc., 2004

Ambrose, Stephen E. *Eisenhower: Soldier and President.* New York: Simon and Schuster, 1990.

American History. *Assassination of JFK.* Primedia Enthusiastic Publications, Inc. 2003.

Baker, Jean H. *The Stevensons: A Biography of an American Family.* New York: W.W.Norton and Company, 1996.

Bamford, James. *Body of Secrets.* New York: Random House, Inc., 2001.

Belfield, Richard. *The Assassination Business: A History of State Sponsored Murder.* New York: Carroll and Graf Publishers, 2005

Bennett, Richard M. *Conspiracy, Plots, Lies, and Cover-ups.* London: Virgin Books, Ltd, 2003

Benson, Michael. *Who's Who in the JFK Assassination.* New York: Citadel Press: Kensington Publishing Corp., 1993.

Beschloss, Michael R. *The Crisis Years: Kennedy and Khruschev, 1960-1963.* New York: Harper Collins Publishers, 1991.

Beschloss, Michael. *Taking Charge : The Johnson White House Tapes.* New York: Simon and Schuster, 1997.

Bishop, Greg. *You Are Being Lied To: The Disinformation Guide to Media Distortions, Historical Whitewashes and Cultural Myths.* "The Covert News Network. New York: The Disinformation Company, Ltd, 2001.

Bishop, Jim. *The Day Kennedy Was Shot.* New York: Bantam Books, Inc., 1968.

Blakey, G.Robert and Billings, Richard N. *The Plot to Kill the President: Organized Crime Assassinated JFK.* New York : Times Books, 1981.

Blum, John Morton. *Years of Discord, American Politics and Society 1961-1974.* New York: W.W.Norton and Company, 1991.

Bonanno, Bill. *Bound by Honor: A Mafiaso's Story.* New York: St. Martins Press, 1999.

Bradlee, Benjamin C. *Conversations With Kennedy.* New York: Norton and Company, Inc., 1975.

Breo, Dennis, L. *The Journal of the American Medical Association : "JFKs Death : The Plain Truth From the MDs who Did the Autopsy.* May 27, 1992 - Vol.267, No.20

Brinkley, David. *Brinkley's Beat : People , Places, and Events that Shaped My Time.* New York: Alfred A. Knopf, Random House, Inc, 2003.

Brown, Peter Harry and Barham, Patte B. *Marilyn: The Last Take .* New York: The Penguin Group, 1992.

Bugliosi, Vincent. *Reclaiming History: The Assassination of President John F. Kennedy.* New York: W.W. Norton and Company, 2007.

Bugliosi, Vincent. *Four Days in November: The Assassination of President John F. Kennedy. New York: W.W. Norton and Company, 2007.*

Chicago Tribune, Friday, July 3, 1992, Section 5, page 3.

Chomsky, Noah. *Secrets, Lies, and Democracy.* Tucson, AZ: Odonian Press, 1994.

Chomsky, Noah. *What Uncle Sam Really Wants.* Tucson, Az: Odonian Press, 1986-1992.

Collier, Peter and Horowitz, David. *The Kennedys: An American Drama. New York: Summit Books, 1984*

Connelly, Nellie and Herskowitz, Mickey. *From Love Field, Our Final Hours with President John F. Kennedy. New York: Rugged Land, LLC. 2003.*

Crenshaw, M.D., Charles. *Trauma Room One: The JFK Medical Cover-up Exposed.* New York: Paraview Press, 2001.

Crenshaw, M.D., Charles. *JFK: Conspiracy of Silence.* New York: Penguin Books, USA, Inc., 1992

Dallek, Robert and Golway, Terry. *Let Every Nation Know.* Naperville, Illinois: Sourcebooks Media Fusion, 2006.

Dankbaar, Wim. *Files on JFK: Interviews With Confessed Assassin James E. Files.* Chicago, Illinois, Independent Publishers Group, 2007-2008.

Davis, John H. *Mafia Kingfish: Carlos Marcello and the Assassination of John F Kennedy. New York: McGraw Hill Publishing Company, 1989.*

Demaris, Ovid. *Judith Exner: My Story.* New York: Grove Press Inc., 1977.

Dempsey, John Mark. *The Jack Ruby Trial Revisited: The Diary of Jury Foreman Max Causey.* Denton, Texas: University of North Texas Press, 2000.

DiEugenio, James and Pease, Lisa. *The Assassinations: Probe Magazine on JFK, MLK, RFK, and Malcolm X.* Los Angeles, CA: Feral House, 2003.

Dobbs, Michael. *One Minute To Midnight: Kennedy, Krushchev, and Castro on the Brink of Nuclear War.* New York: Alfred A. Knopf, 2008.

Donavan, Robert J. *PT-109. John F. Kennedy in WW11.* New York: The McGraw-Hill Companies, Inc. 2001.

Donavan, Robert J. *A Concise Compendium of The Warren Commission Report on the Assassination of John F. Kennedy.* New York: Popular Library, 1964.

Eddowes, Michael. *The Oswald File.* New York: General Publishing Company Limited, 1977.

Epstein, Edward Jay. *Inquest: The Warren Commission and the Establishment of Truth.* New York: The Viking Press, 1966.

Farren, Mick. *CIA --- Secrets of the Company.* New York: Barnes and Noble Inc., 2003.

Fetzer, James H. *Murder in Dealey Plaza.* Peru, Illinois: Carus Publishing Company, 2000.

Fetzer, James H. *Assassination Science.* Peru, Illinois: Carus Publishing Company, 1998.

Fetzer, James H. *The Great Zapruder Film Hoax.* Chicago: Catfeet Press, 2003

Fontava, Humberto E. *Fidel: Hollywood's Favorite Tyrant.* Washington D.C. : Regency Publishing Company, 2005.

Fosner, Eric. *Who Owns History : Rethinking the Past in a Changing World.* New York: Hill and Wang *2002.*

Fox, Sylvan. *The Unanswered Questions About President Kennedy's Assassination.* New York: University Publishing and Distributing Corporation, 1965.

Freedman, Lawrence. *Kennedy's Wars: Berlin, Cuba, Laos, and Vietnam.* New York: Oxford University Press, 2000.

Fritz, Will. *The Kennedy Mutiny: What Really Happened in Dallas on November 22, 1963.* Abridged Edition, 2002.

Furiati, Claudia. *ZR Rifle: The Plot to Kill Kennedy, Cuba Opens Secret Files.* Australia: Ocean Press, 1994.

Fursenko, Alexandr and Naftali, Timothy. *One Hell of a Gamble: Krushchev, Castro, and 1958-1964.* New York: W.W. Norton and Company, Inc., 1977.

Galanor, Stewart. *Cover-Up.* New York: Kestrel Books, 1998.

Garrison, Jim. *On the Trail of the Assassins.* New York: Sheridan Square Press, 1988.

Gentry, Curt. *J. Edgar Hoover: The Man and the Secrets.* New York: W.W. Norton and Company, 1991.

Giancana, Antoinette, Hughes, John R., DM Oxon, MD, PhD, and Jobe, Thomas H. *JFK and Sam: The Connection Between the Giancana and Kennedy Assassinations.* Nashville, Tennessee: Cumberland House, 2005.

Giancana, Sam and Giancana, Chuck. *Double Cross.* New York: Warner Books, Inc., 1992.

Groden, Robert J. *JFK: The Case For Conspiracy.* New York: New Frontier Publications, 2002.

Groden, Robert J. and Livingstone, Harrison Edward. *High Treason: The Assassination of President John Kennedy. What Really Happened.* Boothwyn, PA: The Conservatory Press, 1989.

Groden, Robert J. and Livingstone, Harrison Edward. *High Treason 2 : The Great Cover-up: The Assassination of President John F. Kennedy.* New York: Carroll and Graf Publishers, Inc., 1992.

Hack, Richard. *Puppetmaster: The Secret Life of J. Edgar Hoover.* Beverly Hills, CA: New Millennium Press, 2004.

Hammond Times. Monday, June 29, 1992. Page A1; A7, Indiana.

Harrison, Maureen and Gilbert, Steve. *John F. Kennedy, Word for Word.* LaJolla, CA: Excellent Books, 1993.

Hellman, John. *The Kennedy Obsession: The American Myth of JFK.* New York: Columbia University Press, 1997.

Helms, Richard with Hood, William. *A Look Over My Shoulder: A Life in the Central Intelligence Agency.* New York: The Random House Publishing Group, 2003.

Holland, Max. *American Heritage .* "The Key to the Warren Report" November 1995.

Hosty, Jr., James. *Assignment: Oswald.* New York: Arcade Publishing, 1996.

Hurt, Henry. *Reasonable Doubt, An Investigation Into the Assassination of John F. Kennedy.* New York: Holt, Rinehart, and Winston, 1985.

Jackson, Devon. *Conspiranoia: The Mother of All Conspiracy Theories.* New York: Penguin Group, 1999.

Jeffreys-Jones, Rhodri. *The CIA and American Democracy.* New York: Yale University Press, 1989.

Journal of the American Medical Association. May 27, 1992, Vol.267, No.20.

Kennedy, John. *Profiles In Courage.* New York: Harper and Row Publishers, 1955.

Kennedy, John F. *Why England Slept.* New York: Wilfred Funk, Inc., 1961.

Kennedy, Robert F. *Thirteen Days: A Memoir of the Cuban Missile Crisis.* New York: W.W. Norton and Company, 1968.

Kennedy, Robert F. *The Pursuit of Justice.* New York: Harper and Row Publishers, 1964.

Kessler, Ronald. *Bureau: The Secret History of the FBI.* New York: St. Martins Press, 2002.

Kick, Russ. *You Are Being Lied To: The Disinformation Guide to Media Distortion, Historical Whitewashes, and Cultural Myths.* New York: The Disinformation Company, Inc., 2001.

Klein, Edward. *All Too Human, The Love Story of Jack and Jackie Kennedy.* New York: Simon and Schuster, 1996.

Kurtz, Michael L. *Crime of the Century. The Kennedy Assassination from a Historian's Perspective.* The University of Tennessee Press

Kurtz, Michael L. *The JFK Assassination Debates: Lone Gunman versus Conspiracy.* University Press of Kansas, 2006

Lafontaine, Ray and Mary. *Oswald Talked: The New Evidence in the JFK Assassination.* Gretna, Louisiana, Pelican Publishing Company, 1996.

Lamb, Brian. *Booknotes: Stories From American History.* New York: Penguin Group, 2001.

Lance, Peter. *1000 Years For Revenge: International Terrorism and the FBI.* New York: Harper Collins Publishers, 2003.

Lane, Mark. *Plausible Denial : Was the CIA Involved in the Assassination of JFK.* New York: Thunder's Mouth Press, 1991.

Lane, Mark. *Rush To Judgment.* New York, Thunder's Mouth Press. 1966.

Leamer, Laurence. *Sons of Camelot. The Fate of an American Dynasty.* New York: Harper Collins Publishers, Inc., 2004.

Leamer, Laurence. *The Kennedy Men 1901-1963.* New York: Harper Collins Publishers , Inc., 2001.

Levering, Ralph. *The Cold War 1945-1987. New York:* Arlington Heights, Illinois: Harlan Davidson, Inc., 1988

Lifton, David S. *Best Evidence. Disguise, and Deception in the Assassination of John F. Kennedy.* New York: MacMillan Publishing Co., Inc., 1980.

Lubin, David M. *Shooting Kennedy.* Los Angeles, CA: University of California Press, 2003.

Maars, Jim. *Crossfire: The Plot That Killed Kennedy.* New York: Carroll and Graf Publishers, 1989.

Mahoney, Richard D. *Sons and Brothers, The Days of Jack and Bobbie Kennedy.* New York: Arcade Publishing Inc., 1999.

Mahoney, Richard D. *JFK: Ordeal in Africa.* New York: Oxford University Press, 1983.

Mailer, Thomas. *The Kennedys, America's Emerald Kings.* New York: Basic Books, Perseus Books Group, 2003.

Mallon, Thomas. *Mrs. Paine's Garage and the Murder of John F. Kennedy.* New York: Random House Inc., 2002.

Manchester, William. *The Death of a President, 25 Years.* New York: Harper and Row Publishers, Inc., 1967.

Matthews, Christopher. *Kennedy and Nixon.* New York: Simon and Schuster, Inc., 1996.

May, Ernest R. and Zelikow, Phillip D. *The Kennedy Tapes: Inside the White House During the Cuban Missile Crisis.* Cambridge, Massachusetts: The Belknap Press of Harvard University Press, 1997.

Meagher, Sylvia. *Accessories After the Fact: The Warren Commission, The Authorities, and the Report. New York: Random House, Inc., 1967.*

Melanson, Phillip H. Ph.D. and Stevens, Peter F. *The Secret Service: The Hidden History of an Enigmatic Agency.* New York: Carroll and Graf Publisher, 2002.

Miller, Tom. *The Assassination Please Almanac.* Lincoln, NE: Henry Regnery Co., 2000.

Mills, Judie. *John F. Kennedy.* New York: Franklin Watts, Inc., 1988.

Nechiporenko, Col. Oleg Maximovich. *Passport to Assassination: The Never*

Before-Told Story of Lee Harvey Oswald by the KGB Colonel Who Knew Him. New York: Carol Publishing Group, 1993.

Neurosurgery. "The Assassination of President John F. Kennedy: A Forensic Analysis—Part I." Hagerstown, MD: Lippincott, Williams, and Wilkens, Volume 53, Number 5, November 2003.

Newman, John M. *JFK and Vietnam : Deception, Intrigue, and the Struggle for Power*. New York: Warner Books, Inc., 1992.

Newman, John. *Oswald and the CIA*. New York: Carroll and Graf Publishers, Inc., 1995.

Nightline. ABC News : November 2003. "The Kennedy *Assassination* Beyond Conspiracy.

North, Mark. *Act of Treason: The Role of J. Edgar Hoover in the Assassination of President Kennedy*. New York: Carroll and Graf Publishers, Inc. 1991.

O'Brien, Michael. *John F. Kennedy: A Biography*. New York: St Martin's Press, 2005.

O'Donnell, Kenneth P. and Powers, David F. *Johnny, We Hardly Knew Ye: Memories of John Fitzgerald Kennedy*, Little, Brown and Company

Oglesby, Carl. *The JFK Assassination: The Facts and the Theories*. New York: The Penguin Group, 1992.

O'Leary, Brad and Seymour, L. E. *Triangle of Death: The Shocking Truth About The Role of South Vietnam and the French Mafia in the Assassination of JFK*. Nashville, Tennessee: WND Books, 2003.

Piper, Michael Collins. *Final Judgment: The Missing Link in he JFK Assassination Conspiracy*. Washington D.C. : The Center For Historical Review, 1998.

Posner, Gerald. *Case Closed. Lee Harvey Oswald and the Assassination of JFK*. New York: Random House, Inc., 1993.

Prouty, L. Fletcher. *The Secret Team: The CIA and its Allies*. New York: Skyhorse Publishing, 2008.

Quirk, John Patrick. *The Central Intelligence Agency*. Guilford, Connecticut: Foreign Intelligence Press, 1986.

Quirk, Lawrence J. *The Kennedys in Hollywood*. New York: Cooper Square Press, 2004.

Ragano, Frank and Raab, Selwyn. *Mob Lawyer*. New York: MacMillan Publishing Company, 1994.

Roberts, Craig and Armstrong, John. *JFK: The Dead Witnesses*. Tulsa, OK.: Consolidated Press International, 1995.

Scheim, David. *Contract on America: The Mafia Murder of President John F. Kennedy*. New York: Shapolsky Publishers, Inc. 1988.

Schlesinger, Jr., Arthur M. *A Thousand Days: John F. Kennedy in the White House*. New York: Houghton Mifflin Company, 1993.

Scott, Peter Dale. *Deep Politics and the Death of JFK*. Los Angeles, CA: University of California Press, 1993.

Shaw, Gary J. *Cover-up: The Government Conspiracy to Conceal the Facts About the Public Execution of John Kennedy*. Austin, Texas: Thomas Publications, Inc., 1976.

Sheehan, Neil. *The Pentagon Papers*. New York: New York Times, 1971.

Sloan, Bill and Hill, Jean. *JFK The Last Dissenting Witness*. Gretna, Louisiana: Pelican Publishing Company, 1992.

Smith, Amanda. *Hostage to Fortune: The Letters of Joseph P. Kennedy*. New York: Penguin Group, Penguin Putnam, Inc., 2001.

Smith, Matthew. *Conspiracy: The Plot to Stop the Kennedys*. New York: Kensinton Publishing Corp. 2005.

Smith, Matthew. *Say Goodbye to America: The Sensational and Untold Story Behind the Assassination of John F. Kennedy*. Great Britain: Mainstream Publishing Company LTD, 2001.

Smith, Sally Bedell. *Grace and Power: The Private World of the Kennedy White House*. New York: Random House Publishing Group, 2004.

Sorenson, Theodore C. *Kennedy*. New York: Harper and Row Publishers, 1965.

Southwell, David and Twist, Sean. *Conspiracy Files*. New York: Random House Publishing, 2004.

Specter, Arlen with Robbins, Charles. *Passion For Truth*. New York: Harper Collins Publishers, 2000.

Spies, Karen, B. *United States Presidents: John F. Kennedy*. Berkeley Heights, New Jersey: Enslow Publishers, Inc., 1999.

Stone, Oliver and Sklar, Zachary. *JFK: The Book of the Film*. New York: Applause Books, 1992.

Strober, Deborah Hart and Strober, Gerald. *The Kennedy Presidency: An Oral History of the Era*. Washington D.C.: Bracey's, 2003.

Summers, Anthony. *Official and Confidential: The Secret Life of J. Edgar Hoover.* New York: G. P. Putnam's Sons, 1993.

Summers, Anthony. *Not in Your Lifetime: The Definitive Book on the JFK Assassination. New York: Marlowe and Company,* 1998.

Tague, James T. *Truth Withheld, A Survivor's Story. Why We Will Never Know The Truth About the JFK Assassination.* Dallas, Texas: Excel Digital Press, Inc., 2003.

The Editors of Time-Life Books. *True Crime: Mafia.* Time-Life Incorporated, USA, 1993.

Thompson, Josiah. *Six Seconds in Dallas.* New York: Bernard Geis Association, 1967.

Trask, Richard B. *Pictures of the Pain: Photography and the Assassination of President Kennedy.* Danvers, MA: Yeoman Press, 1994.

Trost, Cathy and Bennett, Susan. *President Kennedy Has Been Shot.* Napeville, ILL: Sourcebooks, Inc., 2003.

Unger, Irwin and Unger, Debi. *LBJ: A Life.* New York: John Wiley and Sons, Inc., 1999.

United Press International and American Heritage Magazine. *Four Days: The Historical Record of the Death of President Kennedy.* American Heritage Publishing Co., Inc., 1964.

Waldron, Lamar with Hartmann, Thom. *Ultimate Sacrifice: John and Robert Kennedy, The Plan For A Coup in Cuba and the Murder of JFK.* New York: Carroll and Graf Publishers, 2005.

Waldron, Lamar with Hartmann, Thom. *Legacy of Secrecy: The Long Shadow of the JFK Assassination.* New York: Publishers Group West, 2008.

Wallace, Chris. *Character: Profiles in Presidential Courage. New York: Rugged, Inc. 2004.*

Wallace, Mike with Gates, Gary Paul. *Between You And Me: A Memoir.* New York: Hyperion, 2005.

Walsh, Kenneth T. *Air Force One: A History of the Presidents and Their Planes.* New York: Hyperion 2003.

Waright, Mike. *What They Didn't Teach You About the 60s.* Novato, CA.: Presidio Press, Inc., 2001.

Warren Commission Report. *Report of the President's Commission on the Assassination of President John F. Kennedy.* Barnes and Noble, Inc., 2003.

Weberman, Alan J. and Canfield, Michael. *Coup D'etat in America: The CIA and the Assassination of John F. Kennedy.* San Francisco, CA: Quick Trading Company, 1992.

Website: McAdams, John 1995-2004. *The Kennedy Assassination.*

Wecht, Cyril, MD, JD, *Cause of Death.* New York: Penguin Books, USA., 1993.

White, Mark J. *The Kennedys and Cuba.* Chicago, ILL: Ivan R. Dee, Publisher, 1999.

Winkler, Allan M. *The Cold War: A History in Documents.* New York: Oxford University Press, Inc., 2000.

Wood, James Playsted. *The Life and Words of John F. Kennedy.* Waukesha, Wisconsin: Country Beautiful Corporation, 1964.

Wrone, David R. *The Zapruder Film, Reshaping JFKs Assassination.* Lawrence, Kansas: University Press Of Kansas, 2003.

Wyden, Peter. *The Bay of Pigs, The Untold Story.* New York: Simon and Schuster, 1979.

Zirbel, Craig I. *The Texas Connection: The Assassination of John F. Kennedy.* Scottsdale, Arizona: Wrightand Company Publishers, 1991.

Breinigsville, PA USA
13 September 2009
224009BV00001B/9/P